France, Fin de Siècle

FRANCE
Fin de Siècle

———— ✳ ————

Eugen Weber

The Belknap Press of
Harvard University Press
Cambridge, Massachusetts
and London, England

Library of Congress Cataloging-in-Publication Data

Weber, Eugen Joseph
France, fin de siècle.

1. France—Civilization—1830–1900. I. Title.
DC33.6.W43   1986   944.06   85-30569
ISBN 0-674-31812-9 (cloth)
ISBN 0-674-31813-7 (paper)

For Joan Palevsky

Contents

Illustrations

France, Fin de Siècle

Introduction

❋

Early in the eleventh century Ralph Glaber, a Burgundian monk, described his world as it had been on the threshold of its thousandth year. Love waxed cold, iniquity abounded among mankind, covetousness stalked abroad, men's souls faced perilous times, manifold signs and prodigies came to pass, and sagacious men foretold other prodigies as great still to come. Since then, no other century had made so much ado about its passing. The French of the 1880s and 1890s referred to themselves as fin de siècle, and since the writ of French fashion swayed the Western World, the term came to mark the close of the nineteenth century as it had not that of any other.

Why fin de siècle, with the evident connotation that not just a century but an age, an era, a way of life, a world, were coming to a close? The nineteenth century had a habit of putting an end to things. Curtains repeatedly fell upon regimes, revolutions, ruling classes, and ideologies, then rose, then fell again; but those whom history allegedly condemned never ceased dying. At the century's conclusion most of the same types of characters who had been around in 1789, or at least in 1802, still hung about the stage, many of their lines still being repeated to similarly mixed reviews. Trying to make ambition look like principle, or principle look like practice, Legitimists, Orleanists, Bonapartists, Jacobins and Liberals, Bourgeois, Aristocrats, Democrats and city mobs, all took their turn in at least one farewell performance before they returned for more. Meanwhile new characters had joined them (the nineteenth century also liked beginnings!), but to an absent eye, or a skeptical one, the charade need not have looked too different.

With hindsight we can see that the First World War brought down the frames of institutions, ways of life and mind, that had been long crumbling. But there was no knowing this before the nineteenth century ended, before the twentieth century faced the possibility of a worldwide war. After that war was over it became fashionable to refer to the years preceding it as the Belle Epoque, and to confuse that period with the fin de siècle, as if the two were one. Perhaps they were; the bad old times are always somebody's Belle Epoque. But the Belle Epoque, named when looking back across the corpses and the ruins, stands for the ten years or so before 1914. These also had their problems, but relatively they were robust years, sanguine and productive. The fin de siècle had preceded them: a time of economic and moral depression, a great deal less redolent of buoyancy or hope.

And yet a lot took place during these two decades that made life better for a lot of people. Not for all. Better alternatives for the many easily turn into less choice for the few. New aspirations can be perceived as threats, especially when the aspiring begin to raise their voices. Transitions can be diversely recognized: as promise, or as menace. Different social groups see the same phenomenon differently. Even beneficent changes can be troubling: access to better food may stir regrets for the old, rough familiar fare; telephones invade privacy; swifter, cheaper transport frightens and pollutes; shorter working hours forecast idleness. Coarse sensualists welcomed the time of modern comforts succeeding "to periods of force and magnificence," delighted to think that it would go down in history as "the century of water closets, bathrooms, and central heating."[1] Sterner observers deplored the softness and the laxness that the new facilities evoked. Coming too thick and fast upon one another, such impressions could be taken for evidence of present corruption, or omens of imminent decay. That is how some of the most articulate among contemporaries perceived and presented them, in the lurid context of military defeat, political instability, private adversity, public scandal, and clamorous social criticism, to stress the *fin* in fin de siècle that made it sound like an unhappy end.

This is what caught my eye about the circumstances: the discrepancy between material progress and spiritual dejection reminded me of our own times. So much was going right, even in France, as the nineteenth century ended; so much was being said to make one think that all was going wrong. That need not be surprising. Public dis-course turns mostly about public matters—especially politics; and the style of politics calls for catastrophic imagery. A great deal of political debate either takes place on the brink of doom or envisions it looming on the horizon. Doom loomed more clearly in fin de siècle France than almost anywhere else at the time. Since contemporary interpreters and later historians pay special attention to politics, this colors their im-pression and ours of years when, as in most times, politics played only a small role on the surface of events. As one shrewd observer of his country put it, "politics does not hold in our lives the place it takes up in the newspapers, in [social] conversations, in the apparent existence of a nation. The public life of a people is a very small thing compared to its private life."[2]

Let me say at once that public life is far from irrelevant, because decisions made at the public level can powerfully affect the private one. Political ideas, though, remained the passion or plaything of small elites, until cheap print and popular illustrations extended them to all. During the last quarter of the nineteenth century political interests and ideologies came to stimulate the general public—more general than it had ever been—pervading popular attitudes and expectations, hence the eventual orientation of the land itself.

The harsh realities of universal suffrage, long eluded, were coming home to roost: lower and lower sections of the middle classes were ruling in parliament; setting the pace in society, letters, arts; tarring politics, so long a sport for gentlemen, with their vulgar brush. The populace, losing respect for their natural betters, bayed for its turn at the troughs of power. The disorderly, volcanic nature of city mobs was nothing new. The claims of organized labor, its disruptive strikes, the politics of socialism in Chamber, Senate, even the Cabinet, were more disquieting. The deferential society tottered. There was no knowing how long it would take to wane.

Still, public events have received a great deal of attention, and read-ers interested in political and economic history of France can turn to many excellent studies. Insofar as I talk of politics, I try to present that aspect of public events that was most likely to catch contemporary attention, and my perspective is not that which comes naturally to those who already know how things have turned out.

Other aspects of public life that I survey are literature and the arts, again, insofar as possible, less from a twentieth-century perspective than from that of the nineteenth century. A good reason for taking an interest in the fin de siècle is that so many literary and artistic movements significant in our time had their roots in the last quarter of the nineteenth century. Here too extravagance and high spirits were taken for signs of degeneration. We know better now: like wine and cheese, literature and art confirm that civilization and fermentation go together. Some splendid works have been written with this in mind. But, however significant they were to become, and however much we may admire their products, such schools and movements were marginal and unrepresentative. The narrow trendy public that appreciated novelty for its own sake and patronized one avant-garde after another was itself marginal, and not necessarily typical even of the wider cultivated public. Though sympathetic to the various avant-gardes that have received their share of attention, I have preferred to focus on more run-of-the-mill activities.

Above all, this book is about the permanencies and the novelties that affected private life. The 1880s and 1890s witnessed novelties of fundamental importance to the future: new ways of heating, lighting, and getting about; better access to water and leisure, exercise, information, and distant places. Telegraph and telephones; typewriters and elevators; mass public transport and that wonderful individual steed—the bicycle; electric lamps (I did my courting as a student in a cafe seductively named A l'Electricité)—all are conquests of the fin de siècle. They may have helped palliate the shortcomings of the political class, but they disturbed the more austere who feared for the national fiber. Yet most who gazed upon or read about such wonders did not enjoy their use, or did so only after long delays. It is important to remember how close to medieval conditions many French still lived; and no less important to know that other possibilities were henceforth available, envisaged, coveted, eventually obtained. If things changed slowly, nevertheless, they changed, and in significant ways. Reaction to change set the character of the period.

As with politics, so with everyday life. It was during the fin de siècle that the virtualities of earlier decades were carried to realization, before the twentieth century made them available to all. Modern productivity, relatively soaring, called up a mass demand from modest customers. It did not better all, far from it; and it doled out its relative plenty selectively, providing more textiles, coffee, newspapers, bread, wine, cheap fares, and music halls than roasts, shoes, art, or decent housing. Still, millions of French now lived as only thousands had fifty years before. We are in the habit of deprecating improvements that affect only some of the people, and not all of them. That is as it may be. But not everything happens at once. That several million of the middle class learned to take for granted new clothes, fresh food, sugar, travel, print, schooling for their children, was no little matter. Equally important, the advances of some pointed the way to others. The less privileged, unlike those of earlier ages, expected to accede to the advantages of their "betters." While their advance proved slow, their right to it was henceforth conceded. Every decade brought them something on account.

Food, clothing, and shelter matter more, or more immediately, than a free press or universal suffrage. When the former concerns do not demand all your attention, you can give thought to the latter. For people of modest means this was just beginning to happen. Food improved; there was more of it even for poorer folk, and more drink too. (It was not until the later nineteenth century that alcoholism became a problem.) Wearing apparel also improved, and became more standardized. Those who mourned the passing of popular costumes had not had to wear them. Those who had worn them preferred ready-mades, which they were beginning to be able to afford. They could also enjoy better cheap entertainment, too vulgar for the cultivated unless they went slumming but a treat for those who had rarely danced even to a fiddle; and colored images—calendars, posters, advertisements—more lifelike than anything that they once had bought at fairs, and far more glorious.

Those details that helped maintain the difference between social orders were being whittled down: literacy no longer set the fortunate few apart; like dress, speech and manners grew (slowly) more similar; and patterns of consumption moved a little closer. Social homogeneity was very far away (it remains so today), though some already were denouncing it as an alarming reality.

Other objects of late-twentieth-century apprehension caused tremors one hundred years ago: pollution, crowding, noise, nerves, and drugs; threats to environment, to peace, to security, to sanity private and public; the noxious effects of press, publicity, and advertising; the decline of public and private standards; the rising tide of transgressions imperiling law and order. The commonweal, then as now on its last legs, looked on itself as into an abyss and shivered.

There had always been innovation; no generation had passed without novelties. Now change became the nature of life, novelty a part of the normal diet, served by institutions like the press and news agencies—dedicated to it, or to its invention when in short supply. The fin de siècle is the age of material novelties, of news, of *faits divers, nouvelles à sensation*—of scoops and beats and bulletins, newsbriefs and sensational tidings; the time when fashions—in dress, politics, or the arts—became clearly defined as being made to pass away: change for the sake of change.

Just because all this sounds familiar, it is good to remember how different it was. The past is another country, and fin de siècle France is a foreign land through which we stroll, recognizing figures, monuments, and landscapes that are familiar: Symbolists, Impressionists, and Neo-Impressionists; the servant problem and the labor problem and the problem of foreign labor; the threat of English words invading the French language (*franglais* had been denounced as early as 1856),[3] that of tourists defiling remote beauty spots, and that of having to get away in summer. We are the more surprised by differences that take us unawares: men lifting their hats in greeting but keeping them on in certain rooms; the cumbrous confinement of women's skirts; ringing coins to hear if they sound true; dueling; the problems posed by walking amid cobblestones, horse-droppings, mud, or dust; the ubiquity of horses and the noise they made; bad smells; the danger from food adulterated by private enterprise or else by swift natural decay before the age of refrigeration; the paucity of clean linen; the rankness and violence of political invective and much of private life.

I restrict myself to surface phenomena, accessible to the inquisitive tourist: us. Profound realities may stir the imagination, but most of life passes on the surface. This is where I mostly look, stopping to examine those aspects of the fin de siècle that catch my attention, attempting to describe and to illustrate them. In the end, you may feel as I do that it is as absurd to expect conclusions *from* historical epochs as *to* them; but that things were not so dark as they were sometimes painted, that the age faced serious problems seriously and generated positive solutions to some of them, that the ultimate French man and woman were those who stood fast and said there was no need to fret: "faut pas s'en faire."[4]

A bad novelist and delightful letterwriter, like so many of his nineteenth-century peers, Prosper Mérimée once declared that what he really liked in history were anecdotes, "and among anecdotes I prefer those where I think that I can distinguish a true picture of the customs and characters of any given period."[5] I tend to agree with Mérimée, as I do with the geographer Vidal de La Blache, who insisted that we should not be afraid to multiply examples.[6] You have been warned.

L'ILLUSTRATION

Prix du Numéro : 75 centimes.   SAMEDI 14 AVRIL 1900   58e Année — No 2981

The stucco figure surmounting the main gate of the 1900 Exhibition was almost twenty feet tall and dressed in clothes designed by a fashionable couturier: Paquin. It soon came to be known as *la Parisienne*.

1

Decadence?

❋

End-of-century trips less lightly off the tongue than fin de siècle. This may be why the term remains associated mainly with France, where it was coined while the nineteenth century still had a while to run. Just what it meant at first was not entirely clear. It could denote "modern" or "up to date."[1] But novelty went with uncertainty and a certain insecurity, and eventually a certain decline of standards.[2] A shoemaker could be praised for being a traditional cobbler rather than fin de siècle.[3] Soon the negative connotations of the term drove all others out. When, in 1891, a judge described young lawyers as fin de siècle, the press found this too harsh, likely to evoke "legitimate protests."[4] That same year, a provincial newspaper's attack on the local prefecture as fin de siècle led to a duel and court action that ended in a fine for the defaming sheet.[5] And when a Paris court judged a blackmailer who lived off his wife's prostitution, it was to hear him explain that he was no more than "a fin de siècle husband."[6] The words were everywhere; they could be applied to anything and everything:

> Fin de siècle! partout, partout
> . . . il sert à désigner tout.[7]

> Fin de siècle! Everywhere
> . . . It stands for all that you might care
> To name . . .

Since art imitates life, when it does not inspire it, literature soon adopted the vision. In 1891 Joris Karl Huysmans (naturally) denounced "the ignoble spectacle of this fin de siècle."[8] But more vulgar, hence more audible, voices intoned the same refrain. An 1888 play called *Fin de Siècle* turns around shady deals, adultery, and murder; a dreary novel of the same title, published in 1889, tells of a rich young man whom boredom, gambling, and misplaced affections lead to suicide in 325 weary pages.[9] As 1890 ended, a new financial weekly, *Le Fin de Siècle,* promised spicy revelations of financial scandals. It foundered with the year, bequeathing its title to a more "literary" review, suggestively illustrated to support its argument that vice is more interesting than virtue. Presumably more representative too: "whoever wants to please today has to be fin de siècle or cease to exist."[10] What were the fin de siècle ideas of this resolutely fin de siècle journal?

"No more rank, titles, or race," explained the editor, François Mainguy, in the first issue. "All is mixed, confused, blurred, and reshuffled in a kaleidoscopic vision." The fin de siècle's character at its most acute was competition, "struggle for life," and, above all, striving to satisfy *les appétits du ventre.*[11]

It would be even more the appetites of the lower stomach that *Le Fin de Siècle* set out to satisfy, competing with *La Vie Parisienne* and other more or less vaguely salacious publications that could afford to rent well-known authors (Emile Zola, Alphonse Daudet, Aurélien Scholl, Octave Mirbeau) at a good fee. In 1893, as a publicity stunt, Mainguy set out to imitate the art students' popular *bal des Quatre-z-Arts,* by organizing a *bal fin de siècle.* His scheme became a great success when the model he hired to represent Beauty was arrested and taken to court for wearing nothing beside (or beneath) a transparent black chemise, while an accompanying nymph was accused of dancing without even that to keep her warm. The *outrage public à la pudeur* brought the girls fifteen and eight days in jail respectively, while Mainguy was sentenced to one month.[12] Circulation soared.

Moral anarchy, or what was so described, subverted ideas and standards hitherto taken for granted, at least in public. There were no more beliefs, vice was everywhere; it was not merely a fin de siècle, wrote *Fin de Siècle,* but a *fin de race:* the tag end of an ailing race (people), "in which only one cult survives, that of love."[13] Love of course meant sex, though not procreation. No wonder that growing numbers, especially within the Catholic Church, believed they saw the Devil's hand behind the accelerating decay. In 1891 the Abbé Jeanin had published *Eglise et fin de siècle,* which decried the decadence of the times. By the end of the century, the end of the world seemed nigh. *The World's End Soon,* Arthur Lautrec promised in 1901; in 1904 Jean Rocroy's more precise *The End of the World in 1921 (As Proved by History)* was printing its 20,000th copy.[14]

One did not have to go so far to appreciate the interest of a time of accelerated change, a society that seemed about to alter in essence as it had in appearance—"a society about to disappear," already agitated and alarmed "by a thousand important symptoms of degeneration."[15] The notion of end, somehow, goes with thoughts of diminution and decay. A hundred years earlier, Sébastien Mercier, dealing with a less hangdog century's demise, had also found misery, gloom, and anxiety predominant; he concluded that it was almost impossible to be happy in Paris. Things had become worse since then: defeat and occupation in 1814–15, defeat and occupation again after 1870, suggested, then confirmed, that France's conquering days were drawing to a close, to be replaced by the new, uneasy experience of decline.

Decadence, sketched by Romantic poets, would be asserted by Naturalist description, hailed by those who savored its concomitant refinements, denounced with bitter satisfaction by those who saw their world unraveling. At midcentury, feelings of this sort appeared to be confirmed by medical research, when Dr. Benedict Morel published his *Treatise of the Physical, Intellectual, and Moral Degenerations of the Human Race and of the Causes That Produce These Maladive Varieties* (1857). The debate was joined around Morel's thesis. "For the last quarter-century," a medical man complained in 1876, all one hears is "We are degenerate! We are in decadence!" As if to confirm this, statisticians tell us that the population is falling, the average height of recruits diminishes, the number of draft rejects grows, morality wanes, crime flourishes, mind and body tend to deformity, cretinism, idiocy, lunacy, and so on. Some of these assertions were demonstrably false, others disputable. Statistics varied, as they always do. But the best that opponents of the Decadence thesis could produce was not a refutation, but arguments that the "pretended physical degeneration" of the French was relatively unimportant when compared to that of other Europeans.[16]

The issue was not one that a scientific approach could settle. The evidence, it seemed, lay all around. Among those who discussed such things, or listened to the discussion, the debasement and decrepitude of the society and of its values seemed beyond argument. The more so when it hit close to home: troubled sleep, troubled digestions, bad circulation, fatigue, and so on. Dr. de Fleury, describing *The Major Symptoms of Neurasthenia* (1901), could only deplore "this discouraged lassitude, this intellectual and physical impotence," that characterized it. Within a decade things had got worse. Neurasthenia, Dr. Grellety asserted, was the *maladie du siècle*. "Neurosis lies in wait for us and weighs more heavily all the time . . . Never has the monster made more victims, either because ancestral defects accumulate, or because the stimulants of our civilization, deadly for the majority, precipitate us into an idle and frightened debilitation." As Pasteur Vallery-Radot remembers, "it was fashionable in 1910 to delight in melancholy."[17] This may explain why a contemporary publicist, reviewing the professions a bright young man might choose, focused on medicine, where "he would find a flourishing career by dint of the anxieties, the neuroses, and the general disorders that reign among the higher social classes."[18]

The higher social classes, or at least their sensitive offspring, knew that tender nerves were evidence of refined sensibilities. Baudelaire had admired the nervousness of Edgar Allan Poe's writing and the nervous intensity of Wagner's music. Baudelaire's admirers venerated the poet's "glorious nervous complaint that would affect all sensitive souls after him"; they sought, like him, to "exasperate their ailment." Félicien Rops, the great etcher, claimed to work with his nerves. Maurice Rollinat's poems *Les Névroses* date from 1883. For Zola, the work of the Goncourt brothers was "a sort of vast neurosis"; and Taine "fits well in our society of nerves." Edmond de Goncourt considered Degas a neurotic. Huysmans' *Art Moderne* (1883) described Berthe Morisot as a nervous colorist, Guillemet as "a packet of nerves under control," and Gauguin as "a skin beneath which the nerves vibrate," while Mary Cassatt offers "a whirl of feminine nerves transposed into her paintings."[19]

This stress on nerves and search for sources of nervous energy went hand in hand with a sense of enervation, loss of enthusiasm, lassitude, *énervement d'esprit,* a general degradation of energy apparently confirmed by the theory of entropy, derived from the second law of thermodynamics. But not only energy seeped away. Health and strength did so too, witness France's miserable performance in the demographic stakes. From the 1880s to the First World War countless voices rose to warn that the country was in danger of disappearing. And, as its numbers shrank, those who were left rotted from the inside.

The hold of the Church had weakened, but the wages of sin, to be paid not in the next world but in this, were no less terrible for guilty and innocent alike. Oppressed, exploited, the people struck back through its womenfolk who transmitted syphilis to bourgeois males. Picked up in the street, the brothel, or the maid's room, their corruption would necessarily affect the "race." The belief that vice carries its own punishment through venereal disease that rots its carrier and his descendants joined with vulgarized Darwinism to suggest that, like families, societies and social groups were subject to degeneration. "The degeneration of the race," André Derain wrote to his friend Vlaminck, "pours out of our every pore . . . We are the mushrooms of ancient dunghills."[20]

In the French version offered by Antoine's avant-garde theater, Ibsen's *Ghosts* spoke no longer about the hereditary effects of syphilis but those of alcoholism.[21] But the vice or alcohol that sapped the ruling classes, depraved and brutalized the lower. If the race ran to seed, the result was further corruption: physical degeneration made for crime; *dégénérescence* and *criminalité* were linked in title after title, as in Zola's saga of the Rougon-Macquart clan. And before long a logical conclusion was drawn: modern man was going against the principle of the survival of the fittest. Some of the very institutions that an advanced society creates cause the decline of the race. Modern man looks after the weak, the backward, the degenerate. Public assistance, asylums, clinics, and hospitals keep people alive—idiots, imbeciles—to breed other degenerates whose survival contributes to the social disaster. Such counterselection should cease: criminals, degenerates, and mental defectives should be sterilized—freely or, if need be, "by fraternal pressure." Else, how can society be preserved?[22]

We shall see that crime played as large a part in the insecurities of the nineteenth century's end as in those of our own; and it figured just as largely in arguments about social deterioration. But the notion of decadence with which that of the fin de siècle is closely associated was not a burning concern of the vulgar classes, rather of the literate few. One theme of this book will be the discrepancy between the concern of the upper classes with decadence (moral, material, social) and the real improvements in living standards, intellectual equipment, and social opportunities that the popular masses were beginning to perceive, even sometimes to experience. An issue that evoked so much attention, even if in limited spheres, cannot be dismissed lightly. The troubles reflected real problems—if not always those on which they were blamed. A hundred years ago, just as today, society bucked and plunged. As living conditions improved for many, others found that life was becoming more difficult. Because the latter were often highly articulate, their views impressed their time—and our memories of it. Nevertheless, like fin de siècle, decadence was not an unambiguous term.

The notion of decadence (from the Latin *cadere*, to fall) is not peculiar to the turn of the nineteenth century with which it is often associated. It was not unknown to Plato, let alone to Gibbon, and it was seen as a present reality, at least by a few, well before the French Revolution. In April 1770 Voltaire addressed it in terms that would continue to be used through the next two centuries. It came, he wrote la Harpe, "through the ease with which we do things and the sloth that prevents our doing them well, through a surfeit of beauty and a taste for the bizarre. Do not expect to reestablish good taste. We are in every way in a time of the most horrible decadence." Facility, laziness, satiety, the disappearance of good taste, and leaning toward the bizarre: a fat boy's rebellion, expressed largely in terms of taste and manners appropriate to a tiny educated and leisured class, demonstrates "the most horrible decadence."

A sense that quality and standards of literary and artistic products had declined could broaden into the belief that the decline in these realms mirrored deeper and more significant corruption, an incoherent literature, art, or politics being the mere reflections of incoherent times. At the fin de siècle men like Charles Maurras, and to some extent Georges Sorel and Charles Péguy, moved from literary to social criticism: confused or rotten minds, they argued, created corrupt products. That was one side of the coin: description or denunciation of decline in certain realms, or in all.

The other side was a glorification of things or attitudes identified with decadence: the enervating artificialities of civilization and refinement; the gestures that demonstrate our triumph over nature and its constricting laws, or over no-less-constricting society and its conventional beliefs. That was the cult of decadence, another pessimism, and one increasingly articulated as the century progressed; but one which appropriated "decadence" for ends it believed or pretended to believe were positive. Corruption in this view, far from being destructive, was a redeeming and invigorating experience, a step toward transcending the stifling mediocrities of everyday convention.

*

Studies of decadence have tended to describe it as the tail end of Romanticism and sometimes to relate the decadents' plaintive tones to the sense of material disgrace following French military defeats in 1814–15 and 1870–71. Certainly the first generation (or tiny fraction of an age-group, for we must remember how few these people were) to show the characteristic symptoms bears out such arguments. Théophile Gautier was born in 1811, Alfred de Musset in 1810. In their twenties, the former articulated the notion, the latter expressed it in memorable terms. In his *Confession d'un enfant du siècle* (1836), Musset spoke about an anxious youth gazing upon a ruined world, living "on remnants as if the end of the world were near." Born too soon in a world too old for them, they found that "all that was is no more, all that is to be is not yet."

Musset's *Confession,* written in the wake of his abortive affair with George Sand, was less a comment on the world he saw than on his own frustration. Not that this makes such feelings less representative— quite the contrary—but it places them in the context of the activities of a rather restricted group in a position to indulge their emotions and to claim for personal, and sometimes fugitive, feelings a significance that was universal—that is, meaningful to people like them. Before writing the *Confession,* Musset had already expressed the gist of his frustration in plays like *Fantasio* (1834), whose young hero's chief complaint was boredom, the specific distemper of those whose leisure is greater than their means to fill it. One can argue that the notions and activities of decadence are closely related to the growth of a leisure class that was socioeconomically irresponsible, frustrated, and *disponible.* Meanwhile, the simple fact of boredom, which looms so large in the experience of nineteenth-century middle classes, must not be lost from sight. From Schopenhauer, for whom boredom is the pervasive terror of mankind, to Huysmans, whose heroes are bored to death (and who may himself have joined the Church because "spleen has no hold on pious souls" whose time is filled with their devotions), ennui is one leitmotif of an era when leisure burgeoned while ways of filling it remained rare. In April 1908 the young François Mauriac, just arrived in Paris from Bordeaux to conquer the literary field, notes: "Weariness, weariness . . . Give my ailment its only true name: boredom."[23]

A nineteenth-century education meant a classical education; and a classical education provided not only a sense of history—as important to the notion of decadence as the more recent experience of Napoleon's rise and fall—but also a wealth of literary references, not least in the realm of the erotic and the lewd. The July Monarchy (1830–1848) seems to have been a heyday of translations and retranslations from the Latin classics, especially those that turned about debauchery and decline. New or renewed versions of Suetonius, Petronius, and Juvenal came out in the 1830s, of Ovid and Horace, Catullus, Propertius, and Tibullus between 1840 and 1845. Amateurs of smutty stories had their play cut out, and moralizers their references brought to hand. This combination of moralism and fun found its symbolic culmination in Thomas Couture's "The Romans of the Decadence." This great painting, exhibited at the Salon of 1847 whose great success it was, had been acquired by the government a year before its completion. Its splendidly ostentatious display of anatomies and activities, both titillating and edifying, was taken as a denunciation of contemporary social decay and welcomed as powerful social criticism by Conservatives, Liberals, and Radicals alike—the best sort of meliorist social art.

The painting, according to the catalogue, was inspired by two verses from Juvenal's Sixth Satire: "We suffer today from the fatal results of a long peace, more damaging than war, / Luxury has rushed upon us and avenges the enslaved universe."[24] It was of course immediately recognized as applying to its own time as much as to the second century of the Christian era. In "Romans of the Decadence," Arsène Houssaye insisted in his memoirs, Couture "depicted the *French* of the Decadence. Can't you just see the French orgy?"[25]

This impression would be confirmed during the two decades of the Second Empire, intensified by the disillusionment that followed 1848. As Charles Maurras observed, universal suffrage has a fault: it is conservative. It conserves the good and the bad. After 1848, as after 1871, universal (or semiuniversal) suffrage did just that, furnishing excuses for dismay, then for cynicism, among its more sensitive supporters.

After 1848, even after 1851, France had taken a great step forward on the road to constitutional liberty; but constitutional (that is, formal) liberty was shown to have little to do with personal (that is, real) liberty, not only for the many, but for many of the more privileged few. Its most visible symbol at midcentury seemed to bear out Gibbon's view that corruption and constitutions went hand in hand. Material progress, painfully discomforting in some of its immediate manifestations, could also appear revoltingly vulgar. The revulsion against a materialism symbolized by greed and money can be properly estimated only by contrasting the dispendious and ostentatious standards of the brilliant second Empire Court and of its satellites ("I am invited to Compiègne," says a lady off for a weekend at court, "I sell a farm") with the enduring aristocratic distate for moneymaking activities.[26] In 1853 the correspondence of Gustave de Beaumont and Alexis de Tocqueville illustrates a gentleman's "extreme, not to say insurmountable, repugnance" for a job, even the directorship of a railway company: "Whoever takes it on, demeans himself." Half a century later the young Pauline de Broglie receives a check for 20 francs from a scholarly magazine that had just published an article on some excavations she had done: "I was struck with consternation! . . . Since I didn't go out alone, I couldn't cash it in a bank; on the other hand, to confess that I had received money was unthinkable! The check remained in my drawer." More explicitly still, a strong-minded country doctor in a fin de siècle novel detests going to his bank and "picking up with clean fingers the abominable metal, motive of every crime."[27]

Real or fictional, none of these characters were decadents. But their reservations reflected an ancient and familiar prejudice against earned money most prevalent among those who enjoy it, and against an overt interest in its acquisition most eloquently expressed by those who need it least. With more opportunities to satisfy greed and to pursue possessions, laments over declining moral values became louder. Those who pursued money most avidly and those who had so successfully pursued it that they could afford to relax agreed on its evils and bemoaned its hold. Balzac's Dr. Bianchon, a character in the Parisian society of *Cousine Bette* (1846), created by one of the most money-conscious novelists of his age, is clear about it: "Once, money wasn't everything . . . Today the perpetual division of estates forces everyone to think of himself from the age of twenty."

One realm where assets mattered was in art. As Flaubert told a friend, worrying about money overloaded the brain with base preoccupations. A private income meant "freedom from care for material things." Scorn for earning money, some source of unearned funds, provides the common characteristic of literary men and literary characters associated with decadence, from the days of Fantasio to those of Des Esseintes. They were, or aspired to be, *rentiers*.

No one has written the history of the rentier, but his figure is surely as crucial to the cultural history of the nineteenth century as that of the bourgeois to social and economic history. Both terms represent notions so broad as to cover a wide spectrum of individuals who could, in the former case, range from young men on an allowance, through gentry or middling folk living on income from investments, land, or urban real estate (often acquired by marriage or inheritance), to soldiers and civil servants retired on a pension, or professional and business people retired on their savings. Once the prerogative of a narrow social caste, the leisured life was becoming accessible to increasing numbers, especially to young men no longer bound to exhausting work. Spared the need to earn a living, the latter spent longer in the indeterminate and undemanding chrysalis stage of student life. Their energies, unfocused by necessity, could be dispersed in the pursuits of "decadence": thumbing their noses at their elders; setting the world to rights or scorning it; perpetuating poetry (less like hard work than prose); and pressing the search for a little fun to whatever excesses they could afford.

Hence the faddish aspect of the rising youth culture of the privileged; hence the striking discrepancy between the literary version of decadence and the material and political progress with which the affirmations or aspirations of decadence visibly clashed. Some of this has been attributed to a cascade of disenchantments: after 1815 and 1830, after 1848 and 1851, after 1871 and from the late 1880s on, old revolutions and new regimes failed to usher in the brave new world they had rashly promised. Such exposure to events in the making would inculcate a sharper sense of history which, in the occurrence, inclined to cynical views that lent themselves to pessimistic interpretation. The realm of politics, in any case, was too demanding to please the frivolous and too imperfect to satisfy purists disturbed by the ethical dilemmas raised by all nonfrivolous political enterprise. The dangers of failure and of soiling one's hands were enough to discour-

age most and drive them into the contempt for political action manifested by Flaubert, Baudelaire, and Valéry. From sanctuary "above the
mire where common mortals floundered," they looked upon what
Eugène Sue had described as "that terrible popular ocean whose tidal
wave could swallow up all of society." In September 1855 Jules de
Goncourt noted in his Journal: "Now that Europe contains no more
savages, the workers will do the job of revitalizing civilization in about
fifty more years. It will be called the Social Revolution."[28]

One other factor complicated this tale of energies unproductively
focused. As Tocqueville found in America, democratic social institutions suggest (and are suggested by) a belief in human perfectibility.
This was reflected not only in the Republican faith in education but in
the ideal, launched in the 1790s, that all careers were open to individual talent. It had turned out that social and economic mobility increased, quite moderately in fact but enough to mobilize an educated
or partially educated troop of aspirants to careers. The young who sang
the "Marseillaise" had learned to believe that

> Nous entrerons dans la carrière
> Quand nos aînés n'y seront plus.*

However, quite apart from the fact that their elders often took too
long to make way (a problem that grew worse with the century), many
aspirants lacked the financial or social capital to satisfy hankerings that
had grown a great deal more exigent than in the 1790s. The figurative
use of *disinheritance* (OED: "to deprive or dispose of an inheritance")
and *disinherited* by nineteenth-century writers such as Balzac and Re-
nan to mean disadvantaged, miserable, or deprived—a usage unrecog-
nized even in the latest edition of the *Oxford English Dictionary* (1961)
and seldom found in earlier French speech—tells something about the
importance of inheritance in the moral economy of France, but also
about post-Revolutionary views of what ordinary human beings could
expect. Like misery, mediocrity no longer was a state to be endured but
the deprivation of better things to which one was entitled.

The essentially static view of society and values, characteristic of a
traditional society that emphasized the adequate performance of duties

---

*A free translation might render this as: How gladly we'll take over / When our elders are
no more.

in the station to which one was born, had been abondoned along with any generally accepted ideal of perfection. Emile Durkheim would recognize that the chief problem of contemporary society was the erosion of moral consensus. Opinions of right, of virtue, of success, had become relative—no more than "opinions." But the notion of success remained, and in its social and material aspects it proved almost as difficult to attain for those on slender incomes and, worse, with dubious access to the crucial advantages of social relations, family background, and a solid socioeconomic base. Many novels trace the downward path of "uprooted" youths, educated beyond their station, whose ambitions outstripped their means. Many careers did so too. Attempts to resolve such discrepancies, when they did not lead to morose reconciliation to a mediocre fate, could lead to social criticism, social revolt, or a desperate rejection of all society.

All these were reinforced in the second half of the century by Darwinian notions of biological preselection. It was not simply that men were unequal, but that inequalities were hereditary. Not meritocracy but predetermined elitism traced the destinies of men and societies. So what was the use of effort? Degeneration lay in wait for the predestined, and the social problem confirmed the personal threat. Revulsion and fear: of masses "democratized and syphilitic,"[29] of democracy, assimilated to mediocrity, to mongrelization, and eventually to "degeneration."[30] They run into each other as through a set of communicating vessels.

The 1840s had seen the popularization of social studies that documented and dramatized widespread misery and its pathological causes: malady and crime. Like malformation and mortality, delinquency and madness became high priorities of public debate, the more challenging for being treated as contagious illnesses for which there had to be a cure. What Roger Williams calls the medical wellsprings of despair could affect more than his exceptional heroes. The guilt and anxiety they produced had social consequences, symbolized by the new professorial chairs set up to study insanity (1878) and the diseases of the nervous system (1882) and reaffirmed by the data which, beginning with the 1880s, compulsory primary schooling forced on the attention of the public.[31] Hordes of "abnormal" children, revealed by new surveys and statistics, testified to an abnormal society, about to be overwhelmed by its misfits, and condemned it as degenerate. Nor did the unexpected scale of physical disgrace revealed by the bustling activity in the realm of public education and hygiene affect the disinherited alone.

The confusion was natural and easy between that hysteria of the lower classes studied and publicized by Professor Charcot of the Faculty of Medicine—"la question palpitante du jour," a contemporary publicist called it[32]—and more fashionable neuroses. One reinforced the other. In 1880 an American medical man, Dr. George Miller Beard, had published a paper on "Nervous Exhaustion (neurasthenia)," which, supplemented by additional chapters on *American Nervousness* (New York, 1881), was soon translated into French (1882). This "nerve weakness," to which housewives and young adults appeared particularly prone, manifested itself in physical and mental lassitude, listlessness, lack of energy and enthusiasm, and a general sense of weariness. What the naive and the uninstructed might take for the familiar lineaments of boredom were being promoted into a neurosis appropriate to the better-off, and one whose symptoms admirably fit the pathology of the decade.

Psychic and physical deterioration alike were blamed on modern— especially urban—living. If society was a living body, social disorders were expressions of malady, connected with a pathology of moral and material corruption: the infection of bodies and minds as of water and air. Conscious of the disgrace surrounding them, city dwellers attributed it to the swift and highly visible changes wrought by industrial growth and speculative enterprise: "a kind of collective neurasthenia . . . A derangement of the collective consciousness."[33]

The new insistence on a higher quality of life, even for the poor, was evidence of improvement. But higher expectations at every level made deviance more depressing, better information made it more ominous, and traditional acceptance more difficult to maintain. Starting with major taints like syphilis and alcoholism, moving on to more general considerations like cleanliness and adequate housing, social solicitude (or anxiety) could lead to initiatives like the fin de siècle's pioneer crusades for garden cities, urban removal, allotments, or even noise abatement. The modern ecological tradition, the concern with pollution and its social fallout, taken up by the radical Left and Right at the century's turn, then by Fascism and National Socialism, only to be inherited by the New Left, the Liberals, and the Greens of the later twentieth century, found its wellsprings in the sensibilities of a "decadent" society apprehensive of "degeneration."

✳

Marx has told us with tautological logic that the dominant ideas of a time are the ideas of the dominant class. In this case, we seem to be talking about the most audible and available members of the dominant classes or, rather, their audible and available offspring, and about a phenomenon that would culminate during a crisis of the economic system (the final decades of the nineteenth century) and benefit from that crisis. Taking 1913 as 100, the French index of wholesale prices fell from 124 in 1873 to 71 in 1896. During the same period, securities with a variable income doubled in value, those with a fixed income (for example, state obligations) tripled in value.[34] So, while goods and services became cheaper, those citizens who could consume them without having to produce them found unusual opportunities to do what they did best: nothing in particular. It was a good case for saying that the economy supports culture like the rope that holds a hanged man. The golden age of decadence was also (and for good reason) the golden age of the rentier: an economic system in crisis, some of whose dominant groups could enjoy it even while they shared in the general mood of depression, showed a fastidious disrelish for bourgeois materialism, and denounced "the competition of greed."[35]

Those who did not choke and rear at rampant materialism, or at the social injustices it seemed to aggravate, were struck by another extremity. Thus, Hippolyte Taine's robust, Americanized, Frédéric-Thomas Graindorge, whose opinions began to appear in 1863 and who found the French overrefined, overcivilized, artificial and decadent: "Paris is an overheated hothouse, aromatic and tainted." Like Théophile Gautier, the Goncourts, Huysmans, and Henri Rochefort, who in 1866 brought out *Les Français de la décadence,* all equated modernity with artificiality and decadence. The latter was not all bad—or necessarily seen as bad; it was a matter of perspective. For this was also the time when the romantic view of genius as derangement of the senses was taken up by scientists like Dr. Joseph Moreau (de Tours): *De L'influence du physique sur le moral* (1830); *Les Facultés morales* (1836). For the next twenty years Moreau busied himself discussing the hereditary nature of degeneracy, a notion that inspired Zola's saga of the

Rougon-Macquarts and led off a long series of works equating genius and madness, such as Cesare Lombroso's *Genio e Follia* (1863), culminating in Max Nordau's *Entartung* (1892), soon translated into French (1893), which depicted "degenerates in literature, music, and painting" and proclaimed Paris the capital of "decadence."[36]

Once more the notion of decadence appears overdetermined: romantic inspirations, reinforced by social experience, merge with the angry disillusions of one more defeat. On September 4, 1870, watching the Republicans take over as the empire collapsed, Edmond de Goncourt had coined the word "mediocracy." A few months later, Jules Ferry wrote to this brother ruing the fate of a country condemned always to find its men inferior to the situations they must face: "There's the implacable sign, the chronic revelation of our decadence!"[37]

The depression of defeat was aggravated by unfavorable comparisons with the newly formed German Reich. Even after Waterloo, the French had continued to think of themselves as the leading representatives of world civilization. Now they felt reason to question this, as others did; and depressing news of their demographic evolution sharpened their doubts. Already inferior in number to the now-united Germans, French population was growing at one-third the German rate, and marriages were steadily declining (by 20 percent between 1872 and the end of that decade).[38] Taine, who had already unfavorably compared French torpor to the primitive vigor of Americans, had also stressed the positive (physical and psychological) factors of social and cultural development: race and environment.[39] He now set out to apply his principles in the study of *The Origins of Contemporary France* (1875–1894), which presented the Ancien Régime, Revolution, and Napoleon as the three agents of the country's "decomposition." Admitting that everything was in a bad way, Taine consoled his readers with the thought that it never had been better, yet people managed to live, some of them quite well. Taine's historical pessimism (for him Roman decadence began when Romulus had murdered Remus) was a bit too general for contemporary political argument, but it reflected a potential mood and affected significant literary and political figures: not only Emile Zola (whose *Thérèse Raquin* [1867] bore an epigraph culled from him), but Paul Bourget, Maurice Barrès, and Charles Maurras.

This is the background to the 1880s which saw the reincarnation of the Jeunes-France of the 1830s in a host of eccentric groups—Hydropaths, Hirsutes, Zutistes, Incohérents—whose names stood for a "programme" of marginality and mystification.[40] Finally, a few months before the appearance of the Symbolist Manifesto, there came the foundation of *Le Décadent* itself, announcing that "*Religion, moeurs, justice, tout décade* . . . Society disintegrates under the corrosive action of a delinquescent civilization . . . refinement of appetites, of sensations, of taste, of luxury, of pleasures; neurosis, hysteria, hypnotism, morphinomania, scientific skulduggery, extreme Schopenhauerism, these are the premonitory symptoms of social evolution."[41] *Le Décadent* never sold many copies, but the attention it evoked in intellectual circles led Edmond de Goncourt to complain that for days on end it provided the only paper he could find in lavatories.[42] Its bombast and extravagance were not very different from those of many predecessors—nor from some of its successors. They related in all cases to social impressions and persistent social realities—the latter best reflected in the *Décadent*'s creator, Anatole Baju (actually, Adrien Bajut, 1861–1903). Baju, the son of a well-off country miller, was a high school dropout who had found a job as a substitute teacher at Saint-Denis on the outskirts of Paris.

This prolongation of earlier trends was marked by the shift from adjective to noun, which could now be used not for pejorative description but to claim an artistic and intellectual identity hitherto unknown, or eschewed. From being decadent, one could now be *a* decadent. Littré's great Dictionary of the 1860s had ignored the word; the 1877 Supplement listed *décadent* as a neologism (it had been used in a parliamentary speech of 1874). By 1895, when the young Paul Valéry passed his examinations for a position in the Ministry of War, his examiner could damn Valéry's essay with a scribbled note: "This [candidate] is a vulgar decadent . . . no good to the Administration."[43]

Then as before the self-styled decadents reflected an abundance of dissenting passions: a reaction against the increasingly democratic society with its engulfing masses and their intellectual limitations; a horror of banality, "the bugbear of this fin de siècle"; a yearning for liberation, sometimes expressed in rebarbarization but more often against the surrounding "barbarians." The latter attitude would be most effectively voiced by a young man born only a few months after Baju, also in the provinces; and who, like Rastignac and Baju, though more successfully than the latter, pursued literary success in Paris. In 1888 Maurice Barrès published *Sous l'oeil des barbares,* the first novel of a trilogy that would express his "cult of the self" against "the vulgar, that is indeed all mankind, a few excepted." Within a decade the cultivation of the self, which recommended escape from stifling humanity, had led Barrès to a cult of the self-within-the-group defined by *la terre et les morts,* the organic foundations of inescapable affinities.

By this time the new Republic affirmed only in the latter 1870s had run into rough weather. The prosperity of the 1850s and 1860s was turning into the long depression whose hold would not slacken until shortly before the First World War. Wages, which had risen steadily between 1851 and 1880, fell or stagnated thereafter, as did most revenues, especially from land. The national investment policy devised as a remedy worked well enough in the long run; in the short run, and as the ripples of economic insecurity spread, it contributed to the general dissatisfaction. Publicized by a new popular press unleashed by the law of 1881 that freed it from government control to attain unheard-of circulation figures, political scandals and corruption illustrated the familiar theme of moral decadence. One reaction to this, extraordinarily influential in the long run, was the foundation of movements and the development of ideologies specifically designed to combat degeneration, decadence, and decline. Men like Charles Maurras and Georges Sorel, haunted by the decay of energy and will, of social and individual coherence, concluded that only action (and reorganization) could revitalize society, remoralize and restructure it. Their novel analyses of politics, directly inspired by their perception of decadence at work but also by procedures of demystification and desimplification characteristic of the age, would not go unnoticed by younger men like Lenin and Mussolini.

Between 1886 and 1888 another Frenchman, Pierre de Coubertin, had reacted to the fears of physical and moral degeneration by advocating the introduction in France of the gymnastic and athletic exercises and the sports on which the England and United States he admired seemed to thrive. His purpose, stated in a lecture in 1887, was "to harden a flabby, listless, confined youth, its body and its character."[44] In 1888 the Ligue Nationale de L'éducation Physique was founded; on its board were Marcelin Berthelot, Georges Clemenceau, Louis

Pasteur, and Jules Verne. In 1894 Léon Bourgeois, past minister in a number of governments and about to become prime minister (in 1895), told the 14th Congress of the Ligue Française de L'enseignement that "minds need hygienists and doctors as much as bodies do." A spate of legislation soon followed to reeducate delinquent, abandoned, or mentally retarded children. In 1895 Coubertin set up the International Olympic Committee, prelude to the first Olympic games of modern times held in Athens in 1896.

Barrès did not think much of games. In 1897 his *Déracinés* (The Uprooted) described the sources of national decadence and prescribed its cure in a new awareness of a commitment to the nation. One more trilogy (*Les Déracinés* was its first part) became *Le Roman de l'énergie nationale,* finished in 1902. The jejune search for titillation, the romantic quest for individual affirmation, the righteous concern for moral regeneration, the social concern for equity and welfare, the "scientific" interest in physical and psychic well-being (or decline) affecting all, seldom heretofore connected, were coming together. They would do so in the nationalist revival that preceded the First World War and that drew its justification from the dictionaries of decadence, decline, and degeneration.

2

Transgressions

---※---

The strongest evidence of ambient depravation and decay was what appeared to be a rising tide of profligacy and crime. The profligacy was most evident in the literary and fashionable circles of Paris, and may well have been largely limited to them. But these circles made the news, and attention focused on them. In the last third of the nineteenth century, news and newsworthiness began to matter more than before. A new kind of newspaper appeared, aimed at a mass circulation to be gained by attracting a new kind of reader with reporting that was lively, racy, piquant, poignant, stirring, appealing, and generally sensational. Begun in 1863, when no French daily printed more than 50,000 copies, the *Petit Journal,* which cost 5 cents when other dailies sold for two or four times as much, soon discovered that a good scandal or murder could boost sales vastly. The presidential crisis of late 1887 allowed it to pass the million mark, and in 1881 it launched a Sunday Supplement illustrated in color that found 800,000 buyers amost at once (a million by 1894). Such success spawned imitators: *Le Journal,* which reached half a million in 1900; *Le Matin,* printing three-quarters of a million in 1905; and, above all, the *Petit Parisien* which overtook the *Petit Journal* to sell about a million and a half by the eve of the First World War.

As the century drew to an end, the wider diffusion of the popular press provided a kind of echo chamber in which the slender voices of a minority were transformed into a clangorous hubbub, and the transgressions of a few bore witness to the depravity of the many. No previous era had been free from vice; but unseemly activities had tended to be carried on with discretion. Now small but vociferous cliques heeded Baudelaire's advice that "Vice is seductive; it should be depicted as seductive." Encouraged by the attention of the yellow press, they flaunted their frailties as exemplary and set out to persuade decent folk (and their increasingly censorious critics) that France was going to the dogs.

The initial evidence was found in drinking and smoking. As the century ended, France led the world in the consumption of alcohol and in the number of alcoholics, with the attendant train of madness, violence, and hereditary ills. Working-class families were just beginning to buy wine to drink with their meals. And while home consumption of wine increased, so did that of other alcohols, aperitifs, and absinthe, drunk only in taverns and cabarets whose numbers were soaring. In 1881 France counted 367,825 dram shops; in 1911, 482,704, an increase of 32 percent. In the twenty years after 1891, 3,300 new bistros opened every year—until there was one for every 82 of France's men, women, and children.[1]

One early-twentieth-century account indicates that some taverns let a patron drink all he wanted for a sou or two an hour: *à la soulée* or *à la rincée*.[2] Nor did drunkenness appear to harm one's reputation: consider the case of a gamekeeper tried in 1898 who, though given to drink, "was well-regarded in his village."[3] Drunkenness provided an excellent defense in court. Murders committed while under the influence drew light sentences—a year or two—or none at all. In 1892 one sot in his twenties, son and grandson of alcoholics, was acquitted of an old woman's murder. Though he was violent and often sozzled, all witnesses agreed as to his sterling character.[4] The foregoing suggests that drunkenness was class-related, ideally a prerogative of men but, above all, of the lower classes.

By 1900 notorious and public drunkenness was accepted as grounds for divorce.[5] Yet one wonders whether it was so regarded among the lower classes. The widely advertised substitutes that pharmacists touted—quina, kola, coca, coka-kola "wines"—were not within the means of poor folk, who stuck to traditional, and more potent, potions. When they could afford it (and sometimes when they could not), townsfolk and villagers consumed prodigious quantities. Small Breton communes accounted for hundreds of liters of pure alcohol in a few weeks of feasting or politicking. Less exceptionally, a survey of 1906 tells us that many Paris workmen drank over three liters of wine a day.[6]

That year, when the Assistance Publique (Poor-Law Administration) issued a poster warning against alcoholism, the Paris federation of wine and liquor merchants went to court demanding damages for the prejudice it caused their trade.[7] Besides, if liquor was bad, the alternatives were no better: women were becoming too fond of "debilitating café au lait," also known as *tue-femmes* (woman-killer) for its reputedly deadly effect on their constitutions.[8]

The medical profession denounced the inordinate consumption of tobacco, which some considered even worse than drink, responsible for physical degeneration, moral abasement, sterility, and excessive mortality. In 1876 Dr. H.-A. Depierris demonstrated in a massive study that smoking provokes loss of semen, a tendency to premature ejaculation, and can lead to impotence—not to mention hereditary effects difficult to imagine in the circumstances.[9]

Smoking meant mostly pipes and cigars. Snuff was being abandoned as old-fashioned and grubby, even while some misguided men were taking up still grubbier chewing, partly as an American innovation and partly as a more republican activity than smoking a pipe.[10] Depierris offered cautionary tales, such as the one about three children who died within twenty-four hours of having their heads rubbed with tobacco liniment to prevent ringworm and, rather more plausibly, of deaths following the use of tobacco in enemas. He added that the fine chestnut trees along the boulevards and in the Tuileries gardens had been withering since ill-bred people had taken to smoking beneath them.[11]

Social relations suffered too, since, as more men smoked, they avoided the company of women where they could not indulge the evil habit. Snuff had been accessible to women and, indeed, some were adopting the habit (with the excuse that it clears the head) as men abandoned it. But women who actively smoked belonged to the lower orders or to the criminal classes. So smoking among the upper and middle classes contributed to the segregation of the sexes and made the smoking-room a necessary part of a wealthy household's organization.[12] By the 1890s one begins to hear of respectable women smoking, but they were either eccentrics or feminists affirming the equality of the sexes. And by that time, men and women in search of dissolution had pushed on to drugs other than nicotine.

Midcentury medical men interested in delirium and hallucinations had experimented with hashish, cannabis, and other hallucinatory

Most cigarettes were rolled by the smoker; age apparently posed no problem.
This Ogé poster advertises a popular cigarette paper. Reproduced from Charles
Hiatt, *Picture Posters* (London, 1895).

drugs. Their writings had piqued the interest of artists and intellectuals on the lookout for new sensations. The 1870s had seen an increase in the use of drugs as they became more available. The war had left a few with a cordite habit, but chloral (prescribed after 1869 to help insomnia) proved far more popular, as did the barbiturates—veronal, gardenal—discovered by the German chemist Friedrich Bayer in 1863. But the great favorite of the epoch was opium, and its derivative, morphine.

Opium, according to Pierre Larousse, was "very frequently used in therapy," as a sedative, as a cure for insomnia, or to ameliorate a variety of pains, dysentery, and diarrhea. So was laudanum, the alcoholic tincture of opium that could be bought in the drugstore or prepared at home, and which was said to provide Clemenceau's favorite apéritif.[13] Larousse, though counseling prudence, included several recipes for opium use in potions, purges, injections, and poultices. Smoking opium had been introduced in the 1840s and 1850s by naval officers returning from the colonies. It seems to have been considered as much a sedative as an excitant, and a serious contemporary source attributed General Boulanger's indecisiveness, when power lay within his grasp, to his dependence on opium.[14] Morphine arrived with the 1870 war in which it had been used as a painkiller; many veterans had become addicted to it. Fashionable circles soon took it up; novelists wrote about it; society ladies got together to exchange injections; jewelers did a thriving trade in silver-gilt or gold-plated syringes; and Alexandre Dumas the younger declared, "Morphine is the absinthe of women." By 1892 it had become "a plague." Even Madame Strauss, widow of Georges Bizet and hostess of a famous salon, ended her life "a bit *morphinomane* to calm her stomach."[15]

There were other drugs, and other addicts. Some were old-fashioned "eaters of dreams" (hashish). Guy de Maupassant preferred ether and introduced its use into fashionable circles. Within a few years the refined were eating strawberries soaked in ether ("No swell dinner without a *Coupe-Jacques à l'éther*," decreed Jean Lorrain); and addicts might consume as much as half a liter a day (the ordinary dose was five to six grams) between swallows of water or taken with brandy. Was it also used in injections? *Le Gaulois* seemed to think so, and to dismiss morphine as old hat.[16] Laurent Tailhade, dedicated to morphine, was also fond of camphor; so in due course was Marcel Proust, who found camphor cigarettes good against asthma. Cocaine, developed in the 1880s, caught on almost at once. Vin Coca Mariani, a medicinal wine containing an infusion of coca leaves, became extremely popular. Or one could be more direct. In January 1886 young Dr. Sigmund Freud and a friend, invited to an evening party at Dr. Charcot's house, arrive: the friend very nervous at meeting the great man, "I very calm, thanks to a small dose of cocaine." The next day, another outing: white gloves, white tie, "a little cocaine to loosen my tongue."[17] Whereas Freud sought to relax, others hoped for an introduction to those uncertain realms and indefinable states of mind that also made for the success of spiritualism, hypnotism, and occultism. As Paul Valéry observed, the very pace of modernity was like an intoxication: one had to increase the dose or change poisons. The refined, dissatisfied with gross naturalism, pursued the stutterings of their souls to ever more ethereal and complex territory: mysticism, neo-Catholicism, a dilettantish quest for the effete and the bizarre that fed on missals, chasubles, ostensoria, lilies, Liberty silks, stained glass, anemia, virgins, waistline dresses, masses plain or black, and novels of J.-K. Huysmans.

The apparent collapse of established ideals, the reaction against scientific materialism and rational explanations, encouraged interest in mystery and the supernatural, appreciation of faith for the sake of faith—and of the sensations faith can spur: *credo quia impossibile*. The religion of the established Church was banal or discredited. Religious observance, when not a political choice, looked much like a social convention. Mysticism offered a means of being religious while being original—a Christian Decadence—and the opportunity to reconcile private obsessions with public ones. Among the scores of late-nineteenth-century esoterists and occultists listed in a recent dictionary of these cults, many were the offspring of atheist or agnostic fathers and pious Catholic mothers, many had been orphaned at an early age, suffered from fragile health (and visions), had dropped out of seminary or school.[18] Some tried to reconcile science and parascience in a grand philosophical synthesis, but most simply grasped the opportunity to reject (and transcend?) the fallen world around without conforming to one of its fallen institutions. So, when Huysmans tired of Naturalism ("this pigsty"), he turned to esotericism and satanism, hoping that he would find there "compensation for the disgusts of everyday life, for the garbage . . . the purulence of a repugnant epoch."[19]

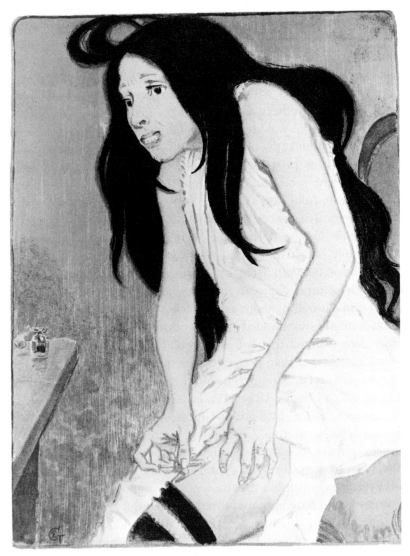

Eugène Grasset, *Morphineuse,* lithograph, about 1890. Grasset was interested in medieval imagery and in the work of the British Pre-Raphaelites.

This was in 1887, the year an annual literary survey noted the progress of mysticism as a mark of the fin de siècle. Within a few years it would be hailed as "the last word in neurosis." Max Nordau's *Degeneration* devoted a chapter to it, and respectable folk took exception to "pornographers, who with their eyes to heaven, preach the Holy Word." Faith, or rather vague religiosities that kept well away from established religion, was chic. *Le Mondain* welcomed the Rosicrucian painting exhibition at the Galerie Durand-Ruél as "a fashionable fin de siècle event in its mysticism." Ladies wore dresses "à la néophyte," gowns "martyre," and "fantom" skirts cut in Liberty silk. The Théatre de l'Art put on Jules Bois's *Les Noces de Sathan,* the Chat Noir cabaret offered mystical songs, Sarah Bernhardt recited the mystery of the Passion at the Cirque d'Hiver, the Salon bulged with Christian paintings, Anatole France recognized "A New Scripture: Jesus in Paris."[20]

The relation between Satan, mysticism, and Liberty silks may not be obvious. It becomes clearer in the light of the contemporary revulsion against arid naturalism and reason and also of the contemporary fascination with the unbounded possibilities of science, whose achievements demonstrated that "all is possible" and that "human powers [went] a lot farther than present experience suggests." These remarks occur in the preface to an eight-hundred-page Treatise of Metapsychics, in which Charles Richet, Professor at the Sorbonne, Member of the Institute, and a distinguished medical scientist, sought to place research into paranormal phenomena on the same plane as "other sciences: physics, botany, pathology."[21]

Belief in telekinesis or ectoplasm seems less naive, Richet pointed out, when you remember that bacteriology, radiology, telephones, or airplanes would have appeared utterly mad in the 1870s. In that context one could more easily believe that human understanding of the universe and of our power to operate in it was destined to extend to areas presently still "occult." Alfred Russel Wallace had defended the spiritist doctrines of Dr. M. H. Rivail, better known as Allan Kardec (1803–1869), whose tomb even today is the most visited of the many monuments in the Père Lachaise Cemetery. Sir William Crookes and Sir Oliver Lodge had helped to set up the British Society for Psychical Research. And Lodge joined Richet in writing a preface to another hefty study of *Metapsychical Phenomena* by one J. Maxwell, M.D., and "Deputy Attorney General to the Bordeaux Court of Appeal," which, among other wonders, discussed crystal ball gazing and indicated where the best balls might be found.[22]

If radioscopy works, why shouldn't crystal balls? If crystal balls, why not devil worship? In 1896 Anglo-Saxon readers were alerted to the latter by A. E. Waite's account of *Devil Worship in France* (designed to defend Freemasonry from association with it), whose preface recorded "as a matter of fact" that "the existence of modern diabolism has passed from the region of rumor into that of exhaustive and detailed statements."[23] In the previous decade the embittered struggle between the Catholic Church and its anticlerical foes—especially the well-organized and articulate Masons—had inspired a covey of works by ecclesiastics who identified their enemies with the devil, or with Antichrist. Then, in the middle 1890s, an inspired hoaxer, using the pen name Léo Taxil, built on this foundation to sell his colorful denunciations of a Masonic conspiracy to abolish the papacy, destroy Christianity, and install the reign of Antichrist. Conducted under the personal supervision of Lucifer from bases in Little Rock (Arkansas), Charleston (South Carolina), and Gibraltar, the conspiracy and the revelations about it captured the imagination of embattled Catholics all the way up to the Vatican, and of non-Catholics too, exciting tremendous interest until Taxil himself denounced it as a pure invention.[24] Harmless, though embarrassing to those he had gulled, Taxil's trickery had helped him to make money and provided his readers with sensations they apparently enjoyed. For us, it provides a glimpse of the extent to which suspension of disbelief could reach in those days, as in ours. If the science of man knew no limits, neither did his credulity.

Pursuit of the infinite could lead too far. In 1895 a young poet, Edouard Dubus, "intoxicated by occultism and narcotics," was found dead in a public lavatory on the place Maubert. In 1898 Barrès's friend Stanislas de Guaita, sorcerer and drug addict, died in more private circumstances.[25] By the turn of the century the popular press had developed an interest in drugs. In July 1903 the illustrated supplement of the *Petit Journal* devoted a color page to opium dens. In 1907 a naval officer was convicted of betraying military secrets to support his opium habit. In 1908 a young German painter hung himself in the artist settlement of the Bateau Lavoir, while under the influence of hashish. This shocked Picasso, who lived there, and his artist friends into suspending their experiments with drugs, though only for a while.

A government decree that same year attempted for the first time to regulate the sale of narcotics.[26] This was far from the end of drugs in France. Their vogue, however, must be seen in perspective. Early in the 1890s Maurice Talmeyr, author of a vapid but successful study, *Les Possédés de la morphine,* had visited a German clinic that treated addicts of every kind of drug—even eau de cologne. The doctor in charge was not very impressed by the situation in France where he found "few, very few," afflicted; he judged the country itself to be far behind Germany, England, or the United States. It may be that, as a fashionable playwright remembers about that time, a lot of people "whose naiveté would make us smile today, believed themselves to be incredibly perverse."[27]

Another aspect of this rather showy perversity appears in Talmeyr's story about a fashionable dinner party, where a slender young vicomte in dinner jacket proceeded to give himself an injection with an enameled syringe while at the table. The aristocratic figure turns out to be a young woman: "Madame de M, qui se piquait et courait les filles" (shoots up and chases tarts). Her act is a great success.[28] Addiction, homosexuality, and transvestism did not necessarily go together, but they moved in the same circles and were part of the same fin de siècle spirit.

Since the seventeenth century, women who wanted to wear masculine garb had to obtain official permission. It is not clear whether George Sand, Rosa Bonheur, or the wife of the explorer Marcel Dieulafoy, all of whom preferred to dress like men, obtained such permission; but they were regarded as exceptional eccentrics. In the country a woman landowner might be found looking over her estate or hunting in male dress, on horseback or on foot. And there were cases, and even more stories, notably during the Paris Commune of 1871, of mistresses disguised as males so that they might accompany their lovers.[29]

More often, though, working women disguised themselves, partly to escape the unwanted attentions of their workmates, but especially to earn men's pay—double that of women. Court records reveal a variety of women—a burnisher, a fireman, a printer, a violin player, and a shoplifter—who were transvestites for utilitarian ends. As one explained with perfect good sense, it allowed a woman more freedom in her trade. On application, the Prefect of Police permitted her to wear male attire.[30]

What was practical for some could be titillating to others, and by the 1890s a number of society women—especially intellectuals—and demimondaines as well, had taken to trousers. Enough for the Minister of the Interior to issue a circular (October 27, 1892) advising all prefectures that "the wear of masculine clothes by women is only tolerated for the purposes of velocipedic sport."[31] We shall recognize in due course the effects of the bicycle on women's dress. But by 1893 John Grand-Carteret had found occasion to depict a whole series of *bicycletteuses* wearing *culottes* on top of their chemise and pantaloons.[32] He soon would publish a whole book devoted to *La Femme en culotte*.

Many transvestites—male, like Major du Paty de Clam who played an ambiguous role in the Dreyfus Affair, or female, like Mathilde de Morny, or Nathalie Clifford Barney, or Rachilde, cofounder of the important literary *Mercure de France* and purveyor of some daring soft porn—were probably or notoriously homosexual.[33] Here too an age-old practice became, for some, a sort of social distinction. Working-class homosexuality had attracted little attention, even though court records attest to its existence to the extent that an "experienced witness" offering evidence at the Seine Assizes in 1903 spoke of the "classic" tendency of criminals to denounce their victims as pederasts.[34] Now, however, fashionable folk were taking it up. Around the Moulin Rouge it was well known that la Goulue (who also kept a pet goat) lived with the plump Môme Fromage. The fashionable Chat Noir offered recitals on the topic. *Fin de Siècle* introduced a regular feature, "Perverse Chronicles," signed by Sappho. This posed problems for the inexperienced, like the banker's wife who explained, "All remarkable women do it. But it's very difficult. One has to take lessons."[35] In May 1900 the Justice of the Peace of Antrain-sur-Couesnon (Ille-et-Vilaine) judged the case of two neighbors who quarreled over their cows. One had capped the exchange by calling the other a sodomite. "Given that the expression 'sodomite' implies obscene and shameful habits," read the judgment, it constitutes an insult; but "given that the man who proffered the insult didn't really know what it meant," it condemned the culprit to a 5-franc fine.[36]

"Sodomite" might be a mysterious insult in darkest Brittany. Along with other fashionable perversions, it had become a familiar notion among the up to date. André Germain, son of the founder of the Crédit Lyonnais and a bright young sodomite-about-town, asks off-handedly about Jean Lorrain, Symbolist and homosexual drug-addict:

In 1903 *L'Assiette au Beurre,* a satirical magazine, focused on
aesthetes: —You're coming to dinner tonight? We're having
Pierre Loti and his latest brother Yves . . .

"Was he coprophagous? Coprophagy was quite fashionable at the
time."[37] But it was probably the idea of coprophagy—as of much
else—that was in fashion. Perversion was à la mode because the fashionable of the fin de siècle were a weary lot: stomachs flagging, livers
worn, palates jaded, their dissipations were limper than their language,
relying on the mind for refinement and spice, seeking out the rare
morbid sensation but seldom able to taste it to the full. The spice of
vice lay in the showing off. When Liane de Pougy had a liaison, she
wrote a novel about it: *A Sapphic Idyll* (1901). Another lesbian, Renée
Vivien, actually translated Sappho; but also wrote and recited poems

—Oh! dear! That's all the exotic flowers you have?

about her lover—Nathalie Clifford Barney, as Jean Lorrain wrote essays about his taste for boys, ether, morphine, and hallucinations.

Occultists, satanists, sadists, masochists, homosexuals, simple erotic dilettantes, common or garden perverts, found that their activities satisfied a certain *nostalgie de la boue* (craving for slime), while bearing witness to a refined sensibility that ordinary sex would not satisfy. Yet the sexual games they played, or toyed with, and, even more, the drugs that opened access to the "artificial paradise" they sought were too expensive for more than the very few: *voluptés de luxe*. They plumbed the depths, perhaps, but did it in good company: the sort that knew how to be scandalous while avoiding scandal, and sufficiently different from the herd as to belong to a distinguished clan.

Sin and vice, at least in certain circles, were no longer forbidden fruit, but the measure of a civilization whose refinement was mirrored in its corruption. It is hard to know whether there were as many lesbians in life as there were in literature, as many sodomites as arrivistes conforming to the moment's fad, as many incestuous passions as there were lines dedicated to them, as many perverts as showoffs of vice. How many Sancho Panzas thought themselves Don Quixotes?

✳

Those who did not share in this pallidly lurid fun were impressed, or depressed, by it because it seemed to confirm the theme of fin de siècle decadence. More run-of-the-mill crimes did so too, and most commentators, as usual, found criminality to be dangerously on the rise. It had been rising since the end of the Second Empire, to a point where the rate of some common crimes had doubled and more. There were almost 30 percent more cases of homicide in 1890 than in 1865, 50 percent more cases of arson, 100 percent more robberies and thefts, over 200 percent more *coups et blessures* (assault and battery).[38] Juvenile delinquency was rampant, shoplifting commonplace (department stores made it easier), assault and murder seemed to be everywhere: poison, acid throwing (this was the heyday of vitriol), hammer blows, knives and hatchets of every kind, canes, cudgels, truncheons, garrotes, lassos, swordsticks, shotguns and revolvers (the latter something of a novelty, at least in the provinces, around the middle eighties). The police, as usual, were accused of being unable to cope. Too few, ill-trained, unpopular, they probably were. The opening twentieth century would see the foundation of private security services, much in demand especially in the worse policed and overburgled suburbs.[39]

Cities and their suburbs were growing, and criminality seemed to grow with them, its incidence shifting from country to town. By the 1880s, when two-thirds of France's population was still rural, well over half of all accused criminals were town dwellers.[40] During the 1880s and 1890s criminals were proportionately more than twice as numerous in towns as in the country; this meant that they attracted far more notice. Statistics are awkward to handle, since definitions of crimes and misdemeanors changed, and those who interpret the statistics do not always agree with each other. The most recent studies, however, suggest that delinquency and criminality rates in the years 1891–1895 were the highest in the century. They decreased for the few years following, to rise again sharply with the new century.[41] These oscillations are more apparent in retrospect than they were at the time. Insofar as they were noted then, they were attributed to economic fluctuations; and most modern scholars agree with this view. Yet even this is complicated by the contemporary advance of alcoholism, which seems to account for the way in which crimes of violence spurted ahead beginning in the 1880s, as did thefts.

Poverty and crime are certainly related, though we do not know to what extent, as proved by the occasional crime deliberately committed to obtain the prison's bed and board (as four unemployed men explained in November 1904 after getting themselves arrested to escape the hunger and cold outside). But need is also relative. Alcoholism is not the vice of unmitigated misery. And, if poverty does not lead to crime, poverty amid more apparent riches does so more easily. It is interesting to note that, while thefts of food and fuel (the characteristic crimes against poverty) varied little during the thirty years between 1870–71 and 1900–01, the nature of the stolen goods altered and their value rose, as more expensive meats (roasts, legs of mutton) and liquor were purloined instead of loaves of bread.[42]

Contemporaries probably paid little attention to this aspect of criminality. What they perceived was the apparent state of diminished order and security in which, as they saw it, laws were broken more often and enforced less. A high proportion of crimes and misdemeanors never came to trial; many of their perpetrators were never caught or, if they were, received light sentences from indulgent juries or a pardon from on high. However exaggerated, such views were close enough to common experience to inspire widespread belief. "The immunity of crimes," a well-known sociologist commented, "is always serious and demoralizing."[43] It prompted strong reactions, like that of the editorial writer who denounced the pressure of "hooligans" and the lightness of the sentences they received when caught and recommended self-defense, the teaching of martial arts, and, if need be, the use of guns against aggressors.[44]

Those who sought to make sense of these phenomena attributed them to the ongoing revolution of rising expectations ("the imitative diffusion of artificial and complicated appetites") and to the absence of common standards. It was banal to say that the poor were readier to claim their share of worldly goods because they no longer believed in otherworldly ones.[45] We cannot know how many had believed in heavenly rewards before, or with what strength such beliefs were held when they were held. More to the point, townsfolk of modest means, many of them immigrants from the countryside, no longer felt the pressure of the small societies they had left behind: constricting, repressive, but stable and orderly. Emancipated from restraints, they lived in a world where almost everything seemed possible, including transgression of the rules of others.

Cities excited greed by their show of wealth and their manifold temptations, unrepressed by the traditional controls that operate in smaller, tighter communities. Since the eighteenth century, urban crowding and discomforts had increasingly alerted the conscience of the rich to the deprivation of the poor. Democratic notions of government by the people, however far from realization, made it more difficult to dismiss the claims of deprived, diseased, and explosive masses to which suffrage vouchsafed a share of power. The organic view of society, which suggested that one morbid member could taint the whole body, intimated new concepts of social solidarity: vice and dereliction concerned more than the parties immediately involved. Crime was a social disease, moral pollution no more a private concern than the pollution of water or air that threatened the well-being of all. As the nineteenth century advanced, social disorders more and more came to be interpreted as maladies, connected with physical infections in a pathology of corruption that seemed as evident in urban decay as in the moral and physical degeneration of the lower classes and of their even more visible betters.

All of this was amplified by a popular press greedy for stirring news items, eager and able to magnify their import and their impact. Disorder, assault and battery, homicide, robbery, beggary, and sexual violence had been the norm of earlier ages. Now they were sensationalized, which made them even more frightening. Disagreements over crime rates continued to engage the attention of specialists, but the publicity given to crimes was greater than any they had received before. So, although crime rates varied, the sense of social anxiety and private insecurity that crime generated went only up.

Henri de Toulouse-Lautrec, *Au Pied de l'Echafaud* (Beneath the Scaffold), 1893. In France capital executions by Dr. Guillotin's humanitarian decapitating machine were conducted in public until 1939. In Paris they took place just outside the walls of La Roquette Prison, in the popular quarter situated between Bastille and the Père Lachaise Cemetery. They never failed to attract large crowds.

✳

Some of the most interesting aspects of crimes and of their records are not necessarily found in statistics. Even when the trends that statistics suggest prove significant—and none would argue that the economic recovery of the later nineties and its consequences did not matter— they are too general to open access to everyday life in its variety. Society is not like an orderly, well-integrated hive, but more like the colorful aggregate of a coral reef, with many formations and many kinds of creature living side by side. A look at some court proceedings reveals a different France from that which we see in Paris and from Paris: a France more varied, and closer to fundamentals, than literature and the literate can reveal.

In sundry parts of France at the fin de siècle many people still spoke no French or spoke it only with difficulty. In Brittany, Limousin, Provence, and even in the north, interpreters furnished a crucial service in the law courts at least until 1899.[46] In numerous cases where in- terpreters are not mentioned, accused and witnesses expressed them- selves in local dialect, and we are often told that they neither spoke nor understood French, or handled it so badly that the language was best avoided.[47] When in 1890 the Haute-Vienne Assizes, sitting in Limoges, heard an eighteen-year-old peasant girl bear witness in a murder trial, the court reporter found it worth noting that "she ex- presses herself in French." Ten years later when, in August 1900, an anarchist unsuccessfully attempted to murder the Shah of Persia, he was first taken for a foreigner. A few days later a Parisian noted in his diary: "The [would-be] assassin is unfortunately French: he is an Au- vergnat. His speech, which had been taken for a foreign idiom, is that of a small village in the Aveyron."[48]

Not only were regions distinguished by speech, but localities, trades, and social classes could be identified by costume and bearing as they had been in earlier times. Simple people rarely dressed like their bet- ters; when they did, it was because they wore their castoffs. Sartorial pretensions excited comment, as in the case of a young man appearing before the Eure Assizes in 1884: "he is only a day laborer, but he coolly wears a frock coat."[49] More often, though, accused or witness wears "the short jacket of the Maraichins" of Vendée, "the dress of a country- woman" or "the pretty little bonnet of the villages along the Loire," the yellow costume traditionally worn by the bakers of Périgueux, the distinctive garb of the peasants of Bresse or of "the comfortable farmers" of Mortagne, the traditional women's costumes which, in Savoy and parts of Brittany, varied from village to village. Masons had their particular costume, as did workmen in the Nord, let alone women in the Pyrenees or the Landes. Better-off peasants had their way of dressing, distinct from their poorer neighbors, and so had the women from Bergerac who tied their scarves in a particular way, the various peasants of Languedoc at least to 1895, and Brittany at least to 1899.

The poor also carried the stigmata of their class: they are described as puny, skinny, sunburnt, dark-complexioned; they look sinister, cunning, sly, shifty, vulgar, stupid, bestial. The better-born have lively eyes, a delicate figure, a fine dark beard, curly hair, and so on. Karl Baedeker, describing the street hawkers of Paris, finds their clean, tidy dress and polite manners worth mentioning because they are "devoid of the squalor and ruffianism that characterize their class." In the same way, when a Breton peasant looks better than he should, the note of surprise is clear: "Born in the region of Léon, the accused looks almost grand in his somber-colored costume." (The Finistère Assizes would condemn him to death in November 1899.)[50]

Fin de siècle France was not only a country where folk could still be identified, as they had been in olden days, by bearing, speech, or garb. While new cults and superstitions sprang up in the cities, and, in Montmartre, Max Jacob prospered as fortune-teller, astrologer, palmist, seer, and manufacturer of lucky charms much in demand by friends like Pablo Picasso and the couturier Paul Poiret, old-fashioned sorcery continued rife in the countryside.[51] Into the twentieth century we come across village witches of both sexes, praised for their services or assaulted and even murdered by those who blamed them for the spells they cast. As late as 1904 the Berry Assizes acquitted a mason from Saint-Georges-sur-Moulon (Cher) who killed a sorcerer who "persecuted" him.[52] By then, however, people had begun to turn to new kinds of witchcraft, such as that which doctors practiced, and to new kinds of amulets and charms. Whereas not so long before they had put their faith in rings like that of Saint Hubert, which preserved from rabies, or those made of quartz or cornaline that cured the wearer's sorrows, they now were buying magnetic rings to guard against migraine headaches and electro-voltaic ones to protect them from rheumatic pains.

No charm could ward off the threat of other human beings. For those who dwelt in isolated places, wandering beggars, above and beyond familiar local ones, were a constant pest and a potential threat. If not satisfied, they might cast evil spells, damage orchards or crops, maim cattle, set fire to ricks or buildings, even cause physical harm. Empty houses of course were fair game. Then as now, not a day passed without some country home being robbed; and scarcely a week without a book or article that addressed the question.

Between the 1870s and the 1890s arrests for vagrancy almost doubled, overworking the courts and crowding the prisons. While the Minister of Justice cautioned magistrates against a zeal that was clogging up the machinery of repression, the local authorities complained about a laxness of repression that left their charges at the mercy of threatening beggars. Around 1899 the Société d'Agriculture evaluated the number of beggars as about four hundred thousand—over one percent of the country's population—contributing to a general sense of insecurity and of the inability to find a remedy.[53] Only the First World War would resorb these wandering masses and, presumably by killing off a large proportion of them, ensure that their numbers never again reached the heights of those days.

But vagrants were not as threatening as one's neighbors; nor, as we shall see, were the latter as deadly as one's kin. The fabled solidarity of small communities operates on two levels: hostility toward outsiders, and interdependence on services mutually rendered. The second is crucial. Neighbors need to have recourse to each other, and often they cannot afford not to cooperate. That does not necessarily mean they do it cheerfully. Mutual aid is based on self-regard that is only sometimes enlightened. Thus, a country magistrate points out that, if attacked, it is useless to try to alert one's neighbors by shouting for their help. Instead, shout "Fire!" and concern for their own safety will bring them out.[54] Yet neighborliness, which makes for mutual adjustment and tolerance at best, often amounted to friction and hatred. Court records bulge with cases of arson, assault, and murder committed by farm servants against their employers, or neighbor against neighbor. Also of course against animals which, being more helpless than most human beings, are better game. This may be why an English resident of France was struck by the proclivity of countrymen for poisoning their neighbors' cats and shooting strays. "I don't shoot for pleasure," a peasant in the Landes explained, "It's to annoy my neighbor."[55]

Still, there could be pleasure in it too, as when young men vied with each other on feast days or at fairs to be the first to kill with a well-aimed stone a tethered goat or a fowl hung upside down, or enjoyed watching the act of *hommes ratiers* who, for a few pennies, bit rats to death. (The prefect of Dordogne prohibited these exhibitions in 1913.)[56] Occasionally things went wrong. In 1912 a wealthy land-owner in the southwest doused his uncle's dog with turpentine and set her on fire amid a circle of interested onlookers: two navvies, one carter, and two children. The desperate animal set fire to one of the young observers, a six-year-old who died of her burns; so, presumably, did the dog. The landowner and his carter were sentenced to two months in prison for involuntary homicide and a fifteen-franc fine for breach of the Gramont Law prohibiting cruelty to animals.[57]

As a report of 1895 described a Norman village, its population was uncouth, churlish, and brutal. One might add that it was also desper-ately deprived, not least on the emotional plane. Consider the case of the twelve-year-old shepherd boy convicted of butchering his employ-er's five-year-old son with a clog (which broke in use) and a blunt knife blade that lacked a handle. The murderer was jealous of the affection shown his victim by a young servant girl to whom he had become attached. Or thirteen-year-old Blanche Deschamps, employed as a weaver in a silk factory at Izeron (Isère), about ten miles from her village home. Terrified of her parents' wrath because, instead of saving all her pay to bring home, she had spent part of it to buy coffee and sugar, she murdered a girl from her village, with whom she shared a bed in the factory dormitory, to steal the money from her purse.[58]

Adult violence reflects the same futility and despair: quarrels over the use of a pathway or a pan, over stray fowl or cattle, over drinks, or a bill, or about a simple song, led to bloodshed and death. When knives, cudgels, or hatchets were not handy, clogs were used, or whatever else came to hand. In 1898 at Vert, in what is now the Yvelines, not far from Paris, one woman battered another woman to death with a frying pan, then set her on fire. In several cases the victims died of bites.[59] A striking aspect of such fights is how often the hammer or stick, um-brella or knife or rifle or clog, spade or pitchfork, broke under the force of the blows. Often those who incapacitated a victim in some trivial tussle went on battering it till it was dead, and sometimes even after-ward, as if the valve of exasperation once opened could not be closed again. Then, the explosion over, they seldom attempted to escape arrest: "It had to happen." As when a wine-grower of the Meuse pitched his three-year-old daughter into the fire, banged her on the ground, finished her off with his fists, then threw her into the tub of dirty washing and crawled into his bed to wait for the gendarmes to pick him up.[60]

Home is always the place where exasperation builds up to its greatest pressure, where long-repressed grudges and frictions most often explode in blows and bloodshed. Over and over one comes across what, in an 1889 case of fratricide, the *Gazette des Tribunaux* describes as "arguments about self-interest and money that divide the families . . . hence the secret hatreds that develop and grow." A lurid illustration of this, among many, appears in the case of Armand Lacoste who killed his mother and threw her in the well because she "favored" his elder brother. The trial revealed a long wake of rancors and threats, beatings, fights, an atmosphere redolent with fear. Yet mother, brothers, and the younger brother's wife went on living together: a certain recipe for trouble, but probably unavoidable.[61]

Only too often husbands maltreat wives and children; couples join to torture their own offspring (in one case because the daughter reminded them of her grandmother); wives murder husbands; stepmothers do away with cumbersome stepchildren (in one case by urging a little boy to look into the well, then heaving him in by his feet); maltreated stepdaughters turn on their tormentors, as when a fourteen-year-old batters her stepmother to death with a stake; she was acquitted.[62] Patricide is no rarer than fratricide, though I have come across only two cases of lads so naive as to kill their fathers in order to gain exemption from military service as the eldest son of a widow.[63] Infanticide, though rife, was not necessarily condemned. In 1890 a poor woman heavy with her eighth child (five more had died in infancy) was acquitted of poisoning her three-month-old: "Good thing he's dead. I'm glad to be rid of him. There'll always be plenty more."[64] In 1901 Parliament, sturdily opposed to abolishing the death penalty, heeded the tendency of juries to pardon crimes of this sort and abrogated the death penalty for infanticide.

We may regard such doings as unexceptional, as they might be today. Yet harshness to one's fellows continued more intensely than we can easily imagine, while harshness to oneself remained the norm. The most common cause of family ferocity was the resentment of useless mouths. Notaries, especially country ones, warned old people against making over their property before death. But some could not help doing so, others had no property as a fragile defense, and still others were hastened to their end by covetous heirs. Over and over one hears the same refrain: "My father and mother are old enough; they have to be killed." The daughter-in-law is murdered because "she's sickly and no help." The old husband is beaten to death: "What would we do with the old man if he were still alive at harvest time?" The mother-in-law is thrown into the well to put an end to annual payments of twenty francs and a bushel of grain. The old father is battered to death with a pestle, a flail, and a rake by his wife, who had long detested him, and his daughter, who wants to avoid the cost of his upkeep.[65]

Quite frequently the victims accept the point of view and share the feeling that a useless—that is, unproductive—oldster is better, and certainly better off, dead. A realistic novel about village life describes an oldster condemned to end his years in his married daughter's house: knocked about, insulted, fed like the pigs on rotten potatoes and on leavings, no bed, no tobacco. "You cost me enough as it is. Go stick some cowshit up your nose!" "Wouldn't I be better off dead?" he asks the village priest. When he is found hanging in the stable (men hanged, women drowned themselves), his children search for his hidden hoard and quarrel and fight when they fail to find it. The village doctor and the schoolteacher agree that this goes on all around: "These peasants are still brutes. A good thing that compulsory schooling has been voted!"[66]

Most French were peasants at the time. And how much better were those who were not? If household conflict and family violence were common, family warfare and its casualties were private affairs, the family name was precious, and for its sake even murder was best concealed. In 1893 a mortally wounded old woman refused to name her murderer: "By thus persisting in concealing the murderer," the examining magistrate commented, "the Widow Tanguy seemed to obey a grave concern. She was determined not to name him for serious family reasons. In effect, was not Jean Combot her son's brother-in-law, and wouldn't his conviction shed shame and dishonor on his kindred?" The following year an old farmer was beaten to death by his son and daughter-in-law who had long tormented him to take over the farm. As he lay dying, "the wretched man tried to avoid answering questions so as not to accuse his children. He died in the night." Several such cases remind us that much remains concealed that we can only guess at, and that the ostentatious unconventionalities which mark the urban fin de siècle were far from popular norms.[67]

It is not my intention to suggest that crimes of the sort detailed above were highly representative, or that family relations were uniformly bad. But if the Republic's schools insisted so much on civilized behavior and on the respect due elders, it may well have been because these did not come naturally. Nor should this be surprising, when poor people—in those days, most people—were hardened by trouble and need, insecurity and fear, their feelings often shriveled and their reasoning capacity limited: "working machines rather than thinking beings," as one syndicalist wrote another in 1905.[68] Deprivation could lead to depravation: not, by the century's end, a very new conclusion, but one that spurred more effective efforts to diminish the former. If the expectation to see delinquency wane along with misery proved false, the sum total of suffering and want declined, and that was a clear profit.

Not all the cruelty and crime were the result of want. Much of both stemmed from envy, greed, or just plain nastiness. But the social laws that came quite late to twentieth-century France—old-age pensions, health insurance, and so on—would help to help the helpless whom a ruthless society, still red in tooth and claw at the century's turn, left terribly exposed.

In the perspective of history what deserves explanation is not the rigor of the times or their violence, but the attempts made to temper both. The nineteenth-century obsession with cruelty and violence, its growing revulsion toward them, the refusal of nineteenth-century men and women to accept what earlier ages easily took for granted, bore witness to a sensibility more finely honed; to gentler, more compassionate standards, less harsh than in the past and less ready to accept harsh treatment of others. Such standards had to trickle from the sensitive few to the hardened many, to be inculcated by schools and literature, to be enforced in court and in the street, before they became anything but eccentric. Before one can instill rules of social conduct there has to be agreement upon what these are, and such agreement was still being forged. Nor did it last very long. Just long enough to leave the later twentieth century with the nostalgic delusion of a vanished norm, when what it thinks it remembers was a brief exception.

3

How They Lived

---※---

Space is something that man conceives only imperfectly, especially when his perception of it is slender. The notion of distance is relative: the familiar is closer than the dimly perceived faraway. In 1891, when Thomas Hardy published *Tess of the d'Urbervilles,* he commented that, "to persons of limited spheres, miles are as geographical degrees, parishes as counties, counties as provinces and kingdoms." Fourteen years later, in H. G. Wells's *Kipps* (1905), the people of Folkestone still look upon London as a far-off country. The same was then true of France, where an old Norman woman, whose son had died during military service soon after 1900, explained that "he was serving in Beauce," and, remembers Jean Follain, "for her the Beauce was as mysterious as India."[1]

From this point of view, despite half a century of railroads, fin de siècle France was still a congeries of idiosyncratic neighborhoods, as far away from each other as mutual ignorance could make them, and even farther from the capital, which many perceived as something out of a fairy tale rather than a modern metropolis of stone and brick and mortar. That was especially true of those rural parishes where two-thirds of the French still lived in 1891. In the last year of the nineteenth century hardly more than 35 percent of the country's population could be found in towns of more than 5,000 inhabitants;[2] and we shall see how little most of these conformed to our present idea of an urban center. The ones that came closest, great cities like Lyons, Marseilles, and Rouen, were few and, in the old-world optic still obtaining, far apart. Not setting the general temper, not representative of the national atmosphere, but standing out as exceptions, envied by some, irrelevant to most.

Then there was Paris, which, a country magistrate observed, "throned royally" over the rest. "You cannot imagine," wrote young Paul Valéry from Montpellier to Pierre Louÿs in Paris, "what a few pages . . . from Paris mean, from Paris, which is alive and intelligent"; Montpellier quite evidently was neither. Paris was a continual feast, an "electrical machine" that instilled nervousness and fire; and it was an emancipation, a dream, two young girls from Limoges reported back. What charmed them specially was "that no one spied upon anyone."[3]

The contrast between metropolis and provinces, what the English long called "the country," went back a long way and was not limited to France. But nowhere else was the contrast as acute, or felt as keenly, as in France. The very term "la province" echoes with negative connotations. True human activity was concentrated in Paris. "Provincials and peasants," Edmond de Goncourt noted in 1881, were simply "natural history." That peasants were uncivilized boors went without saying, but few could bear not repeating it. J.-K. Huysmans expressed himself pungently. A cavalry officer billeted in the mining country of the Nord compared it to Africa: "you might think yourself in a black village." A medical man reporting from the Vendée in 1911 found it still only partly civilized. An urbane magistrate who admired city workers ("frank, generous, vital") dismissed peasants as savage brutes. Anarchists and Socialists seem to have shared these prejudices, which reflected not class but place of residence.[4] The war between country and town, the mutual dislike and suspicion townies and countrymen entertained for each other, continued vigorously into the 1950s and, some would argue, continues still.

Less obvious, in some ways less expected, was the contempt big-city folk of every social stripe, especially Parisians, felt for the lesser towns. Amiens, in Huysmans's *Les Soeurs Vatard* (1879), is as "amusing as a prison gate." Jacques Chardonne's Barbezieux is described as fixed in a stifling gloom. A 1901 guide to over three hundred French garrison towns offers confirming glimpses. At Saint-Dié (Vosges) "diversions are rare. In this respect Saint-Dié is like all small provincial towns." At Macon the main streets, only the main streets, are paved—but ill paved with shingle from the Saône. Worse, there are so few people to see that one sees the same faces all the time. Roanne "offers nothing of interest.

The society of Roanne has few diversions, parties are rare, social relations slack." At Belley, where no street is paved, there is a little promenade where the band plays on Sundays; but only market days introduce a little life. At Issoudun, the chief subprefecture of the Indre, a muddy, ill-built town, there are practically no diversions and social relations are nonexistent. The inhabitants appear indifferent or hostile to strangers. The short boulevard is hardly frequented, but there is a pretty little public garden where the band of the 68th Infantry Regiment plays twice a week. When, as at Le Blanc, the place is "quite pleasant and the inhabitants affable," communications are difficult and butchers offer beef only once a week. In late-nineteenth-century Abbeville (pop. 20,000), a contemporary remembers the compartmentation of social life: nobles, grands bourgeois, professionals, tradesmen, each keeping to themselves, avoiding their neighbors or greeting them in terms of a civility strictly measured to fit their station. "Understandably," most young people dreamed of getting away.[5]

Larger centers shared in the general dreariness. Most reportedly had narrow, winding, awkward streets, so difficult to negotiate that the last sedan chairs did not disappear until the late 1880s. That was when, really about the turn of the century, urban improvements straightened the streets, razed the decrepit old houses and the constricting city walls, put up new buildings, and provided new means of public transport which both pleased and offended: "the victory of Jewish bazaars over old timber dwellings," grumbles a man from Bourges.[6] It was not Jewish bazaars but the new municipal passion for clearing out the old—historical monuments and tumbledown hovels alike—that spurred parliament to legislate the preservation of monuments. But many hovels survived. Raymond Abellio, born in 1907 into a modest family only one generation removed from the land, remembers the family home in a suburb of Toulouse: two rooms for his parents and grandparents, two for his father's sister and her husband. No electricity, no gas, just candles and petrol lamps; no running water, but a public fountain a hundred yards away; no windows, only the door to let in light and air. In their apartment the fire burned in the hearth all year round, as much for light as for cooking. The uncle and aunt had a small charcoal stove, "symbol of comfort, even of luxury."[7]

Yet these meager boroughs, where during hard winters, like that of 1879, wolves still roamed the streets, were centers of activity, disseminating goods, education, information. They housed not just the market and the courthouse, the post office, telegraph, and sometimes the barracks, but schools, theaters, bookshops, through which the culture, fashions, ideas, and politics of the metropolis reached the rest of France. Seen from the perspective of Paris, provincials were clods indistinguishable from the general ruck that found its place only in natural history. Seen from the grass roots, the little town was the representative of the modern world, urban and urbane; its inhabitants were city folk, who on Sundays went "to drink a glass of milk on some farm . . . far away . . . in the countryside . . . five hundred yards from the little town."[8] That was where one could find paved streets, though not too many and stretching not too far, and sometimes even a sidewalk. That was where the first street lights were to be admired, though only in the center, for a few hours on moonless nights during the winter months.

The nineteenth century was the age of the conquest of darkness; but many lesser urban centers acceded to light that was better than primitive at the fin de siècle or later. Facilities in the home remained scant. Most houses were badly built, and the wind passed round and under ill-fitting doors and windows. Not everybody enjoyed even candles, let alone lamps. For poor people the hearth was often the only source of heat and light. Even the better-off had little heat. Elizabeth de Clermont-Tonnerre recalls that heating in her father's house was turned off in March.[9] Poorer people had nothing to turn off. They might buy a pound of coal (six lumps) for 10 centimes (2 sous) and use it while it lasted to warm themselves at the same time as the soup. It is not surprising to find the less well-off wearing as many layers as they could to keep out the cold, which must have been as fierce indoors as in the open. Court records reveal the tendency to multiply shirts, smocks, skirts, anything one could find. A case of attempted fratricide judged in 1884, where the knife was deflected by five layers of clothing, does not appear exceptional.[10] But people seem to have taken cold philosophically. Water was more difficult to do without than heat, and the problems of getting water, then disposing of it, presented a major challenge for every urban center into the twentieth century.

In 1886 the Prefecture of the Seine, which essentially managed the Paris area, forced the owner of a building to install a water conduit. The water of the neighboring well was not safe, the nearest public

In 1907 *L'Assiette au Beurre* celebrated the spread of modern
comforts into the suburbs of Paris:
—So you've left Saint-Ouen for Ivry?
—Yes, it's more distinguished round here and, besides, we've got
gas lights.

fountain was a long way off, public sanitation called for a standpipe in
the building.[11] Polluted wells and ill-accessible fountains were nothing
new; public sanitation was, as, even more so, were the changes being
imposed in its name. "The day will come," an architect had written
wistfully only a few years before, "when 'waste' of water will become
synonymous with cleanliness and hygiene. [Before this happens, how-
ever] hygienic 'waste' will have to become a habit."[12] By the 1890s,
though "waste" was still avoided, water consumption had risen. But

the water piped to Paris homes often came directly from the polluted Seine. Given its evil reputation, "the wise housewife sends her maid to bring a provision of water from the fountain." Comfort and hygiene, an article about Paris water declared, were modern notions, scarcely familiar in 1892.[13]

If these conditions obtained in the capital, the situation elsewhere is easy to imagine. The prefect of a Breton department described the contaminated wells and streams from which everyone went on drinking.[14] What else were they to do, when all traditional sources of household and of drinking water were heavily polluted? Rivers that served as sewers also carried the soapy water of washhouses and the industrial waste of the factories along their shores. Wells were tainted by seepage from middens, cesspools, graveyards. Growing awareness of this—not unconnected with the stink that proclaimed some streams to be more of an open sewer than the city streets—turned the fin de siècle into the age of public fountains.[15] Paris was more fortunate than most places. In 1872 the English philanthropist Sir Richard Wallace had endowed it with one hundred fountains that bubbled with drinking water and whose graceful bronze design by Charles Lebourg can still be seen. But many country towns waited years for one. Some never had more than one. And since few houses, even in larger towns, boasted running water on the premises, large numbers of women and maids crowded round the fountain as early as four A.M. to get a bit of the rare commodity it dispensed. They often had to walk three or even five hundred yards with their jars and buckets. A marble plaque in the town hall of Villefranche-de-Rouergue reads: "In grateful homage to the Republican Municipal Council elected in 1884, which brought drinking water to the town. Work began in 1887." That achievement may not be unrelated to the fact that the first Republican to represent an area traditionally "white" in politics would be elected in 1898.[16]

The water problem preoccupied every municipal council, whatever its hue. The faster a town grew, the greater its trials. Nice, Marseilles, fell steadily behind the needs of their inhabitants. Saint-Etienne did not get a stable supply until 1949. By the twentieth century half the households in Angers subscribed to the water service, but this did not extend to the suburbs which, like other neighboring communes, got it only after the First World War. In Indre-et-Loire, upriver from Angers, only 8 percent of the communes enjoyed drinking water in 1950, and fin de siècle Tours was often short of it. Nor were the viaducts and pipes that brought water from afar always safe. Typically, at Besançon, which piped its drinking water from the Arcier River (its own stream, the Doubs, being much too dirty), contaminated waters were probably responsible for typhoid epidemics in 1886, 1893–94, 1901–02. The widespread suspicion of water from tap, fountain, or well would encourage all who could afford it to drink safely bottled mineral water; it would justify another French tradition: the low regard in which H_2O is held.[17]

The disposal of used waters presented problems even more obstinate than their obtention. Practically to the end of the century, great cities like Rouen, Bordeaux, or Rennes, as well as lesser ones, saw their household garbage, sewage, and kitchen waste discarded in the gutters, chamberpots emptied in alleyway or street, the contents of cesspits removed in open tipcarts. Sewers and drains, where they existed, emptied into the local stream. In 1892 the national Commission on Public Hygiene commented on conditions in Rodez, Millau, and the Aveyron Valley, hard hit by typhoid fever: "The dirt of the people, of the homes, and of the water has propagated the [typhoid]." It noted the filthy streets, "where many inhabitants empty chamberpots and kitchen waste," the pigs in possession of the center of town, the river a running sewer, the village streets vast heaps of manure, the fountains and wells full of organic matter. No wonder that typhoid fever remained endemic in the noble episcopal city of Rodez![18]

The situation was complicated by the fact that many towns continued partly rural. In 1889 a Pyrenean subprefecture such as Oloron counted 16 percent of its electorate as farmers and farm laborers. But even urban centers like Toulouse retained a strong rural imprint, and everywhere townfolk kept poultry and pigs, goats and cows, close to the house. Beehives were commonplace, despite desultory municipal ordinances.[19] Butchers slaughtered cattle in or outside their shops, so that the gutters ran with blood; offal and even carcasses might be left in the roadway for dogs to despatch.[20] Municipal slaughterhouses were slow in coming, even in larger towns like Besançon, and slower in lesser ones like Langres, where one finally opened in 1901. Vivonne, whose council talked about building a slaughterhouse in the 1890s, actually built one in the 1930s. So, while the Paris police sought to prevent dogs from defecating on the sidewalk (it has given up!), many

provincials continued to slaughter their pigs in the backyard and sometimes in the street, where alive they had benefited from the general filth
and their remains contributed to it.[21]

The travelers who expressed regret at the passing of medieval streets
and structures gave little thought to the conjunction between the pes-
tiferous and the picturesque. Many things were performed in the
street, as they had been for centuries, including the natural functions of
men and beasts. In Finistère the prefect had to admit that people
"satisfied their needs pretty much everywhere." There and elsewhere
dung might well be swept from the street to feed the green plants in
the home; but there would be much left over, and sanitation left a lot
to be desired. Direct-to-sewer drainage (the famous *tout-à-l'égout*) was
much discussed, but little developed until after the First World War,
except in Paris. There the prefect of 1884, Eugène Poubelle, had already prohibited the traditional discarding of refuse in the street and
required the use of newfangled garbage cans which rag- and bone-
pickers, fearful for their trade, maliciously named after him. The name
stuck, and French garbage cans are still known as *poubelles,* just as
French *pissotières* were long known as *rambuteaux,* after the name of
their inventor—also a prefect. But when in 1894 another Prefect of the
Seine decided to introduce direct-to-sewer drainage, the bitter legal
battle dragged on into the twentieth century.[22] By 1903 only one Paris
house in ten had been connected to the system.

If one considers the scarceness of water and of facilities for its evacu-
ation, it is not surprising that washing was rare and bathing rarer.
Clean linen long remained an exceptional luxury, even among the
middle classes.[23] Better-off buildings enjoyed a single pump or tap in
the courtyard. Getting water above the ground floors was rare and
costly; in Nevers it became available on upper floors in the 1930s.
Those who enjoyed it sooner, as in Paris, fared little better. When the
Duc de Broglie, one of the richest men in France, bought a luxury
mansion in the capital in 1902, the house had no bathroom, no *cabinet
de toilette* ("naturally," the duke's daughter comments), and one water
tap per floor.[24] About the same time, a sumptuous home on the avenue
de Iéna boasted one bathroom and three lavatories where, toilet paper
being unknown, one used "small cloth serviettes folded in four."[25]
With water brought up by carrier costing 10 cents the bucket, about 5
francs the cubic meter, it was too precious to use in many water closets.

The number of lavatories in the Iéna mansion was exceptional at a time when two out of every three lodgings in France had no lavatory at all.[26]

What limited lavatories also put a crimp on washing, and baths especially were reserved for those with enough servants to bring the tub and fill it, then carry away the tub and dirty water. Balzac had referred to the charm of *rich* young women when they came out of their bath. Manuals of civility suggest that this would take place once a month, and it seems that ladies who actually took the plunge might soak for hours: an 1867 painting by Alfred Stevens shows a plump young blonde in a camisole dreaming in her bathtub, equipped with book, flowers, bracelet, and a jeweled watch in the soap-dish.[27] Symbols of wealth and conspicuous consumption.

Recourse to home-delivered baths had been imported from Germany under the Restoration, but cost tended to restrict their use. By the fin de siècle, ambulant bathmen, mostly sturdy Auvergnats who could carry a tub and warm water up to an apartment and down again, were familiar figures; giving them false orders was a favorite schoolboy joke.[28] Yet see how exceptional and complicated the process still continued to be—and in the highest society. In 1898 Pauline de Broglie, then ten years old, caught the measles. When she had recovered, the doctor prescribed a bath: "It was a terribly complicated business, and it was talked about for several days. Naturally there was no bath tub in the house. No one in my family ever took a bath. We washed in tubs [low round basins recently imported from England, which can be recognized in the drawings of Degas] with 2 inches of water, or else sponged ourselves down, but the idea of plunging into water to the neck struck us as pagan, almost wicked!" So a portable bath was hired, placed before a fireplace in which a fire had been lit (in June), and the tinplate was lined with a sheet; the little girl got into it with her nightshirt on.[29]

The daughters of a rich provincial family, on the other hand, seem to have had baths "once a month in summer, *never* in winter," though it is not clear whether the circular tub they used was a bathtub or a basin. They soaped themselves through their bathshirts, "for never would we have allowed ourselves to be naked to wash!" When changing the chemise, they closed their eyes and crossed themselves. "I grew up without ever seeing my navel." Such reminiscences confirm the experience of Elinor Glyn's Elizabeth, whose (noble) French godmother was shocked to hear that she goes down to the *salle de bain* every day ("no one else seemed to use it") and especially distressed "that there never were any wet chemises" and Elizabeth got into the tub *toute nue* . . . "deplorable immodesty." Elizabeth understood: "I suppose a nice big bath is such a rare thing for them that they are obliged to make as much fuss as possible over it."[30]

This gives us an idea of the situation in the world of the Guermantes (Pauline de Broglie's aunt Elizabeth Greffulhe was Proust's Duchesse de Guermantes), and we might consider another comment of the clear-sighted Elizabeth: "It appears you do not wash much till you are married, it is not considered *bien vu* . . . But it must be a bother picking up a taste for having baths and things afterwards."[31] At the very time when Pauline had her first bath, Captain Dreyfus was being tried for the second time, in Rennes, a city of 70,000 which boasted thirty tubs and two private homes with bathrooms. In a public lecture course Vacher de Lapouge had affirmed that in France most women die without having once taken a bath. The same could be said of men, except for those exposed to military service.[32] No wonder pretty ladies carried posies: everyone smelled and, often, so did they.

Things were going to change slowly, as new products came into general use. Zinc and enameled metal permitted the spread of jugs and basins and tubs and bidets that no longer had to be made of porcelain, which was too expensive for most. Still, washing, in the modern sense, was not a nineteenth-century commonplace: hair, for example, was washed seldom, if ever. The Comtesse de Pange recalls: "At seventeen, I had very long hair which, when loosened, wrapped around me like a mantle. But these beautiful tresses were never washed. They were stiff and filthy. The very word shampoo was ignored. From time to time they rubbed my hair with quinine water."[33] Some women might have their hair washed by the *coiffeuses à domicile,* who came in the morning to perpetrate the edifice that ladies carried around during the day.[34] Less exalted creatures carried lice and fleas. Jules Renard's autobiographical Poil de Carotte and his brother came home from boarding school with their heads full of lice.[35] In the countryside lice and fleas and scabs were so common that popular wisdom considered them essential to the health of children.

Teeth were seldom brushed and often bad. Only a few people in the 1890s used toothpowder, and toothbrushes were rarer than watches.[36]

Dentists too were rare: largely an American import, and one of the few such things the French never complained about. Because dentists were few and expensive, one would find lots of caries, with their train of infections and stomach troubles. Between bad teeth and overcharged stomachs, it is likely that most heroes and heroines of nineteenth-century fiction had bad breath, like their real-life models.[37]

They would smell in a more general way also, because their heavy suits and dresses could not be dry-cleaned, and their underwear (if they wore it) was seldom changed. Jules Renard seems to have been particularly sensitive to smells: at the theater he notes (as I did in my youth), "it doesn't smell of roses"; a sixteen-year-old country girl smells like someone "who never undresses to sleep. A mixture of hay and sweat." His old servant, Ragotte, emits "that odor of scraped leather that comes from people who never wash." The local schoolteacher's wife "smells of dirty underwear, never brushes her teeth."[38] Olfactory sensibility had risen out of nothing to become a predisposition particular to the nineteenth century. Flaubert at midcentury, traveling in a public coach, had grumbled at the way his proletarian neighbors stank to high heaven.[39] The passages where Huysmans and Zola glory in scents and odors strike me as the opposite extreme of the same sensibility. Awareness of smells seems to have been particularly strong at the turn of the century, as new standards clashed with traditional habits. Even Nietzsche (in *Beyond Good and Evil*) sensed that "what separates two people most profoundly is a different sense and degree of cleanliness." Yet in 1900, when *La Nouvelle Mode* recommended baths for health, for beauty, and even for cleanliness, it had to admit that "few families enjoy the means to have even a broom in their apartments."[40]

The broom, where it existed, was generally wielded by a servant. The multiplicity of household chores—doing the laundry, baking bread, fetching water, coal, or logs, making clothes, mending, darning, taking care of poultry, of horses, let alone of fireplace, floors, and furniture—ensured that everyone who could afford it had a servant, and often more than one. Household servants—maids, butlers, coachmen, cooks—represented 8 percent of the active labor force.[41] The effects of these resident aliens on family life have not begun to be estimated: whether on the manners and behavior patterns of families with limited privacy; or on the language, beliefs, and prejudices of the children they brought up.

Alphonse Daudet has written searing pages on the subject of the "savages" inserted into urban homes, "with their rough voices, their incomprehensible speech, their strong smell of the stable." However much you wash them or teach them to speak French, "the [country] brute will reappear. Under your roof, at your hearth, she remains the peasant, the enemy." Hostility of this sort was returned with interest, and one child growing up at the turn of the century has recorded the repressed hatred and malevolence of servants for the rich and the less rich they served. Can you imagine, asked Alphonse Daudet, leaving your child in the hands of such brutes? Brutes or not, many, perhaps most, children of the middle and upper classes were so left. Daudet warned that many survived only as "dreadful monsters . . . with rustic manners . . . speaking barbarian patois."[42] The question remains (and deserves) to be asked: from Alfred de Vigny to Jean Giraudoux and Simone de Beauvoir, how much of the cultural baggage of the upper classes was instilled by nurses and by servants? Perhaps quite as much as they got from schools.

The influence working in the other direction is easier to discern. Servants acted as crucial intermediaries between town and country, as between rich and poor. They copied their employers' dress, manners, mannerisms; they conveyed money, secondhand clothing, printed matter, or novelties back to their village or small town; and news, and general information about urban consumption and life styles. The woman of the village or of the working class who spent some years as maid or cook in a neighboring chateau or hostelry, or in a town household, returned home—generally to marry—with different tastes, standards, and expectations from her neighbors who had missed such an experience. For one thing, she cooked better; for another, she was probably cleaner.[43] Around 1900 a Parisian noted that a maid newly arrived in town could not even distinguish between what is dirty and what is not: "For the distinction is not evident for everybody, and it has only started to be made during the last few years."[44]

Such distinction had grown to a great extent out of the urban realization that overcrowding, congestion, criminality, disease, mortality, were connected and that, although for the most part they affected the lower orders, they also threatened others indirectly. The miasmic theory of disease suggested that sickness arises from decaying organic matter which creates the miasma that carries disease. If bad smells did not cause disease, they appeared to be connected with it; and the smells in turn were evidently connected with dirt. Clean streets, clean water, clean air, began to look highly relevant to the welfare of those with the time and energy to worry about such things. And the welfare of those with neither time, energy, or concern was quickly recognized as related. In 1879 a Jules Verne novel described Franceville, a model modern city, where children were trained to "rigorous cleanliness" from the earliest age, and streets never allowed to look as normal streets looked at that time. "Clean up, clean up, unceasingly destroy . . . the miasmas that constantly emanate from an urban center."[45]

Medicine, and following medicine the public, were beginning to recognize that many maladies were social problems, not just in their effects, but in their origins. Tuberculosis—which dominated the later nineteenth century as cancer does the later twentieth century—was as readily, and as dogmatically, linked to alcoholism as lung cancer is to smoking.[46] Typhoid fever was more evidently linked to polluted waters. In the 1880s the Minister of War, concerned for the welfare of the conscript army, and after him the Minister of the Interior, moved into action;[47] municipalities were encouraged to purify and filter local waters, improve drainage, clean up the streets. About the same time, medical and sanitary measures reduced the danger of cholera, whose vibrio was isolated in 1883. The cholera epidemic of the mid-1880s killed only half as many as its predecessor of the 1860s had done; that of 1892, only one-third as many as died six years earlier.[48] One of the great dreads of earlier times waned with the century.

So did another, less spectacular but more deadly: smallpox. The Franco-Prussian War had triggered a European pandemic that left half a million dead. The German armed forces, like the British, had introduced vaccination against smallpox in the first half of the century, so far more French soldiers died, and more French citizens, than German ones. Drawing their conclusions, the Germans made vaccination compulsory for all in 1874. The French lagged in the name of liberty and went on dying at higher rates than other Europeans, except Russians, Italians, and Iberians. But the army adopted vaccination in 1883, and in 1893 it became compulsory (and free) for children in any town with a population over 5,000.[49] In 1900 *La Nouvelle Mode,* always alert to the latest fad, reported on a novel fashion: "This is done in parties, as if one was going to the theater . . . one organizes an intimate luncheon;

the doctor arrives at dessert, the vaccine in his pocket . . . It's the last word."[50]

The later nineteenth century was the great age of German medical and chemical breakthroughs. The French had their own hero in this realm: Louis Pasteur, whose discoveries after 1870 would be colored by his patriotic desire to affirm French science against the German. Personal genius or patriotism, Pasteur left his mark on crucial aspects of everyday life. He improved the fermentation and preservation of milk and milk products, wines, vinegars, and beers (requesting that beers brewed according to his formula be called "*bières de la revanche nationale*"), devised a water filter, developed vaccines against anthrax and hog fever, sheep pox, poultry and cattle maladies. Finally, in 1884, Pasteur found the remedy for rabies—a major terror of the countryside. By 1886, of 1,235 French children treated for rabies at his laboratory, only 3 had died—and they had been bitten in the head.[51]

Probably more effective than even Pasteur's work in improving public health was the steady amelioration of the average diet. In the last half of the century the quantity of bread, wine, and potatoes annually consumed in France grew 50 percent, that of meat, beer, and cider doubled, that of alcohol tripled, that of sugar and coffee quadrupled. Bread, which had accounted for 20 percent of the average household budget in 1850, counted for only 9 percent in 1900. Even those poor working girls—seamstresses, milliners, shop assistants—known as *midinettes* because their midday meal (repas de *midi*) was no more than a snack, could find 15 sous for a *dinette* consisting of a plate of meat, one of vegetables, cheese, wine, and bread. In 1902 the Vicomte d'Avenel remarked that it had become practically impossible to find black bread (symbol of poverty and backwardness).[52] Even the poor now ate the white bread that used to be the prerogative of princes. A study of a Breton, hence backward, department at the beginning of the twentieth century dismissed the food as monotonous and badly prepared, but noted the shift from rye bread, oaten porridge, and buckwheat cakes to white bread, potatoes, coffee, and meat at all meals.[53]

Peasant thrift was and still remains proverbial. Describing conditions in his rural Gascon family home, *after* the First World War, Pierre Gascar remembers that they lived in the Middle Ages: indifferent to comfort, to hygiene, let alone to any decoration, "with a simplicity close to indigence," the only difference being that, although they ate frugally, they never went hungry.[54] Sober country housewives shunned fresh bread because one ate too much of it, preferred rancid butter because the taste was stronger and one used less of it, put salt into coffee because it cost less than sugar, and generally maintained a regime that an English observer described as a continuous fast. The appearance of meat on peasant tables on other than feast days deserves to be regarded as one of the great events of Western history. In 1907, in a Nièvre village less than 150 miles from Paris, Jules Renard recorded an old woman returning from the market proclaiming her surprise: "The world is becoming carnivorous!" There were now five butchers where there had been one, and even the poor were shifting from a herbivorous to a carnivorous diet. Peasants' regular access to butchers' meat reflected a progress so recent that on special occasions roasts and hashes were served without vegetables, because the humble vegetable one ate every day "would show lack of regard [for guests] and lessen the festive atmosphere." Still, townsfolk continued more carnivorous than rurals, and miners or industrial workers just up from the land, eager to stress their difference from the rusticity they had left behind, marked it in the food they consumed, and especially in the quantity of meat they put away.[55]

If food continued to be a problem for rich as for poor, it was henceforth rather by the accentuation of age-old frictions connected with trade, the marketplace, and, increasingly, shops. Everybody cheated on weights and measures, almost everybody on quality. Eggs were hardly ever fresh. Sausage or minced meat contained almost everything but what it was supposed to. Wine, when not watered, was chemically adulterated. Milk, when it was not watered (with polluted water of course) was cut with plaster, lime, chalk, white lead, or dried ground brains. The rich got their wine in barrels or sealed bottles, their milk from goats milked at the kitchen door. One understands better the prevalence of urban stables whence came milk on the hoof, as of poultry yards; and the contemporary return to breast feeding by the baby's mother rather than by a nurse whose own milk might be suspect in the light of modern ideas of hygiene. The poor, however, had little choice and, for them more than for most, shopping was an adversary relationship, every act of buying a potential conflict.[56]

Always short of cash, the poor bought everything in small quantities, and frequently on credit. Inevitably the goods they bought were overpriced and often of poor quality. Another factor made life difficult for buyer and seller alike. Cash itself was short. Coins were so scarce that, even in Paris into the late 1890s, Roman or medieval coins discovered in some excavation were occasionally accepted as small change.[57] More often, foreign coins in copper or in silver were used to supplement French ones. The smallest available coin was the 5-cent piece, the sou, hence the long-lasting tendency to speak not of the relatively new-fangled francs, but of 20 sous, 100 sous, or whatever a coin's sou equivalent might be. (Thus, 5 francs would be cent [100] sous.) Hence also the fact that prices necessarily were quoted—and rose—in multiples of 5 cents, no less. Worse, the copper sous in circulation were worn and few. Around 1890–1900 workingmen were paid in badly worn 50-cent coins or rolls of sous that included foreign coppers struck cheap in Greece, Italy, or Argentina.[58] Naturally the workmen and their wives paid for their purchases with these coins, and traders raised prices to offset their loss. Friction was inevitable.

Between 1900 and 1913 the value of French coins in circulation rose by nearly one-third, from 6.7 to 9 billion francs. But this did not suffice. Unable to provide sufficient currency (no one of modest means willingly accepted paper bills, the smallest of which, anyway, was worth 50 francs), the government oscillated between tacit tolerance and prohibition of the foreign coinage. Banning the latter met with limited success. In 1888 Paris bus conductors were refusing to accept coins from Argentina, Chile, and Peru.[59] In 1896 a prohibition of foreign sous provoked rioting in Marseilles. The law of 1897 renewing the privileges of the Banque de France required it to sort out small coins and make sure that those circulating in the provinces would henceforth be "as good as those in Paris"—which was not saying much. Guy Thuillier estimates that in 1914 foreign coins still accounted for 15 percent of the small coins in circulation.

Far more than that must have been worn, defaced, abraded, or simply counterfeit; and this held even more true of silver 5-franc coins. Between 1878 and 1909 about one-third of these were of foreign provenance—mostly Belgian, Italian, or Austrian—and the often justified suspicion that such silver evoked led to its depreciation. Speculators in Spain counterfeited 5-franc coins whose silver content cost about 1 franc, sold them in France for 3 francs, and let enterprising speculators offer them at 3.75 francs, for use as New Year tips (*étrennes*) to domestics, postmen, newsboys, and young relatives.[60] No wonder that what Thuillier dubs "monetary mistrust" became a long-standing trait of business dealings during the fin de siècle and beyond! Into the 1930s people treated all coins with diffidence, rang them on metal or marble slabs, tested them with their teeth, continually suspecting the tricks of others, continuously driven to tricks of their own. Not the best way to conduct relations, either human or commercial.

Nevertheless, the fact that between 1900 and 1913 the total French money supply rose from 16 to 27 billion suggests that there was more money around, some of which trickled through to those who had been least used to handling it. The economic recovery of the opening years of the twentieth century accounts for the Belle Epoque. But even before that, and despite the hard times associated with it, the later nineteenth century is the time when the laboring classes (to use the words of Yves Lequin) graduated from misery to precariousness.[61] There is, by the end of the century, greater employment security, the real value of wages rises, food comes to account for only one-third of an average family's budget, ready-mades toll the knell of the rag merchant and his trade in cast-off clothes; and of course, as buying power grows, so does relative deprivation. The workmen's new Sunday suits were going to be sported more often at socialist meetings than in church. But to the outsider's eye things were clearly improving. In 1893 John Grand-Carteret was impressed by the novelty of relative well-being among the disinherited, and by their *embourgeoisement*. "In our day of perfect equality and of emancipation by money," the only way of establishing social distinctions would be by looking at people's features, their white skin, the way they wore their clothes. Grand-Carteret was premature but prophetic. He was also typical of the many among the upper classes (a term by which I mean simply above the lower classes) whom "the invasion of the popular masses" made uncomfortable.[62]

Other aspects of modernity caused uneasiness. In 1888 Albert Robida's *The Nineteenth Century* began by declaring that, "nearly all centuries end badly, ours appears to follow the common law." According to him, the nineteenth century would breathe its last "in an indigestion of iron and steel and chemical products," not to mention the money and the explosives which he considered as destructive as the rest. The present "era of scientific barbarism" was bound to end badly.[63] Brilliant draftsman and cartoonist, one of the pioneers of science fiction, Robida was at one in his grumbling not only with the reactionary aristocracy, but with the equally reactionary rustics who attributed bad weather to the wireless telegraph and looked on new means of transport as vehicles of hell. Since such a point of view is not unknown today, a swift glance at some of the novelties that evoked it might not come amiss.

The rhythms of human life had always been set by light and lighting. Farmers and artisans began and ended their day (mostly) in relation to sunrise and sunset. The timetables of great collective institutions—convents and colleges, hospitals, prisons and barracks—were dominated by the need to save light. Government offices ran on the *journée continue,* usually from 9 A.M. to 4 or 5 P.M., until better lighting and public transport at the end of the century made them shift to the more familiar pattern of the lunchtime break. The slow advance of electricity capped a long evolution in which artificial light (oil, gas) artificially stretched time and began to support the tendency to bend time to our convenience, to regulate it, to divide it, and homogenize it.

The French Revolution, which grappled with so many things, had tried to rationalize time, but local usage, different from place to place, outlasted the Revolution. It was only the railways that forced people to accept the notion of standard time. In most places, as at Bayonne in 1865, the city hall clock showed Paris time, the cathedral clock kept its own. Most of the people, who were illiterate, took no account of hours and minutes. Train timetables imposed a precision nobody had bothered about before—the telegraph in the railway station made the precision possible—as well as a degree of homogenization which would have been irrelevant under earlier conditions.* After midcentury the habit of considering not just hours but minutes spread. And in the 1890s sports and sporting contests began to suggest counting in

---

* In 1891 a respected scientist commented on the law that had just imposed a standard time throughout France: "The railroads have set their timetables and their station clocks by Paris time, to the effect that every town has found itself with two different times of day: local time and station time, the two differing more than a half-hour at Brest." This was denounced as a tyrannous imposition on a defenseless public. C. Wolf (de l'Institut), "Le Temps local et l'heure universelle," *Revue pédagogique,* October 15, 1891.

If life improved for some, not everybody noticed it. This Steinlen drawing translates the traditional image of poor children gazing longingly at a toy store window into something more realistic: a barefoot boy glowering at the footgear that he covets but cannot attain.

seconds as well. Of course the chronometers one can see in people's hands in some of the cycle-racing pictures of Toulouse-Lautrec were very rare; but watches had been almost as rare until the 1860s. Watchmakers were few, sundials many; in a number of provincial towns men set their watch by the sundial, until the railway-station clock provided something more consistent. After the 1860s watch prices began to go down and public clocks multiplied; but in 1914 watches were still a rare and prized possession, passed down from father to son, with members of the lower classes owning one only exceptionally (army substitutes, or children's nurses). How else explain the vogue of a gold watch on retirement?

Trains, which so fascinated Impressionist painters and filled their canvases with steam, are part of the great nineteenth-century revolution in which men grabbed for mastery of space as well as time. We have no historian's history of trains, let alone of their effects in expanding the horizons of our fantasies. But Stephen Kern's *Culture of Time and Space* (1983) tells us how their magic affected the century's view of nature and the world. Of history, too, as in the picture Flaubert's Pellerin painted in 1848: "It represented the Republic, or Progress, or Civilization, in the person of Jesus Christ driving a railway engine."[64] The triumph of the trains and their general acceptance meant that technological innovations, once regarded as toys or nuisances, were recognized as powerful levers for manipulating both the physical world and life itself.

One clear instance of this can be found in urban transportation, where electrification of street railways begun in the United States in the 1880s spread to Europe in the 1890s, cutting costs, hence fares, by half or better and tripling the number of users within a year of its being introduced. Not only in Paris but in major provincial cities the streetcar revolution allowed schoolchildren, housewives, and workmen (the last-named further encouraged by special low fares), who had once walked to ride, permitting families of modest means to take a Sunday outing, introducing the age of "cheap, mass-oriented urban transport."[65] Then, in 1900, the first Paris Metro line opened and proved phenomenally successful, despite somber warnings against the danger of electrocution, asphyxiation, and pickpockets, which made it known at first as the "Necropolitain." The pickpockets are still with us today. So, once more, are the automatic turnstiles which had to be replaced within the first few months by human controllers to punch tickets and discourage gate-crashers. The other dire predictions proved false; and, while the number of subway travelers soared (from 15 million in 1900 to 312 million in 1909), that of tram riders held firm, somewhere below the 300 million mark. The more public transport was made available (at reasonable cost), the more the public used it. "Today," the Vicomte d'Avenel rejoiced in 1905, "duchesses and millionaires rub shoulders with cooks and clerks."[66] Whatever millionaires might choose to do, cooks and clerks were certainly better off.

By that time, when most (though certainly not all) provincial clocks marked the hour of Paris, well over ten million telegrams were being sent every year. In 1901, when Marconi's first wireless radio signal went from Brittany to Newfoundland, appropriately opening a new era along with a new century, the wonders of electricity were no longer new. Bell's telephone and Edison's phonograph had been admired at the Paris Exhibition of 1878, along with other marvels, such as Pictet's machine for making artificial ice, and the giant head of Bartholdi's Statue of Liberty about to be shipped off to the United States. As early as 1884 a cab with two electric lamps pulled by a horse with an electric headdress was advertising the electrical jewels of Mr. Aboilard.[67] In 1886 Villiers de l'Isle Adam's *Future Eve* celebrated electricity's glories and those of Mr. Edison. The Exhibition of 1889 was illuminated by gas; but its centerpiece, the Eiffel Tower, depended on electrical elevators. The Exhibition of 1900 took place under the sign of electricity. Camille Saint-Saens wrote a hymn to its glory, and "The Heavenly Fire" was performed by a mass orchestra and chorus in a free concert. The *fée électricité* was as much a presiding figure of the show as the twenty-foot stucco Parisienne that rose over the main gate dressed in the latest fashion by Paquin.

By 1900 Paris boasted nearly 350,000 electric lamps; not terribly many, perhaps, for a city of over two and a half million. And few were to be found in ordinary homes; most were in theaters, hotels, railway stations, department stores, government offices, and expensive shops.[68] The use of electricity in the home was associated with showy ostentation. When Marcel Proust's Madame Verdurin buys a town house that is to be lit entirely by electricity, "even to the rooms, each of which will have a lamp and a lampshade," this is "evidently a charming luxury." The Broglies' Paris house had no electricity until after the First World War; many homes installed it only in the reception rooms.

We have to remember that for a long time electrical power was not

Théophile-Alexandre Steinlen, "In the Omnibus" (*Gil Blas,* 1894).

Maurice Delondre, "In the Omnibus," 1890 (Musée Carnavalet, Paris).
These pictures illustrate the new democracy of public transport, where elegant
ladies and men of the world rubbed shoulders with the lower classes.

very reliable: it worked badly and broke down often. But the problems
of electricity were less concerned with production than with distribution. The latter was hampered by the high tax placed on electrical
consumption, which discouraged its use, especially in private homes
where costs could not be passed on to customers. While outside France
the price of power fell with increased consumption, in France the cost
per unit remained stable or fell very little, ensuring that electrical light
bulbs would be few, weak, and turned on as seldom as possible.

Still, there was a special excitement and prestige attached to electricity that fostered its acceptance. At the very time when city dwellers
were becoming concerned about clean air, electrical power seemed to
promise a pure, almost sinless source of energy. Gas was associated
with coal, fire, dirt, eventually hell; electricity with water, glaciers, and
the wonderful *houille blanche* (white coal) of water-power. When the
electric chair was introduced in New York State in 1889, electrical

companies protested, arguing that it would make electricity appear too dangerous for public use. French enthusiasts, however, denied the possibility of a lethal electric chair: electricity could not kill.[69] It was, as a guide to the 1900 Exhibition would describe it, a magic fluid; but its sorcery was white, not black. The magic of electricity fitted the contemporary interest in paranormal phenomena like levitation, turning tables and telepathy. Its therapeutic possibilities, stressed by Roentgen's discovery of X-rays, were nothing less than fascinating. Mechanics and magic had long been studied—and practiced—as parts of the same organic whole. In the eighteenth century Mesmer's magnetism had provided a more "scientific" competitor for occultism. We need not be surprised to encounter fin de siècle magnetic clinics that promised to treat nervous or organic maladies, with no recourse to drugs, by magnetism and electrotherapy; or swindlers brought to court for healing by (electrical) magnetism and by spiritualism all sorts of ills, including paralysis.[70]

The telephone too would offer fresh opportunities to criminals to show their enterprise: the first telephonic swindle appears to have been judged in 1888.[71] Crooks were not the only ones to benefit from the telephone. In 1878 the selection committee of the electrical section of the Universal Exhibition almost refused to accept Alexander Graham Bell's invention, regarding it as a fraud or toy. That very year, however, Jules Ferry was writing to his brother about the new marvel's progress.[72] Soon afterward music lovers who visited the Electrical Exhibition of 1881 could listen to a whole performance relayed from the Opera, a mile away. The *théatrophone,* by which one could dial a play, recital, or the sittings of the National Assembly, was an instant success among those who could afford it. Its installation immediately doubled the number of telephone subscribers to 2,442, and it continued to delight connoisseurs (Proust discovered *Pelléas et Mélisande* on the theatrophone) until killed by radio in the 1930s. At a more mundane level, the telephone appeared in police stations as part of the fight against crime,[73] though it seems to have done so only after its adoption by the criminals.

Polite society proved relatively slow to accept the phone, and President Grévy took a lot of persuading before he allowed one to be installed in the Elysée Palace. Only a few people, like the Comtesse Greffulhe, appreciated "the magic, supernatural life," the telephone

Jules Chéret, *Théâtrophone,* 1890. The possibility of listening to the latest play or opera over the telephone was demonstrated as early as 1881. In 1884 the introduction of telephone booths made the service available to nonsubscribers, though evidently only prosperous ones. It continued to be used until radio rendered it out of date in the 1930s.

afforded. "It's odd for a woman to lie in her bed," she told Goncourt, always grouchy about novelties, "and talk to a gentleman who may be in his. And you know, if the husband should walk in, one just throws the thingummy under the bed, and he does not know a thing."

One recent view suggests that the instrument was regarded as an intrusion into private living space; and it is true that the telephone impinged on privacy at a time when formal "calling" was the recognized form of sociability. The informality of the device troubled many; its location was generally inconvenient; and answering it appeared a servile gesture. As Degas told Forain when the latter was called away from the dining table: "Is *that* the telephone? They ring, and you go."[74] The telephone remained suspect for a while: good for giving orders—to servants, stores, or subordinates, for idle chatter, for amorous or adulterous trysts. This low esteem helps to explain why in 1900 there were only 30,000 telephones in France, when New York City's four largest hotels boasted 20,000 among them.

More likely, the same Malthusian attitude that sapped the swift development of electricity applied to the telephone as well. In 1881, as in 1971, would-be subscribers in France were more numerous than actual installations. In December 1881 one-third of postulants, in December 1882 one-tenth, still awaited a line. Bad organization, poor equipment, the determination to invest little and charge a lot, and the state's eagerness to tax conspired, as they so often do, to give the French a telephone network incomparably worse than any that could be found in comparable lands. In the year 1905 the Paris-Marseilles circuit alone broke down 204 times, and service was interrupted for 123 full days. In 1909 the Telephone Subscribers' Association published a pamphlet denouncing *L'Anarchie téléphonique*. In 1921 some country towns still lacked the half-century-old facility. Even so, the number of subscribers continued to grow and, as it did, the first telephone books appeared (the initial *Bottin* came out in 1889), followed by telephone numbers.[75] The shift from calling subscribers by name to calling them by number was of course denounced as depersonalizing and demeaning.

That was the trouble with scientific progress: it devalued old wisdom and hoary certainties; it threatened established attitudes and securities; it encouraged new insecurities, which science fiction reflected as clearly as political rhetoric. Most of the late twentieth century's familiar themes were being proclaimed during the late nineteenth century: science, industry, and machinery poison mankind, crush it, or turn it into a mechanical contraption. The electrical power domesticated by man does not bring freedom but a new kind of bondage. The new appliances, the paraphernalia of modernity, enslave their users. Valuable activities are threatened by new goods. In 1892 Robida published a novel about the twentieth century: *The Electrical Life.* It opens in 1954 with an engagement trip to a national park established in darkest Brittany, where industrial and scientific innovations have been prohibited and where the young lovers, among other things, admire the last postman, preserved as a rare specimen. Since everybody "telephonoscoped" or at least phoned, "only perfect ignorants" still bothered—or knew how to—write.[76]

Robida's mid-twentieth-century world includes test-tube babies and emancipated women, cassettes, electrical typewriters and electrical trains, air travel and helicopters, but also overpopulation, dangerous pollution, every kind of warfare, on land, in the air, on and undersea, and a thriving arms trade in bombs and machine guns, armored vehicles and artillery, not overlooking the possibilities of chemical warfare. We have become used to man's imagination at its most fertile when dealing with possibilities of destruction. To a degree this has always been so, but only to a degree. The possibilities of destruction that were revealed to the fin de siècle fueled a peculiarly pessimistic vision of the future that fitted its glum vision of the present. Thoughtful folk of the late eighteenth century, when they looked forward, tended to see vistas of progress and a glorious dawn. Their 1900 heirs preferred to shade their phantasies in darker hues. When, as the twentieth century opened, the Vicomte d'Avenel set out to describe the mechanisms of modern life, he wondered if one still dared to speak of Progress. Once vaunted, the notion of advancement as something beneficial was now being traduced. Yet the new was no closer to reality than the old had been; it was simply a point of view. Never, added Avenel, has the French people been as well off as it is now, and never has it felt more sorry for itself. "Its grievances have grown along with its well-being; as its circumstances improved, they were judged to deteriorate. The character of this century, favored above all others, is to be displeased with itself." It was a fair assessment of a moment's mood, which would become the pervasive spirit of the new century.[77]

✻

It would be wrong to close this chapter on an equivocal note—even though my book is bound to reflect a degree of indetermination. My view, like Avenel's, is that the fashionable perception misjudged and misrepresented reality. While the experience of progress was not an unqualified success, it involved far more than its detractors were (or are) willing to allow.

Charles Péguy, born in 1873 to a poor widow who earned her living by mending chairs, was to become one of France's national poets. Not long before he died, in the first weeks of the 1914 war, he declared that the world had changed more since he went to school in the 1880s than it had changed since the Romans.[78] Péguy is a good example of the well-known phenomenon of upward mobility through education. But if we go beyond the familiar stereotypes (no less true for being stereotypes), we can consider some other things that the slow spread of literacy, and the gradual passing of illiteracy, meant for ordinary people.

Illiterate people, like Péguy's grandmother who never went to school, had always been aware that they were at a disadvantage. Jules Renard's maid, Blandine, thirty-seven, who never wrote home to her family in her native village, explained: "It bothers me to have strangers write [my letters]."[79] Illiteracy placed one at the mercy of others. Strangers could learn one's secrets: the record of loans, the details of wills, one's financial situation. Tenants and sharecroppers found it hard to confirm accounts or agreements. Wills, contracts, deeds of sale, voting bulletins, could not be checked, or shipment manifestos filled in. After the 1880s school-taught reading and writing offered emancipation from a kind of dependency we seldom bother to remember. Writing provided a new level of individual autonomy. As it progressed, migrant workers could write their own letters home, swains could write their own love-letters, and one result was the disappearance of the public letterwriter. A few survived in the Paris of the 1880s, and even into the twentieth century, when their stalls could still be found near prisons or railway stations. They continued to operate in country fairs and in 1913 could commonly be found, at least in western France. But they were going out.[80]

Writing is hard to learn. But a boy with a "good hand" was sure to get a job. For this reason in the second half of the century more parents sent their children to school—even before the 1880s made elementary education compulsory and free. More children in school meant fewer children in factories (where under-thirteen-year-olds were prohibited by a law in 1892) and fewer beggars on the street: a way of legislating deferred gratification. And so the lower classes learned to write; and some of them also began to learn shorthand, which developed after 1860. Then, in December 1886, Edmond de Goncourt visited an American lawyer on the avenue de l'Opéra to discuss the sale of American rights for one of his plays, and noted that the contract, instead of being written out, "is printed on little pianos."[81] Office equipment never looked back.

We take for granted many things that were rare, or simply not available. We know that they were not available, but most of the time we do not think about it, or about what it implies. Not least, the difference in dress and bearing, as in spoken language, that we observed existed between classes, between regions, between rural and urban populations: a set of differences which educational and material opportunities would slowly whittle down. But there are less momentous instances of the growing availability of goods and facilities affecting the most commonplace aspects of conduct and turning the exceptional into the banal. The problem of keeping food fresh was solved only very recently, and our memory has quickly adjusted to the fact that we no longer have to boil milk as soon as it is bought to keep it from turning. Yet before refrigeration, meat, milk, and fish frequently turned bad in summer, involving both serious waste and risk of poisoning.

When one reads about a character looking at himself or herself in a mirror, it is well to stop and think that until late in the nineteenth century the casual glance or the graceful pose were largely reserved for the better-off. In her Nièvre village Ragotte has only one mirror, the size of her hand. Her daughter, a servant in Paris, would send her a bigger one. In Maupassant's *Bel Ami* (1885) the hero owns only a shaving mirror, and an early scene of the novel depicts the revelation that comes to Georges Duroy when he sees himself in a full-length mirror.[82] A generation before, the wealthy farmers who attended Madame Bovary's wedding had cut themselves shaving in the bad light.[83] A lot of men shaved, a lot of women put up their hair, looking in a windowpane. What would mirrors do to their self-image? Let alone to their kemptness! A lot of men continued to cut themselves, as in *Madame Bovary,* until American safety razors with exchangeable blades came onto the market in the 1920s, putting an end to a familiar middle-class figure, the barber who shaved one at home, as well as to a familiar instrument of crime and suicide.

The mass production that enemies of modernity vilified meant, among other things, ready-made clothes, cheaper and more accessible linen, more and better underwear. The problems and costs of laundry meant that these were seldom changed. Among the lower classes shirts would not be changed for a week, sometimes two. Even among the better-off, the older generations that died out with the century often made the day shirt do double duty as a nightshirt. Into the 1930s waiters remained just about the only members of the petty bourgeoisie to boast freshly laundered shirts. Others relied on detachable collars and cuffs. The white-collar worker probably wore his *faux-col* over a shirt that was less than pristine. But the opportunity to change even that was offered by celluloid, a plastic developed in 1870 to replace expensive ivory billiard balls, and only later adapted to collars and cuffs—a reorientation that testifies to changing patterns of consumption, aspiration, and propriety.

Can we locate, trace, and evaluate the factors of this change? School, domestic service, military service, greater exigencies of the upper classes from the lower, greater aspirations and expectations of the lower classes themselves, and so on. At any rate, the threshold of shame and disgust—what Norbert Elias describes as civility—had been raised another notch. A whole range of perceptions and discriminations would be adjusted because of that, through the nineteenth century, and after.

Does all that amount to more than a collection of anecdotes and, worse, of trivia? Maupassant did not despise trivia, the "steady stream of small facts from which the overall meaning . . . will emerge."[84] A lot of life is about things so trivial that we do not bother to record them— only sometimes to note their absence, as with manners. But the *petite histoire* is made up of details, and it can surely help to make vaster and more important processes clear.

The preceding pages suggest some obvious questions. What, for example, can we tell from dress or cleanliness or sanitary facilities, about relations and definitions of class, and their evolution in the nineteenth century and beyond? We seem to move from an age when sumptuary and physical class distinctions become less visible, to the point where new and subtler distinctions have to be invented. Shaw's *Pygmalion*, first staged in 1914, called attention to the fact that anyone could be taught to be a lady. A quarter of a century before that, Philip Gilbert Hamilton had remarked on the number of French middle-class women who "spoke quite as well as ladies of rank!" By that time new commercial enterprises, especially the great department stores like Boucicaut's Bon Marché limned in Zola's *Au Bonheur des dames,* had already established that clerks could dress and behave like gentlefolk. Ready-made clothes helped, and soon it became fashionable to claim that it was hard to tell masters and servants apart. Few really believed it. More modest but more promising (or more ominous, according to your point of view), the true change was that differences long taken for granted were perceived as surmountable, not only in the exceptional sense to be found in picaresque situations where servants dress up as their masters, but as a socially significant possibility and, eventually, expectation. Norms of dress, consumption, and bearing, which once differed according to social or physical location, became more alike, tending toward the superficial similarities of the later twentieth century. At least on the material plane, the republican ideal of equality tiptoed toward partial realization.

So did the nineteenth-century ideal of improvement. Shortly before his death, a provincial tinsmith testified to this from the standpoint of one who had lived through the last two-thirds of the century: "Certainly we are advancing rapidly toward a better future. When one sees the great things that have been accomplished during my lifetime, one has to rejoice over those that await us in the future."[85] Though written only three months before the outbreak of the 1914 war, Louis Marcelin's words remind us that the perspective of the workingman could well be sharply different from that which sensitive intellectuals have passed down to us.

To stay on the level of the commonplace—quite literally at the grassroots—let us glance back at Péguy's grandmother, and his mother too. All her kind, at least in the countryside, wore clogs, *sabots,* well past the century's end. By 1900 or so most people could also afford a pair of shoes, which they would wear to town, to fair, to fêtes, but the rest of the time they shuffled and clattered about. Their heavy footwear gave them a particular gait and an easily recognizable carriage. The shambling rustic might wear city clothes and keep his (her?) mouth shut, but he stood out among those not of his own kind.

This was still true when Pierre Jakez Hélias grew up in the 1920s, but it changed in the following decade or two, and perhaps Hélias could claim as much for his lifetime as Péguy for his. At any rate, "today," Hélias tells us, "the young peasants no longer walk like their fathers. That is because they wear different shoes; the roads are tarred; there are not so many slopes. Nor is their bearing like that of the old peasant. That is because they use different tools. They move faster."[86] There is the steady stream of small facts Maupassant had called for. To me, it seems to testify for change. And perhaps for progress.

4

Affections and Disaffections

---※---

Hoary convention decrees that one look back fondly upon the years spent growing up. The family nest, brimming with affection, symbolized things as they should be: warm, secure, and caring. Such nests surely existed, beyond conventional generalities, but one suspects that they were not the norm. The ideal in the home, or the society that prolongs it, appears to be less one of harmony than of unity imposed from outside or above. Family relations are adversary relations. French literature is curiously rich in works denouncing the conscious or unconscious cruelty (not to mention indifference) of parents to children, of spouses to each other, the hatred of relatives at loggerheads. The documents confirm these negative impressions. The family sheltered less tenderness than tension, suffering, and more or less covert violence.

Whether because one or both parents died or because the parents worked, ordinary children were often farmed out with wet nurses, foster parents, or family members: a kind of abandonment no less depressing for being temporary (as a rule), and likely to deprive children of parental affection at a crucial age. The eight-year-old orphan Pierre Fournier, who grew up to become the journalist and novelist Pierre Gascar, was boarded out with his father's family in the Perigord. He remembers a general absence of warmth or affection, personified by his grandmother, who did not seem to love anybody. He assumes that "her coldness stemmed from an incapacity to express feelings by language, gestures, or looks. Her existence had been too hard, too sad, too irritating, for her to learn to show tenderness, if she had ever felt any. In brief . . . an inhibition of affectivity."[1] The stunted affectivity that Gascar discerned in his foster family must have existed in many others, especially when further cramped and chafed by abandonment in early youth, by deprivation of tenderness, by the absence of vicarious intellectual indications of warmer alternatives. School texts, the theater, and literature intimated that more affectionate relations were possible. An easier life, greater tenderness in the home, eventually moderated a harshness directed as much toward oneself as toward others. But that took time.

Marriage for one thing was not about pleasure, less about love, but chiefly about working and living together as best one could.

> Lie together, eat, and drink,
> That is marriage, I think

declared the Poitevin proverb. No more than that. Flora Tristan, great friend of the oppressed, had to admit that "there are very few workers' households where happiness prevails." We have already seen what to make of in-laws: "The best-off wife," the proverb asserts, "has neither mother-in-law nor sister-in-law" to cope with. "A son-in-law's love is like the winter sun, but look out for the daughter-in-law."[2]

Nor did smaller urban households fare better. A recent article by Harry Eckstein describes lower-class families as authoritarian and family relations among the poor as unlikely to produce a sense that one had any hope of influencing the powers that govern life. An unpredictable succession of cuffs and cuddles, kicks and kisses, breeds a sense of helplessness and anxiety, irritable distrust and aggressivity. People become suspicious, easily feel slighted, and are easily roused to aggression. The better-off have options, hence something to discuss. The poor regard talking as useless, which it usually is. "If discussion occurs at all, it generally takes the form of quarrels—struggles for domination or autonomy." "One takes what one can, suffers what one must"—and hits back as one may. Some aspect of this analysis seems to apply to much French experience. A workingman remembered no expression of affection in the home, only frequent quarrels, beatings, fights. A schoolteacher's son, more discreetly, recalls good moments to have been scarce and brief. "It never lasted. Large families endlessly secrete quarrels and trouble." Even apparent calm concealed intimate enmity. "All her life," Raymond Abellio recalls, "my grandmother was sustained by the hatred she bore her husband, a hatred never wasted in words or in invective and which, compressed, lived in her as a reservoir of energy."[3]

We have seen in another context that those who smarted most were of course the weakest. But there are degrees of defenselessness, and if the old and useless were more likely to suffer, "women and children first" is a good description of the priorities of popular martyrdom.

Among the peasantry things were simple. A southern proverb, "Lei femmas non son gents," tells us that women are not people: not "individuals" in the legal sense, but also not worth taking into account. Witness the tendency of fathers to count only their sons as offspring: "Ask a father who has daughters only how many children he has; he will almost always answer that he has none."[4] The widespread practice whereby women took their meals standing up, while men sat down at the table, has been explained by practical considerations. This makes some sense but not enough. Even when women sat at the table, they seldom or never touched meat—that was reserved for men, "who needed strength." The housewife was the last to help herself to food, even after the farmhands.

Another practice affords less debatable indication of women's status: the ritual of churching the mother after childbirth. The new mother was considered unclean; she ate apart and forbore touching anything her contact might soil or defile, even her own children. This taint was not removed until she was strong enough to make her solitary way to church and wait in its porch to be raised up by the priest before whom she knelt for purification and benediction. By 1900 the *relevailles,* waning in urban centers, were still common in the countryside, demeaning women in their most natural function.[5] And relevailles were not the only testimony to the low esteem in which women were held.

As in England, the French countryside was acquainted with an informal kind of divorce: wife-selling. Though illegal, conveyances of this sort, which usually took place in the marketplace or an adjacent cafe, were sanctioned by popular acceptance. At mid-nineteenth century a man near Rive-de-Gier (Loire) tried selling his wife along with their furniture for 110 francs the lot, failed to get his price, then made a deal for 100 francs with 50 more to follow. When the local *notaire* refused to register the sale, the parties recorded it before three witnesses at a cabaret. An English student of the practice cites four nineteenth-century French cases that had been noted by the London *Times,* but he concludes that in England by the 1880s the institution was confined largely to the industrial North. Whatever went on in England, at least one Limousin peasant seems to have sold his wife after the turn of the century. We hear that the bargaining took several hours, and lots of people looked on.[6]

For all that such actions were probably decided by mutual agreement, they still appear demeaning. Women could be sold like cattle at a fair. Men never were, at least not in this sense. And some cattle were better off than women. As the Hautes-Alpes proverb had it: "Better a mare at Talissieux than a woman in Bion." In part this was a matter of labor. Jules Michelet had described peasant women as *négresses blanches*. Half a century later a publicist insisted that they died of overwork.[7] So did their menfolk, but at least these ate and drank more, and were hit less often.

Wife-beating was one symbol of male preponderance. Proverbs again record the popular wisdom: "Women are like cutlets. The more you beat them, the tenderer they are" or "Asses, nut-trees, women: no good comes from any of them but by the stick." Wedding songs referred to wife-beating as current and natural. Folklore, which has nothing to say opposing it (except perhaps that "Beating your wife is beating your purse"), punished the reverse—the husband beaten by his wife—by public humiliation.[8] Naturalist novelists have noted violence against women as a lower-class habit in country as in town; and readers of Zola's *L'Assommoir* will remember that one of Gervaise's dreams was that some day she might live without being beaten. When in 1884 the Finistère Assizes judged a man who beat his wife to death, the village mayor, in the course of giving evidence, described "the daily violence exercised especially upon their wives" by most of the local men.[9]

Drunkenness did not help, and drunkenness was increasing. Jéhan Rictus, the slangy, moving poet of Parisian lowlife, described the effects:

> Quand qu'y n'a bu, y d'vient méchant
> M'man dit toujours qu'al'le plaqu'ra
> Mais avant y l'estoubira
> Pis nous . . . y nous en f'ra autant.[10]

> (When he has drunk, he gets nasty,
> Mother keeps saying she'll quit,
> But befor' she does, he'll stomp'er
> Then us—he'll do us in as well.)

Drunk, or simply exasperated by hardship and endless frustration, men came to blows at the slightest provocation. They could as easily turn against their family, more accessible and less likely to retaliate. The last was not always true. Women responded in kind when they could do so, preferably with poison, the weapon of the weak: arsenic, copper sulfate, vitriol, mercuric chlorides, hemlock, or even phosphorus from the heads of matches. Most wives of the lower classes seem to have lived in fear of blows, but many a husband ate and drank in fear of poison, and some succumbed to it.

Physical violence, at home as in the street, was "natural," came easily, and ceased to be taken for granted very gradually. School and mimicry of the upper classes slowly taught that restraint and self-control could proceed from something other than fear: good manners and social virtues. This had occurred first among the upper and the middle classes, where by the nineteenth century the social graces had been assimilated as marks of proper breeding. It gradually worked its way down to the lower orders, as these acceded not just to education but to a modicum of space, comfort, and security that relieved some of the tensions under which they labored and provided slender opportunities for privacy, for relaxation, for civilization.

Such material change came late. Until it came, sometimes after the Second World War, household tensions remained intense, and opportunities to escape them slight for the less-well-off. Household duties were heavy, and they were not improved by frequent pregnancies. Trapped in domesticity in the suburb of Argenteuil, Karl Marx's eldest daughter, Jenny, who died two months before her father, in the winter of 1883, had borne six children during eight years of marriage. In one of her last letters to her sister Laura, she wrote: "I do believe that even the dull routine of factory work is not more killing than are the endless duties of the ménage. To me, at least, this is and always has been so."[11] Laura herself had three children in three years and saw them all die. No wonder women aged quickly, a fifty-year-old woman being considered old, another provoking comment for being still alert though over forty.[12] No wonder either, that the reinstitution of divorce in 1884, however hedged by formidable formalities, caused a sensation; and that within twenty years the ratio of marriages to divorce or legal separation had soared from 93 to 1, to 23 to 1.[13] But divorce, though it released a few, did not solve the problem of the many. Edmond de

Goncourt in his *Journal* for 1893 mentions the little girl of twelve who, in despair because of her gender, said a novena to become a boy.[14]

If life was hard for members of the middle-class, how much worse for those who faced more difficult conditions? Until 1914 poor women traditionally sold their tresses for the few sous that would bring them bread or some coveted luxury, like a length of calico or a kerchief. Wigmakers from all of Europe flocked to the Café de France at Limoges to attend its *Bourse aux cheveux* during the midsummer fair, where a kilo of hair sold for about 100 francs, until Chinese competition brought down the price. Following the economic upturn of the 1890s, the hair trade declined, shrinking back to poorer regions like Brittany, Auvergne, and the wine-growing South during the bad wine years.[15] But the problems of poverty continued for many, and marked even those for whom conditions improved. For those who had known the miseries of the depression, scrimping and pinching remained the rule: "*il n'y a pas de petites economies*" (there are no small savings). There was more meat, there was more wine, the prayer for one's daily bread was more readily answered. But lighthearted laughter did not come easily, or did not come at all. As the son of a fin de siècle artisan remembers: "My mother did not appreciate humor. She never laughed. The past weighed too heavily upon her."[16]

If the children of the poor soon learned about the realities of life, those of their betters were revolted when they discovered some of them. In 1904 a nineteen-year-old girl in her third year at a teachers' college became engaged to the son of her godfather: "Taking advantage of our being alone in a room, he kissed me. I was so affected that I fainted." There would be worse to come. In 1891 the highly respectable *Revue des Deux Mondes* published a story which mentions a wedding night: "from this moment there rose between them that fatal shadow that hovers thereafter over all of life, [the shadow] of an inexcusable rape, the irretrievable misunderstanding of the first embraces."[17] Disgust or pleasure, in any case, were secondary. For most men, and perhaps most women, motherhood was woman's major function. Even a sympathetic medical man writing in 1900 had to declare that "for the woman, maternity is the greatest and the noblest function; it is so to speak, her whole function. Thus, it is with good reason that physiologists and medical doctors have correctly and briefly put it: 'woman is but a womb . . . a uterus.' Woman is not a brain, she is a sex." Evidently, as a twentieth-century mother warned her daughter on her wedding eve: "A woman must accept everything her husband wants. It's hard because there are men who want it every day."[18]

Even when they were not repellent (and many a bride had been brought up to find them so, and many a groom to make them so), such demands could lead to conception; and repeated pregnancies endangered life and health. So, many a wife set out to discourage her husband, or even to suspend sexual relations altogether, as Adèle Hugo did with her Victor after their fifth child. It was more comfortable (and safer) to be a grandmother. The notorious profligacy of nineteenth-century husbands perhaps may be attributed less to ungoverned lust than to compliance with a spouse's wish.

In 1876 Germaine Boutelleau, exhausted after bearing her first child, had told her husband: "Georges! if you don't mind, we will adopt the others."[19] Her next and last, the future novelist Jacques Chardonne, would be born eight years later, a tribute to Georges's ingenuity—or to Germaine's strength of mind. If one may believe Chardonne's twentieth-century views on lovemaking, relative abstinence may not have been too hard to bear for men who regarded intercourse as a frustrating and fatiguing experience, let alone for women to whom it offered fateful consequences and little fun: "the woman is never satisfied . . . the game isn't worth the candle." In Chardonne's novels, as in old popular myth, the raptures of the flesh are reserved for women, which tells us little about the women but a good deal about the men. If literature gives the impression of a fin de siècle society seared by sex, the reality may have been quite different. One last revealing remark from Jacques Chardonne: "Sex is not very important. The trouble lies somewhere else: there is no love, or it is not what one would wish it to be."[20]

By 1884, when Jacques Chardonne was born at Barbezieux (Charente), much of the bourgeoisie, at least outside strict Catholic circles, was committed to family planning, often to contraception in one form or another, none entirely satisfactory. Births per 1000 population fell 27.4 percent between 1870 and 1914. During the first ten years of the twentieth century alone, the decline was 13 percent. Since village women tended to look to the bourgeoisie for models, bourgeois practices encouraged or sanctioned lower-class ones. This is not to say that peasants had waited till then to limit their families; in some parts of

France they had begun to do so before the Revolution. Late marriage, chastity, abstinence, weaning delayed because women didn't "take" with a child at the breast, were as much part of the peasant armory as of the bourgeois; and there are tales of mothers-in-law intervening (remember the crowded quarters on a farm) to limit marital sex.[21]

As the nineteenth century drew to an end, however, the more primitive and frustrating contraceptive techniques of the past were being replaced by the more bourgeois practice of coitus interruptus. Hardly very satisfying for most women, let alone for men, it did at least permit the serious limitation of conceptions. As a result, marriages which had been long avoided in order to avoid unwanted children were growing more general and being entered into at an earlier age. Between 1861 and 1931 the proportion of married women grew 12 percent; their fecundity fell 43 percent. When the century ended, Alphonse Bertillon, among others, was warning that more people were dying in France than babies were being born: "One doesn't have children because one doesn't want children." Certainly no more than two. "It is unseemly to go beyond this," and considered a breach of good manners by the son-in-law (note here the maternal family's novel interference). "Maternity no longer imposes respect." Women, Bertillon explained, were becoming more active: they worked, they wanted to be free, they even flirted. Worse, "they have abandoned the modesty reserved to the wife, now exempt from the respect by which her husband distinguished her from cynical mistresses." Wives too now sought "ennervating pleasures, the spice of embraces," and, when they obtained them, were surprised to conceive.[22] The next step was likely to be a pursuit of enervating pleasures while avoiding the surprises of conception. So even partial emancipation from biological destiny would be a step toward emancipation from social destiny. One can glimpse the source of Bertillon's discomfort as of Chardonne's glum view of sex: women of their class were no longer willing to limit their choice to abstinence or pregnancy. They sought pleasure on their own terms, with no painful consequence. This privilege had so long been reserved for men that there was something unsettling about women's pretentions.

*

As the last few paragraphs have intimated, the woman question, even in those dark days, was not all black. Women of the upper classes might sometimes be forlorn, but they were not bereft of influence—even on their husbands. Women of the lower classes were often oppressed and exploited, but they did their best to join the oppressing and exploiting classes, and sometimes succeeded. The woman question continues debatable, its aspects changing according to point of view and subjective interpretation. Among the upper classes, like a modern sovereign, the wife does not govern, but she often rules within the limits of rules that have been made by others. She has no power but can bestow honor, friendship, social acceptance, and standing. Among the lower orders the man rules, but the wife often governs, as mistress of the household, of the family budget, and of the cash—if she can get her hands on it.

In 1884, Henry James, passing through Tours, hired a horse-trap from a woman who managed a livery stable. He found occasion to note that "there is, in fact, no branch of human activity in which one is not liable, in France, to find a woman engaged . . . They are very formidable. In France one must count with the women." An Englishman long resident in France compared the lot of French women, especially of the working classes, with that of their English sisters; he found the former to be far better off: "In France it is the women who rule, and it's right that it should be so, considering their physical and intellectual superiority." The workman, clerk, or counter-jumper, Robert Sherard explained, usually handed his wages over to his wife, who gave him "a small allowance of pocket money." The woman then dispatched the household budget as she pleased, and bought a dress or hat if she thought she could afford them, with no reference to her husband, a thing no English working wife would dare to do.[23]

In this same vein, it is striking that of the three heroines of a recent book on justice under the Third Republic[24]—Thérèse Humbert, the force behind a major financial scandal, judged in 1902; Meg Steinheil, the brain behind an unsolved double murder, judged and acquitted in 1908; Henriette Caillaux, acquitted in 1914 of shooting the editor of the *Figaro*—none resembles the traditional image of the helpless woman: the milk-white lamb that bleats for man's protection.

I am inclined to believe that, among the better-off, the proportion of scatterbrains and vacuous flibbertigibbets was high, higher than it need have been. But, then, they had been deliberately bred to it, like the pretty goose of noble Lorraine blood whom Captain Esterhazy of

Dreyfus fame married in 1886, whose vapid snobbery and propensity to ennui provided some small retribution for his sinister excesses.[25] The education inflicted in the convents and private schools to which the daughters of good families were condemned left many girls unable to carry on an intelligent conversation and deepened the intellectual gap between the sexes which the eighteenth century had begun to close. No well-bred girl would be allowed to read a novel or go to the theater without parental censorship; few could go out at all without some kind of chaperone. Marriage came as emancipation, but by then the harm had been done. Men and women who dined at the same table, separated after dinner. Men and women of social orders where this did not obtain, similarly divided into the separate worlds of kitchen and cabaret, *lavoir* and blacksmith's shop.

As long as maternity and household chores designated a woman's particular sphere, a degree of division was not unnatural. But education and social conditioning conspired to emphasize the difference, which increased in a vicious spiral. Defined as mindless, too many women were trained to mindlessness. Their menfolk, discouraged and equally conditioned, fled from their mindlessness instead of attempting to change it. The only men who did not flee were priests, who offered women attention and a sphere of activity denied them almost everywhere else—a proclivity that further increased the division between the sexes.

The impression that, as Steven Hause and Anne Kenney put it, "attendance at Mass was a secondary sexual characteristic of French women" would have unfortunate effects on their political fortunes.[26] Parliamentary majorities, however much they disagreed on other things, continued to believe that giving women the vote was tantamount to handing the country over to a retrograde Church. This left the women at the mercy of the Roman Law and of its 1804 incarnation, the Napoleonic Code, than which (at least from women's point of view) few churches could have been more retrograde. The Code treated women as minors. They were denied the vote, could not witness civil acts, serve on juries, take a job, or spend their own money without their husband's consent. Their adultery was treated as a crime, whereas husbands' adultery was not even a misdemeanor. At last, in 1903, one eccentric magistrate refused to find a woman who had left a brutal and alcoholic husband to live with a decent man guilty of adultery, despite a law which the judge denounced as anachronistic and unjust.[27] But he was an exception.

Because, in René Viviani's wise words, legislators make the laws for those who make the legislators, the women's suffrage movement was caught in a bind. Without a vote they could exert little pressure on legislators, and legislators would not give them the vote. French feminist and suffragist traditions went back a long way. But their adherents were few and divided and almost all of them were to be found in Paris. That was bad, but ambient prejudice was worse. Discussing women's rights, the widely read *Petit Journal* (May 3, 1897) compared the horrid circumstances obtaining in Colorado, where women were free to vote, to sit on juries, and allegedly to serve in the National Guard, with those in France where women were wives and mothers first of all, honored for it and enjoying the men's protection, even against themselves. The *Petit Journal*'s readers were invited to look on the women of Colorado as Spartans did upon the drunken helot: as a horrid example that would remind them of the order and common sense they enjoyed at home.

A suffrage bill introduced in 1901 by an obscure deputy was never heard of again. And when, in October 1904, the feminists organized to heckle government celebrations of the hundredth anniversary of the Napoleonic Code, their feeble demonstrations flopped. Characteristically, the manifestation that drew most attention occurred during a ceremony at the Sorbonne, when Caroline Kauffmann interrupted the dignified proceedings by shouting "Down with the Napoleonic Code," while her hired man inflated and released balloons into the auditorium. This sort of thing was not calculated to make a deep impression, either on the general public or on the police court magistrate who dismissed her case.[28]

Nevertheless, spasmodic legislative initiatives were chipping away at the Code. In 1884 divorce had been made possible though difficult; in 1886 women were enabled to open savings accounts without their husbands' consent; in 1893 single or separated women were granted full legal capacity; in 1897 all women were recognized as eligible witnesses in civil actions. That same year married women were allowed to dispose freely of their own earnings, and even to seize the husband's pay if his contributions to the household were deemed insufficient. They would shortly gain the right to initiate suits concerning family property and to be consulted on property sales. Though all this may read like a meager harvest, clearly things were looking up.

History is lived by all, perceived by some, made by few. The history of women's emancipation in France lies less in the chronicle of political advances, which materialized only after the Second World War, than in sporadic steps toward more equal access to professional careers, many of which were taken during the twenty years preceding the First World War.

The relation between women's liberation and their access to paid employment is an ambiguous one. In 1900, 45 percent of all French women worked outside the home, and working women represented nearly two-fifths of the active population. That did not represent liberation: it was merely proof of the need that drove women, like men, to find a way to keep body and soul together. Equal pay for equal work would be long in coming. And not even that can make dreary repetitive labor other than what it is: a necessity. What nineteenth-century liberationists sought, as twentieth-century ones still do, was interesting, satisfying work, when most labor is neither—in other words, access to higher education and to the careers this opens up. In that connection, the first bottleneck women had to negotiate was the baccalaureate, which permitted entry into a faculty of the university. By 1905, 1148 girls had achieved the baccalaureate, and nearly two-thirds of these attended some university course. But it was slow going.

The ruling Republicans were well aware that education was the key to conquering minds and hearts. They no more ignored the problem of women's education than their opponents did. But the education offered by all parties would be separate and unequal. Women would benefit from a school system appropriate to their minds and needs— for one thing, lacking Greek and Latin—and preferably they should be taught by women who had themselves been specially and separately trained. By the 1890s women had won acceptance to higher education. Their problem was how to obtain the same education as men.

The argument that woman's place was in the home could only with some difficulty be raised in opposition to her sharing in the tasks of healing, with which she had been associated for centuries. Midwives apart, however, those drawn to lay cool hands on feverish brows long gravitated (or were oriented) to religious orders. Admission to medical studies, hence to the medical profession, was opened only through the intercession of Empress Eugénie. In 1869 four women students were admitted to the Medical School in Paris, which granted the first M.D. to a Frenchwoman in 1875. Bordeaux followed in 1884, and Montpellier in 1888. The first women *externes* in Paris hospitals appeared in 1881, *internes* in 1886. But most women medical students between 1868 and 1888 had been foreigners (of Eugénie's first four, only one had been French), and women in medical practice remained few: seven in all of France in 1882, ninety-five in 1903—one-third of them in Paris. As late as 1928, when the French medical corps counted 28,380 members, only 556 were women, and well over half of them practiced in the Paris area.[29]

Other faculties were slower to accept women. The Sorbonne allowed a girl to enroll in the Faculty of Letters in 1883; the Law Faculty admitted a woman in 1884; the first doctorate in the Sciences would be awarded in 1888; in Letters in 1914. But when, in 1882, Camille Claudel, a sculptress of great talent, sought admission to the School of Fine Arts, the director, who appreciated her work, refused: "I can't afford to start a revolution in my school."[30] Claudel had to continue in a private atelier for young women, as did most aspiring artists who could afford it. Paul Dubois, director of the Beaux Arts, knew whereof he spoke. In 1896 (the same year life-drawing classes in private academies were integrated at last) the Ecole des Beaux Arts announced that women students would be admitted to its classes and to competition for the prestigious Prix de Rome. The following year the first women students to tread the sacred precincts of the Beaux Arts set off a riot that ended with the intervention of the police and the temporary closing of the Ecole. The school reopened and women students stayed on (that first year forty-seven competed for admission and ten got in); but their right to compete for the Prix de Rome was rescinded and not restored until 1903. The first woman to win one of the coveted prizes and attend the Villa Medici would be a sculptor, Mademoiselle Heuwelmans, in 1911.[31]

The experience of the Fine Arts was not exceptional. Male students, ready to riot in the best of circumstances, greeted the appearance of women in their preserves with hostility. At the Sorbonne in 1883 their demonstrations had forced the cancellation of the course in which the first woman admitted was enrolled. In 1885 the admission of women to the prestigious *concours d'internat* had been greeted with noisy demonstrations, and the first candidate for an internship had been burned in effigy. Candidates for the doctorate in medicine faced the hostility of examiners eager to discourage others from following in their footsteps. "I don't see what you expect to gain from your studies," Professor Charcot told Blanche Edwards, when she got hers in 1889.[32] Law students were more disruptive, and in 1892 Jeanne Chauvin, the first woman to defend her dissertation, was forced to complete the public examination *in camera*. In 1897 she demanded admission to the bar and the right to exercise the profession for which she had qualified. She was refused, went to court, and lost on the ground that the legal profession should be reserved for men, who alone exercised civic rights. In 1900, finally, a special law permitted women to practice as lawyers. By 1910 the Paris bar counted seventeen female lawyers.[33]

On Christmas Eve 1900, a fortnight after Chauvin finally gained admission to the bar, a women's magazine, *La Nouvelle Mode,* looked to the century that lay ahead and found it unpredictable but for one thing: "the new evolution of women," no longer passive but henceforth militant and counting on their own efforts to affirm their personality and win their independence.[34] *La Nouvelle Mode* may have been premature, but its previsions would be vindicated.

✻

Such forecasts would be seriously borne out, in this as in other domains, only during and after the First World War, when women were admitted into engineering and technical schools and to the agrégation examinations which opened the way to teaching positions in higher education. But if, as the Comtesse de Bassanville asserted, dress is to the body what education is to the mind,[35] we can trace a similarly hesitant and jerky evolution in another crucial realm: fashion. If the record of the fin de siècle is as ambiguous in this as in other domains, here too it marks at least several liberating changes.

Fashion in traditional society is functional only in the most symbolic sense. In the kind of world where idleness is vital to social prestige, the apparel of the fashionable declares that, heedless of practicalities, its wearers can afford the superfluous, the futile, or the merely enjoyable. Frail footwear, gossamer materials, precarious headgear, proclaim their own uselessness and the incapacity of the wearer to perform demeaning physical tasks. The less functional the raiment, the more prestigious it looks. Simplicity, dear to revolutionary ideology, is worshiped only briefly and soon discarded for the flounces and furbelows that suggest affluence.

By the end of the century the time had passed when, as in the fastuous 1860s, a *robe de bal* was worth the price of a farm. But ball-gowns for the dressy, such as Mademoiselle Otéro or Liane de Pougy might wear, still cost from 900 to 1600 francs, a good deal more than their maids' annual wages. And many a dressmaker's bill soared into tens of thousands. Most women in country or town, if not too poor, owned two dresses: one for everyday, preferably in some drab serviceable color; and one for Sundays and great events, which was usually the marriage gown, eventually dyed black, in which they expected to be buried. But the well-dressed, then as today, needed far more. The rule laid down by a fashion treatise of 1866 held good thirty years later: a woman of the world needed seven or eight *toilettes* a day.[36]

The more useless and hemmed about the wearer, the more incapable of free and easy movement, the more genteel he or she must be. This principle dominated feminine fashions of the nineteenth century: delicate slippers, voluminous skirts, unstable coiffures, hazardous headgear, hobbled those who could afford them and culminated in the crinoline whose scale prohibited access to vulgar public transport and sometimes passage through ordinary doors. Nor were such fashions reserved exclusively for the very few. They trickled down to the middle classes and also, by way of hand-me-downs and the thriving old clothes' trade, to servants, urban workingwomen, and even to the villages where so many domestics were recruited. By the 1860s chroniclers of fashion were claiming, with some exaggeration, that the crinoline hoopskirt had reached remote country hamlets.[37] It was certainly discomforting a lot of women and inconveniencing a lot of men. Then, having helped launch this awkward monument, Empress Eugénie led a movement toward simpler attire. Holidays at the seaside, in the mountains, in the countryside, excursions in search of fresh air, were better enjoyed in less expansive robes.[38] Introduced for the summer "season," the *petit costume* was soon brought back to town as vastly more convenient, even for society ladies, but still more so for the bourgeoises who followed their lead and for the workingwomen who wore their castoffs.

Then came the war of 1870, defeat, the Third Republic, and a

René Péan was Jules Chéret's brother-in-law, and an able watercolorist in his own right. The great department store Aux Trois Quartiers, founded in 1829, still stands by the Madeleine, as it did when Péan advertised it in the late 1880s.

"seriousness" appropriate to more difficult times. Republican simplicity was supposed to contrast with flashier imperial forms. No longer would the duchesse de Mouchy wear two millions' worth of diamonds at a ball, as she had done in 1869. The way to wear a beautiful dress, declared the wife of a great newspaper editor, is to forget you are wearing it. Or one might add, at least forget the price. Yet postwar austerity did not last long: accessories first, then dresses, resumed the bent toward conspicuous consumption; sleeves, collars, bustles, and muffs again caused problems at carriage doors, in theater stalls, on sofas.[39] Finally the first important step toward lasting improvement was taken. In 1885 Redfern the couturier (like several other Paris dressmakers, an Englishman) created the *tailleur,* or tailor-made costume: plain wool, plainly cut jacket, plain collar, no ornaments. This was a costume you could walk in, convenient for travel or on the city streets, even for working in; it was appropriate to the new *indépendance d'allure* which foreign influences were inspiring.[40] It also reflected the growing interest in hygiene; the reaction against overeating (now denounced as gastrolatry) and toward greater sobriety in diet; and with this a changing ideal of femininity, from the opulence and pallor of the midcentury to a slimmer, healthier type of beauty, less plump, more sportive.[41]

The new, more slender lines, though honored largely in the breach until the 1920s, were to affect other aspects of feminine apparel. As the mass of superimposed petticoats receded, so did the pockets sown into them or the "horrid satchels" of canvas or linen, hanging from the waist and hard to locate amid the folds.[42] No longer would women have to tuck up their skirts and fumble, when looking for a key or for a handkerchief. Ladies, henceforth, would be equipped with the handbags which Frenchwomen had adopted once before: to go with the straight dresses that had come in, in the 1790s, during the Diréctoire. Discarded at the Restoration, when skirts had swelled once more, reticules or *ridicules,* offspring of the humble drawstring bag, now returned for good, henceforth to be carried in the hand, to be adorned and filled, to be forgotten, and increasingly to be snatched away by thieves.[43]

More interesting, as bulky petticoats and panniers ebbed, other articles of underwear acquired more importance. Octave Uzanne, writing in 1898, felt that the special characteristic of contemporary women was the luxury of their underwear—considerably developed in the past fifteen years, "in response to the severity, the simplicity, the sobriety of outer garments," and especially of the "English costume, the *costume tailleur.*" Having abandoned outward ostentation (Uzanne exaggerated a good deal, but his standard of comparison remained the crinoline!), all jolly luxury now took refuge with the undies. So apparently did color, which a chronicler of 1896 interpreted as a recent "modern taste, born no doubt of the nervousness that torments our imagination."

Such male views seem to be confirmed by an article of the same year in *La Nouvelle Mode,* which referred to the current efforts to render underwear "as little voluminous as possible—given the fashion of ever more clinging skirts. A whole school of very elegant women who count the millimeters of their waists and the centimeters of their hips" has managed to combine chemise, drawers, and small underpetticoat into a single garment made of cambric or, if one were chilly, of China silk. This was the *combinaison* (combination), imported from the United States. The corset went directly over it, the underskirt was buttoned onto the corset, a little *cache-corset* in lawn (fine linen) went over the lot, then everything was ready for the dress. "It is difficult to dress more lightly," *La Nouvelle Mode* opined, but ladies given to chills had better avoid such excessive divestiture.[44] It is clear from this that simplification was relative, and that the silks, cambrics, and fine linens offered plenty of opportunity for creativity.

They also provided an open invitation to greater cleanliness, which seems to have counted among the rarer refinements of the modern age. Octave Uzanne, writing in 1894, noted the novelty of the concern "for the most intimate cleanliness" shown by fashionable women at least, for it went along with luxurious lingerie. Was his observation representative? It was certainly new. We have seen that people were grubby, did not smell sweet, nor seemed much to mind it. As the proverb had it, the more the he-goat stinks, the more the she-goat loves him. That this could also work the other way is attested by frequent references to that *odor di femina,* the effluvia of armpits, and so on, supposed to drive men mad with passion. But even among the more sedate, shortage of water and feminine modesty long combined to make washing rare. A manual of elegance for ladies ordered its readers to shut their eyes while washing their private parts. This cannot have been a serious concern, since thorough ablutions were largely left to women of ill repute. Most of the rest followed the medieval Salernitan precepts of hygiene: "[Wash] the hands often, the feet rarely, the head never." Forain's sybarite affirmed that, whether he needed it or not, he always took two baths a year.[45] Few of his fellow French of either sex could claim as much, and a few years before 1914 the father of a boarder at the lycée of Aurillac (Cantal), learning that his daughter attended the public baths weekly with her fellows, wrote a letter of protest to the headmistress: "I didn't entrust you my daughter for *this!*"[46] Yet even such a letter is evidence that cleanliness forged ahead—slowly, like everything else, hesitating before established prejudice reinforced by antediluvian facilities. Nevertheless, it pressed forward impelled by new medical and didactic norms, by the dictates of fashion, and by the rules of conspicuous consumption that made freshly washed linens a rare, hence desirable, luxury.

Two items among those listed by *La Nouvelle Mode* also became the subject of further evolution, along with much debate. One was drawers, or underpants, also known as tubes of modesty. Drawers had been a novelty, imported from England at the beginning of the century to be worn by little girls, whose skirts were shorter, and left to them for threescore years thereafter. At mid-nineteenth century, underdrawers did not figure among the items in a proper young bride's dowry. But the crinoline, with the mishaps to which it was prone, encouraged sporadic adoptions. Adding to the undergarment jungle, drawers were awkward, and the slits they occasionally had made them potentially more indecent than their absence would have been. This may be why prostitutes were quick to adopt them—a further argument against their being worn by honest women who, when they did wear them, preferred the closed model, buttoned at the side. Still, in certain circles drawers were considered symbols of purity; by the 1880s many well brought up girls were wearing them, at least in Paris. In 1892 Yvette Guilbert was singing

> Ell'n'voulait pas avant l'mariage
> Quitter ses pantalons fermés;
> Ça vous prouv'bien qu'elle était sage,
> Sa mère ayant su la former.[47]

> She never dreamed before her wedding
> To yield th' impenetrable pantaloon;
> It goes to show she was a good girl:
> Her mother taught her not to spoon.

It is not clear how many women continued to wear drawers once they were free to go without them. A student of the question in 1906 believed that many among the bourgeoisie did not; and that "women of the people" never had. One of Colette's heroines explained that she preferred to feel her thighs soft against each other when she walked. More basically, as four young washerwomen tried in 1895 for flaunting themselves a bit too visibly declared: "Your Honor, it costs too much!"[48] Before underpants really caught on with women, skirts had to get a good deal shorter, and this they did not begin to do till 1915. On the other hand, if underpants took their time, overpants appeared as early as the 1880s. We shall learn about this in due course, à propos the bicycle. But all seem to agree that cycling costumes affected fashion considerably. They probably furnished one more argument for wearing drawers. But they also put many young women into breeches, bloomers, and other sporting gear, taught them the convenience of pockets, spared them the need to raise their skirts, and gave them a taste for costumes in which they could sit, walk, or lean back more easily—let alone pedal.[49]

Above all, they helped to free women from the corset, or at least they set them on the road to freedom. If pants were a luxury, and a dubious one at that, corsets were regarded as a necessity at almost all levels of society. "A self-respecting woman," *Fin de Siècle* decreed, "must have a morning corset, a dress corset, and a bathing corset."[50] This last, in heavy tulle or some light tissue, stiffened only with light stays, should still be strong enough to squeeze the waist tightly beneath the swimming suit. Corsets were big business. Under the Second Empire Paris had counted over 10,000 women corsetmakers, selling about 1,200,000 corsets every year for as little as 3 to 5 francs or as much as 200 francs, for a general turnover of more than 10 million francs. All this for the capital alone, where the relevant figures had grown by about one-third at the turn of the century; it would have been still higher but for the new disfavor with which the garment met.[51]

Colette recalls "the time of the great corsets which raised the breasts high, crushed the behind, and hollowed out the stomach." Germaine Gallois, a contemporary actress, never accepted a "sitting" role. Sheathed by a corset that began under her armpits and ended close to the knees, two flat steel springs in her back, two others along the hips, a cord between the legs maintaining the edifice that was held together by six meters of stay lace, she stood up, even during the intervals, from 8:30 P.M. to midnight.[52]

Even less majestic structures could be a torture to wear and a menace to the innards they compressed. Women would hide in the shadows of theater or opera box to slip off their corset, roll it in a newspaper, and breathe more freely; but many had no opportunity for relief. This mattered little apparently, until the cycling fad emphasized the corset's constriction and led thousands of young women to rebel against a grave impediment to their liberty to pedal. One cycled best in trousers, and trousers preferred no corset. Even without trousers, constrictions made pedaling difficult. The journal of the Touring Club de France in 1895 advised its women readers to abandon the traditional corset for a more rational foundation garment and, if they needed it, a brassiere. Riding bicycles had already revolutionized fashion, argued Dr. Gache-Sarraute. If it could lead to corset reform as well, it would benefit all humanity. The corset hampered women's breathing, their digestion, and ultimately their fertility, placing them in "an unjust and illogical state of inferiority."[53] Dr. Gache-Sarraute was right, but the benefit she sought, like many others, was slow to come about. Medical theses were still arguing the case against the corset shortly before the First World War. The corset, Dr. Ludovic O'Followell affirmed in 1908, caused nervous dyspepsia, insomnia, heartburn, and, through the cordials taken to relieve this last, could lead to insidious alcoholism. It also occasioned "all those bothersome gurgles" that sometimes rose to the level of "sinister plashings that spring from the depths of your stomach and make you pale and shudder with shame and horror." In this time of feminine revindications, opined O'Followell, when the natural being revolted against the conventions that deformed it, the corset, symbol of slavery that "add[ed] to the natural inferiority of women," was "a new Bastille to be demolished."[54]

O'Followell's eloquence bore testimony to the frustrations that the corset's adversaries encountered. But the Bastille was crumbling. In a few years, thanks to the war and to postwar fashions, it would be in ruins. The bicycle had played a great part in this; so had medically and socially inspired arguments for healthier bodies and more rational dress; so had the great couturiers, from Redfern to Paul Poiret. Unmoved by considerations of comfort or hygiene, dressmakers then as now concerned themselves with fashion—that is, with styles whose chief characteristic is that they go out of fashion. As Cocteau has said, "la mode, c'est ce qui se démode." The frills and flounces that had given women of an earlier age "the appearance of being composed of different pieces poorly fitted together" were discarded in favor of more fastidious harmonies; showy materials and garish colors fit for parvenus were replaced by discreet effects seen only by the eyes of connoisseurs. Proust's Marcel dressed his Albertine in subdued shades and materials that only an aesthete like Charlus could "appreciate at their true value."[55]

Everything suggests that fashion remained equivocal as ever. Writing about the years when his clients replaced the corset with the brassiere, Poiret would boast: "I liberated the bust, but I hobbled the legs . . . Everyone wore the narrow skirt." In the same vein, the loosely pleated robes of Fortuny, admired by Proust's painter Elstir in *Remembrance of Things Past,* hung in natural folds and dispensed with corsets, but they imprisoned their wearers in heavy folds of brocade and silk.[56] Conspicuous uselessness continued à la mode. The role of fashion in women's liberation remains uncertain. Still, *La Nouvelle Mode* of 1900 correctly noted a change: sports, diet, and hygiene had altered habits and manners. Women were trying to lose weight, they were eating less, they were crying less, they were fainting less.[57] If women no longer suffered from the vapors, this may have been due to less constricting garb. It was certainly due also to loosening social constrictions. And to a changing image of themselves that was reflected in and by the images of fashion.

5

The Endless Crisis

Emile Verhaeren, the Belgian poet, enjoyed the 1900 Exhibition and "the motley show that this hour of an ending century offered." He also praised the courage that the French had shown in preparing for it over a five-year period, "through the dangerous days, the controversies, and the dangers of war, through international hatreds and covetousness."[1]

As an elementary text put it, since 1871 Europe (meaning France) "has lived under the threat of a new war, always possible."[2] The dangers of war had been most evident during an incident with Germany in 1887 and, more recently, in 1898, when summer and autumn had seen France and Britain come close to conflict in Africa, where a French column commanded by Captain Marchand had reached the Upper Nile at Fashoda, even as Kitchener marched south from Egypt into the Sudan. France was not prepared for war overseas, or on the seas. The crisis had been settled at the cost of one foreign minister's disappearance and of a modicum of French pride. But it confirmed ancient hostilities. Not Germany alone but Britain, and Britain primarily, were the enemies of France. As the eminent founder of the Ecole des Sciences Politiques demonstrated in a book written under the influence of these events, it was hopeless to think that France and England could ever attain a mutually sympathetic understanding.[3] This point of view would fade after the rapprochement of 1903 and the Entente Cordiale of 1904, but it never disappeared entirely, as was evident in 1940—and since.

Nevertheless, since 1870 the official enemy had been the Germans: official in textbooks, which reminded the new generation and its parents that the Treaty of Frankfurt "is a truce, not a peace; which is why

La Porte Monumentale de la place de la Concorde.

since 1871 all Europe lives permanently under arms."[4] Official also in
the courts of law which had to consider just how insulting or discredit-
able it was to call someone a Prussian. At Lille in 1887, at Douai in
1890, at Sceaux in 1898, the courts had held the allegation that a
person or a firm was Prussian to be defamatory, "given the state of
public opinion in France concerning the Prussian nation." Only at
Boulogne-sur-Mer, in January 1900, did the court decide that "to call
someone a Prussian does not qualify as abusive language . . . It would
be different if the expression was dirty Prussian."[5]

Defeat was also felt as a personal loss, a kind of dishonor, remembered by men like Paul Cambon, walking around Versailles with his
brother Jules in 1897 and feeling that the splendors of the palace were
tarnished by memories of the German presence there: "between the
glorious France of yore and our France there is this . . . disgrace, this
flaw . . . like a burn that doesn't heal."[6] But the Cambons, like Paul
Déroulède, the nationalist poet and founder in 1882 of the Ligue des
Patriotes, had been in their twenties at the time of defeat. Their genera-

tion and those of their elders—Henri Rochefort, Juliette Adam—
remembered the "terrible year" and the loss of the eastern provinces in
a way young folk did not. Even Cambon suspected that the young of
the century's end felt nothing about 1871, or about revanche, and the
observant J. E. C. Bodley concurred.[7] At the *Nouvelle Revue,* which she
kept going with her money, Symbolists and Decadents scoffed at
Juliette Adam's old-fashioned chauvinism. Young intellectuals looked
on revanchists as ridiculous, and within a few years their avant-garde
views would make their way among the general public. By 1905 an
Englishman long resident in Paris noted that people no longer remembered the war and that talk about *la revanche,* quite common in the
1890s, was now restricted to a few.[8] In 1905 this too was about to
change. Before it did, however, the growing indifference to the humiliation and loss suffered in 1871 appeared to furnish further proof of
decadence, just as the defeat itself had done: grist to the mills of
nationalist pessimism.

As always, foreign affairs loomed less large than internal ones, and
foreign conflict chafed less than conflict at home. Accounts of the
Third Republic which mark only its major crises lose sight of the fact
that its existence, practically to the First World War, was one long
crisis, every lull overshadowed by disbelief that it could last, every
relaxation of tension flouted by some new alarm.

The hesitant new Republic proved more resistant than most people
hoped or feared. In retrospect, it had a lot of luck: Napoleon III's heir,
the Prince Imperial, was killed in Africa in 1879; the heir of Charles X,
Henri de Bourbon, Comte de Chambord, stuck resolutely to antediluvian views that discouraged his supporters and discredited the idea of
monarchic restoration. By the time he died in 1883, the Republic had
settled in and royalism, though fashionable in some quarters and frequently disruptive, was never again a threat. Active and sometimes
effective as critics and troublemakers, royalists would never again make
policy, let alone form a government. But they continued numerous in
the army, the administration, the Church, and the schools that the
Church controlled, spinning out a sense of uncertainty by their insistence that the Republic was no more than a temporary interlude. In
1882 young Pierre de Margerie, seeking to take the entrance exam for
the foreign service, was asked to declare his loyalty to the Republic.
His father, dean of the Catholic University of Lille and a man of

conscience, was torn: the Republic was a form of government he did not hate in theory, he said, but which he abhorred as a Frenchman because it brought misfortune to France, and as a Christian because he could not admit its legitimacy. On the other hand, he reasoned, many graduates of Jesuit schools had signed declarations of loyalty, and the Minister knew perfectly well what their assurances were worth. Since the Republic colluded with its enemies to let them into its service, why should one scruple over an oath? Margerie entered the service of the Republic.[9]

The Republic knew what it was up to. In the long run, monarchism persisted as an eccentricity rather than a political force. For example, the young Elizabeth de Clermont-Tonnerre, whose aunt, the Duchesse de Choiseul (a Republican), had given her a little necklace of red, white, and blue pearls: "But it is *tricolore,* I cannot wear a republican necklace." Or the Marquis de Farges, condemned to five days in jail and a 15-franc fine for having called the "Marseillaise" a "filthy" song.[10]

Furthermore, just as the Republic was finding its feet, politics was becoming considered a profession unfit for decent people. Here too the pernicious American influence denounced in other contexts was making itself felt. Henry James, in Paris in 1876, had noted an eminent literary critic's complaint: "We are Americanizing!" Did he refer to the elections of that year, or to the way that they were being fought? A journalist was clearer: "We are beginning to imitate the United States," the Bonapartist Fidus wrote, "by leaving politics to people who are little esteemed and who will end by being a little despised." Within ten years, another man of letters, having tested the political waters, testified that Fidus was right: politics in France, said the critic Jules Claretie, is the business of people who have nothing else left to try, when it is not a springboard for young men who have not tried any-thing yet.[11] Unfortunately, politics proved to be the business of others than politicians alone.

The Republic had started with one more advantage. In late spring 1871 the Commune of Paris had been put down in fire and blood, its hopes of social revolution scotched. Edmond de Goncourt, embittered but farsighted, had commented that such a bloodletting, "by killing off the battling part of the population," delayed the next revolution by one generation. "The old society has twenty years of peace ahead." He was a bit too optimistic and, anyway, memories faded slowly. In 1879, when the exiles of the Commune began to trickle back, some Paris shopkeepers, expecting the worst, hid their valuables and laid in stocks of food. As late as 1883 a Parisian recorded that the anniversary of the Commune had just passed in peace: "this evening we are still alive! Our homes haven't been burnt down!" The diarist could afford to be ironic, but he had to admit that "lots of people are afraid of the revolution awakening."[12] Within a decade his fears had spread, and with better reason. As memories of the Commune faded sufficiently to revive in fresh, exciting form, the social atmosphere grew more tense. A Swiss banker could not help noting, "In France, there's constantly something in the air . . . the atmosphere is charged with electricity."[13]

After years of uncertainty, during which the provisional had become chronic, the elections of 1876 returned a Republican majority. Tension between this and the conservative (actually monarchist) president, Marshal MacMahon, grew steadily worse. Henry James, writing to the *New York Tribune,* reported the intensity of political debate, the sharpness of political divisions, and his impression that "No French people are Republicans—at least no one that one meets." But Republicans there were in number, even though James did not frequent their kind. And since history is made with memories, many remembered how a similar clash of wills a quarter-century earlier had ended with Louis-Napoleon's coup of December 2, 1851. By the end of 1876 Cambon, then Prefect of the Doubs, was telling his mother that the country was in a state of revolution, which could end in gunfire. Would the Marshal attempt a coup?[14] On May 16, 1877, he did, although his action remained within constitutional bounds and open violence was avoided.

Although no barricades went up and no shots were fired, the political class knew that the electoral battle of 1877 continued the long French civil war, by other means. The royalist bishop of Poitiers, who was a man of principle, pointed out that true coups are made for someone or something, not, like MacMahon's, against. But he was one coup behind. Henceforth, all sides were apprehensive, all persuaded that time was running out before the enemy struck the first blow. MacMahon's was a preemptive move. It failed. But it testified, if testimony were needed, that politics were to be treated as a matter of life and death, that political crises could inspire still more attempts to resolve them by extralegal means. The language of politics, extraordinary in its violence and scurrility, confirmed this.

In fact politics continued to be, as they have been since representative assemblies first appeared, a matter of wheeling and dealing. This too was grist for the mill of those for whom porkbarrel politics confirmed the corruption of parliamentary institutions, reflected and advanced the decadence of French society, and justified the violence of their own reactions. How could one respect the authorities and the laws of a corrupt society?

If 1877 had broken the precedent of 1851, it set a precedent of its own: in 1878 the humbled president hosted the first International Exhibition since 1867; it proved, as an English journalist put it, that "Paris was herself again." Gustavus Augustus Sala could not know that such recovery rites would become a habit, and that exhibitions would follow crises in 1889 (after Boulanger), in 1900 (after Dreyfus), as in 1937 (following the strikes of the Popular Front). Or perhaps it was not that exhibitions followed crises, but that crisis had become so endemic that no decade would pass without one. Since the first Revolution, no regime had lasted more than twenty years. Why should this one be different?

At the beginning of July 1886 the British ambassador to France remarked that the Republic had lasted sixteen years, "and that's about the time which it takes to make the French tired of a form of government."[15] Within a few days the military review that marked July 14 seemed to confirm his words: the Minister of War, General Georges Boulanger, was cheered with a frenzy that forecast a new threat to the established order. Limned in cheap images and broadsheets, consecrated in popular songs, Boulanger became "Général Victoire," symbol of national pride, soon to be denounced by Bismarck as the greatest danger to Franco-German relations, by good Republicans as a music-hall conspirator—a *Saint-Arnaud de café-concert*. But even those who sneered knew that Saint-Arnaud, as Minister of War, had helped carry out the coup of December 1851, and that the popularity that makes music-hall heroes could lead to greater heights, perhaps even a Boulangist coup. In spring 1887 a convenient change of government forced the general out of office, and a convenient provincial posting sent him out of Paris just a few days before the next July 14 parade.

The brushfire seemed damped when, that October, a political scandal fanned it back to life. As with many such affairs, its immediate cause was accidental. One lady of dubious reputation had borrowed a dress from another and would not return it. The lover of the despoiled lady denounced the borrower to the police for trafficking in decorations. Soon the police discovered what many had been whispering for years: generals and senators were heavily involved in the sale and purchase of honors and favors, especially the revered Legion of Honor, whose ultimate source lay in the presidential palace, where the President's son-in-law, Daniel Wilson, had his office. Before President Charles Grévy, who had been reelected to a second term just two years before, was persuaded to resign, all Paris was in an uproar, plotting and threatening insurrection. By late November the boulevards were black with shouting crowds, carriages were being toppled over, old Communards tried to march on the Hôtel de Ville and had to be dispersed on the rue de Rivoli, new revolutionaries held meetings in the Hôtel de Ville itself, the patriotic and gymnastic clubs of Déroulède held themselves ready for combat, and anxious (or hopeful) eyes were cast on the army barracks to see whether the army was likely to intervene.[16]

It was hard to tell how much of the unrest was directed against Grévy, tarred by his son-in-law's discredit, and how much against Jules Ferry, the strongest figure in Republican ranks, who seemed destined to succeed him but against whom too many hatreds coalesced. The extreme Left detested Ferry for his role as Prefect of the Seine during the siege of Paris and the Commune that followed; the nationalists denounced him as an agent of Bismarck for having diverted national energies from the Vosges to colonial enterprise; the Catholics would not forgive the patron of the secular—"godless"—school and, even less, the man who had been married (and, worse still, continued happily wed) in a civil ceremony. Within forty-eight hours of Grévy's reluctant decision to resign, dated December 2 as if to show that the chance of a coup does not return on every anniversary of Austerlitz, a successor had been found in the person of Sadi Carnot. "Anything but a civil war," Clemenceau had advised, "let's take an outsider." The "outsider" would be selected not because of his high character or of the historical associations of his name (his grandfather, Lazare, had been "The Organizer of Victory" under the First Republic) but, as Clemenceau, never short of the mot juste explained, because of his "perfect insignificance." Detractors would claim that what Clemenceau really said was "We shall vote for the most stupid," which he denied.[17]

Yet it does seem as if democracy, at least in France, preferred mediocrities to lead it. Perhaps it felt safer that way.

One short-lived result of the Wilson scandal was to call attention to the French democracy's penchant for distinctive decorations. "*Vieux décoré*" became an insult, and one enterprising man was sentenced to three months in jail for selling an imaginary decoration: the *ordre de la Mélusine*. But such discredit did not last long. Indeed, since a decree of March 1891 confirmed the wearing of decorations or rosettes without the actual cross or palms attached, the Frenchman's beribboned buttonhole may be to some extent a re-creation of the fin de siècle.[18]

For the moment, the first concern of Carnot and of his friends was to defend the established disorder against the rekindled popularity of General Boulanger, who was garnering the votes of all the discontented and the support of all the regime's enemies from monarchists to Communards. Boulangism, declared *l'Univers*, the leading Catholic newspaper of the day, was ceasing to be a farce and becoming a force. It was futile to remind the general that, at his age, Napoleon was already dead. By Easter Sunday 1888 Cambon could see no way out of the situation but "a dictatorship . . . demagogy inside and war outside." The republic seemed doomed. Again. The military governor of Paris, expecting a kidnap attempt, had his office doors secured with extra-heavy bolts.[19] Flaubert's old friend Maxime du Camp reflected bitterly that it would probably be his fate to die under the rule of Boulanger: "Like Peru, Haiti, Mexico, France slides toward intermittent Caesarism." When two aging statesmen met in the Senate, the royalist Louis Buffet urged Jules Simon (the Prime Minister whom MacMahon had dismissed on May 16, 1877) to draw his salary and have some ready cash in hand in the event of a coup: "Tomorrow we may be in prison." Cambon noted sadly that "this sort of joke is a good reflection of the general state of mind." Later economists would suggest that this was when the middle classes again started to keep their cash close by, for fear of social turbulence.[20]

When, in January 1889, the string of Boulanger's electoral victories culminated in a spectacular triumph in Paris, everybody—the government, Boulanger's friends, and the crowds in the streets—expected him to march on the Elysée. But the General proved a paper tiger. Indecisive, intimidated, and distracted by a passionate love affair, he fled the country, appropriately on April Fool's Day. A few hours before his departure the Eiffel Tower was inaugurated. Because its elevators were not working, the president of the Seine General Council (the same Edouard Jacques whom Boulanger had defeated in January) and the president of the Paris Municipal Council accompanied Gustave Eiffel up 1792 steps to raise the tricolor flag over the tower that men of taste denounced as a monstrosity. Throughout the summer visitors flocked to the Exhibition, which at least one observer had expected to be opened by Boulanger not by Carnot; arrests were made for subversive cries of "Vive Boulanger!"; but when the elections came in September the leaderless Boulangists were crushed.[21]

Yet the concerns that Boulangism represented lived on: dissatisfaction with a regime denounced as inefficient, corrupt, and unprestigious; political opposition from the Right, from the Left, from patriots calling for national regeneration, from Catholics revolted by a godless regime, from anti-Semites demanding "France for the French," from moralists disgusted by the decay of private and public morality. In 1897 the acute English observer J. E. C. Bodley commented on the curious French insistence on associating "purity of morals with the Republican form of government, for which history furnishes no justification," but which he traced to the high Plutarchian standards that the first Revolution had tried to set.[22] Whatever the inspiration, good Republicans were more shocked by Republican immorality than by that of the unconverted, and newly horrifying revelations did not improve their conscience.

Soon after the Boulanger scare there came, in 1891–92, the collapse of the Panama Canal Company. This organization, having devoured over $300 million, carried with it in its fall the savings of thousands of small investors, the fame of Ferdinand de Lesseps, builder of the Suez Canal and one of the Republic's last surviving heroes, the good name of Gustave Eiffel, and the remaining shreds of the prestige of the political class.

The Panama scandal was a Republican debacle. Over a hundred deputies, senators, ministers, and ex-ministers were implicated in the company's dishonest and demeaning shenanigans. All that the Republicans could think of to palliate it was to point out that they were not the only, or necessarily the greatest, thieves around. Louis Barthou, a future prime minister, advised his rural electors: "Look and see on which side the greatest thieves are to be found." Perhaps, after all, as

Denis Brogan said, if Republicans were thieves, their foes were fools, and "a peasant electorate prefers a knave to a fool."[23] Even more likely, the politics of Paris were of slight concern to the rest of the country, its crises had a metropolitan rather than a national impact. Even so, the echo of Parisian doings, filtered through the talk of provincial cafés and clubs, was emphasized by the rhetoric of a popular press just beginning to be read more widely, magnified by the prestige of the capital, and brought home by the dire financial losses caused by the Panama bankruptcy when times were hard anyway. Descriptions of the late-nineteenth-century political scene remain to a large extent descriptions of Paris. But this grows steadily less true as politics come to concern ever broader sections of the population, the sense of the regime's discredit and its fragility grows stronger, and the perceptions of Paris trickle through the lesser urban centers even into the countryside.

Few seem to have believed that such a frail and rickety regime could continue much longer. Even Bodley, although he insisted that "outside the trifling circles of the capital . . . and among the general public" one found only indifference to political movements, actors, and activities, had to conclude that when parliamentary institutions were not respected, they could not be regarded as permanent.[24]

This is not a political history of the Third Republic, but an attempt to convey the lack of respite, the persistent sense of insecurity, and the ambient disgust with political life. The country stumbled from one crisis to another. By the end of 1892 the *Gazette des Tribunaux*, no radical sheet, commented that "the measure of scandals is running over." No wonder that an old royalist who found the fin de siècle atmosphere "anxious, agitated, and inclined to pessimism," asked himself whether society was not sliding down the steep slope of dissolution.[25]

One more factor of anxiety and disquiet had been slowly developing. Since the late 1870s social and socialist agitation had begun to gather speed. In 1880 the pilgrimage to the *mur des Fédérés* at the Père Lachaise Cemetery, where the last fighters of the Commune had gone down, had become an annual ceremony honoring henceforth not criminals but martyrs. A decade later, on May 1, 1890, Labor Day was introduced from the United States, a kind of annual rehearsal of revolution, alarming to well-thinking folk, encouraging to workers conscious of their reviving force, exciting to those bourgeois with a social conscience—the sort of men in whom Cambon deplored "the weepy socialist sensibility fashionable today."[26]

✳

French socialism in the most general sense was more a matter of sensibility than of doctrine, partly because the country knew not one socialist doctrine but many. A united socialist or labor movement did not exist before the twentieth century. Beginning in the 1880s, the most forceful and visible section of the extreme Left was also the least organized: anarchism. Where socialists wanted to capture the state on behalf of the oppressed, anarchists sought not the capture of the state, but its abolition. True anarchists in a revolution, explained Jean Grave, one of their ideologues, should not stupidly proclaim a new government but shoot whoever tries to set one up. This sensible appreciation of how easily reformers turn into oppressors went along with distrust of all instruments of repression (army, police, bureaucracy, church, and schools), of private property, and of capital—which could result only from the appropriation and accumulation of the value created by the work of others, that is, from theft. Most visibly, though, the anarchists were activists. Rejecting the patient preparation of revolution, let alone of elections and reforms by legal means, they argued that insurrectionist deeds were the most effective propaganda. Whatever its effectiveness, propaganda by deed evoked the sympathies of many and the attention of all.

Convinced anarchists were few, and during most of the 1880s their propaganda remained on the verbal level.[27] Because they criticized property, the police, and military service, sometimes in inflammatory terms, anarchists often appeared in court charged with advocating murder, arson, pillage, or desertion. None of this, however, aroused much interest until the bombs began to explode in a vicious crescendo of repression and revenge. May 1, 1891, had seen anarchist riots in Paris; those arrested had been roughed up by the police before being tried and sent to jail. In 1892 the homes of legal officials involved in that trial began to be blown up; and Paris lived in terror until the author of the explosions was denounced by a waiter before whom he had disparaged the government ("What do you care who governs you?") and the army ("a lot of idlers").[28]

François-Claudius Koeningstein, a thirty-three-year-old dye worker, smuggler, and counterfeiter, who called himself Ravachol, declared that he had wanted to "terrorize in order to call attention to us, the true defenders of the oppressed." As he went on trial in Paris, in April 1892, a violent explosion in the restaurant where he had been arrested blew off the owner's legs and wounded a great many others. Condemned to hard labor for life for the bombings, Ravachol was then tried again at Saint-Etienne for five murders, a series of thefts, and a grave-robbery committed, as he explained, for the good of the cause; he was sentenced to death for the murder of an old man.[29] Shortly after his execution another bomb exploded, this time in the Chamber of Deputies (December 1893), wounding several legislators. Auguste Vaillant, the twenty-two-year-old leather worker who had thrown it, was tried in January 1894. He explained in court that in his view neither crime nor criminals existed, everything being attributable to the milieu and the [dis]organization of society. A society as rotten and unjust as the present one had to be changed by any and every means. On February 2 Vaillant was executed; on February 16 Emile Henry, son of a Communard, threw a bomb into the Terminus Café, killing two and wounding more. The Terminus, at the Gare Saint Lazare, was not frequented by many exploiters of the people, but by a lot of their lackeys. As Henry explained, not just the bourgeois had to be punished, but all those who accepted the existing order, especially those small employees "who hate the people even more than the bourgeois do . . . the pretentious and stupid clientele of the Terminus."[30]

Condemned to die in April, Henry was executed in May 1894, while bombs were going off, it seemed, in hotels and restaurants throughout Paris. Fear turned folk back to religion: "We've never sold as much fish as this last Easter Week." On June 24, in Lyons, a twenty-one-year-old Italian, Santo Caserio, shouting "Vive la Révolution! Vive l'Anarchie!" stabbed President Carnot to death with a six-inch knife. Carnot had refused to pardon Ravachol, Vaillant, and Henry; now Caserio too would die, unpardoned, two months after his prey, last victim of this two-year frenzy.[31]

Would the murderous spiral have stopped without the *lois scélérates*, the villainous laws, passed after Carnot's murder? They made advocating anarchism an offense, ruled that anarchist trials could no longer be held before a jury, and removed all possibility of propaganda, including press reports. Caserio, we are told, was interested only in the statement that he planned to make in court, as his predecessors had done, evoking the admiration of men as eminent as the geographer Elysée Reclus. The new law prohibited the publication of his words, and let him die without an echo. One notes that the Radicals who condemned the *lois scélérates* in the harshest terms, maintained them when their turn came to govern the country.

Was it the repressive laws and their execution that discouraged further bombings, or a waning of public sympathy? In February 1894, as the Seine Assizes tried an anarchist who had murdered a policeman, the press found reason to comment that the public was growing tired of such affairs.[32] For one thing, trial evidence made it fairly clear that the terrorists were trying to work out their personal problems even more than those of society. Ravachol was a professional criminal; Vaillant an unmistakable ne'er-do-well who changed women as easily as jobs. The twenty-year-old cobbler Léon-Jules Léauthier, condemned to life at forced labor for trying to murder the Serbian Minister in Paris with a shoemaker's knife, blamed the social organization that prevented him from consuming according to his needs; it turned out that he never lacked work but never delivered it on time or did slipshod and ill-finished work.[33]

More ominous, out-and-out rogues were adopting the language of principle to justify their crimes. One of the first to do this, in 1887, was Clément Duval, who robbed the apartment of a woman painter (Proust's friend Madeleine Lemaire), set fire to it to cover his traces, then stabbed to death a policeman who tried to arrest him. Duval proclaimed "the right of those who have nothing to take from those who have" and described his arson as the act of "a convict setting fire to his jail." As for his encounter with the policeman: "He arrested me in the name of the law; I struck him in the name of liberty." It turned out that one of Duval's fences, who was a member of the anarchist group "The Disinherited of Clichy," enjoyed an annual income of 1,600 francs from stocks and bonds.[34] The trial records of the late 1880s and early 1890s abound in thieves and murderers claiming the right to repossess the property of others, by force if need be. One of the more appealing among these was a member of an anarchist gang caught expropriating one more bourgeois after a long series of robberies and break-ins. "Your name?" asked the judge. "I am the son of Nature."[35]

By 1894, whatever sympathy folk might have felt for such children of nature was waning fast. In the popular nineteenth arrondissement of Paris, between La Villette and Batignolles, a crowd beat up a drunk after someone shouted "He's an *anarcho!*" "It wasn't a good thing to identify oneself as a libertarian," a liberal policeman remembered.[36]

There would be more bombs, more alerts, more murders and attempted murders. In 1900 a young anarchist with a previous record of homicide attempts tried and failed to kill the Shah of Persia. In 1905 a bomb thrown at the King of Spain and the President of the Republic, who were returning from the opera, missed them but left twenty wounded. A Corsican policeman expressed it poetically when he said that every government advanced along an avenue of daggers and of bombs. When the first Fauve paintings appeared in the Salon of 1905 and critics described Derain's brush as dipped in dynamite, readers understood that this was not unmitigated praise.[37]

Around the world, other public figures were being murdered by anarchists, but these were last hurrahs. The modern world was leaving anarchists behind—at least the violent ones, at least for the moment. But the terrorists had found a style that suited the 1890s. Defeated Boulangists, ruined holders of Panama stock, frustrated enemies of the regime—or of the world that changed without regard for them—all felt that the anarchists were paying off their grudges. Not everyone expressed appreciation as did Laurent Tailhade: "What matter the death of vague humanities, if the gesture's fine!" Yet it is significant that Tailhade's bitterness against the ambient turpitude and philistinism, so apparent in his poems, came in the wake of losses suffered in the Panama and after a costly divorce. Though he lost an eye in an anarchist bombing, Tailhade stuck to his guns. In 1912 he was still singing the praises of the *bande à Bonnot,* a professedly anarchist robber gang. Brave as one of Arthur's knights, the master of poetic invective averred that Bonnot had died as Roland or Siegfried died, heroically.[38] Other allegiances proved less lasting, especially those among young and idealistic intellectuals who were inclined to rebellion by temperament rather than philosophy.

Through much of the 1890s the up-to-date young "Ravacholized."[39] For Léon Blum, a whole literary generation "was affected or at least tinged by anarchist propaganda." As early as 1891 *Le Figaro* had warned against anarchists in morning coats, *gens du monde* who found nothing better to do than play with fire: socialism, Boulangism, revolution, and anti-Semitism, the Théatre Libre and talk of blowing up

Paris all could enliven the conversation of jaded salons.[40] Paul Adam, who fell out of Boulangism into anarchism, then into skepticism, denounced "The New Anarchist," who dressed *à l'Anglaise,* owned impressionist and pointillist paintings, collected first editions of Marx and the decadent poets, subsidized terrorist magazines and organically grown vegetables, played around with explosives, and hired an English governess for his children.[41] It was fun to break windows that took too long to clean. But fashionable anarchism was going to decline, once the Dreyfus Affair confused anarchists with unfashionable Jews and Dreyfusards. Also because, as they perceived the oppressed accept their lot or yearn to join the oppressors, humanitarians shifted their attention from others to the self, and then to the transcendence of the self: mysticism. But that was in the future.

One of the anarchists' admirers, the Hellenist Pierre Quillard, had published an *Eloge de Ravachol,* which compared the robber-hero to Saint Francis of Assisi. Quillard was a Symbolist poet (he is better remembered as the 1899 editor of the anti-Dreyfusard *Monument Henry*), but others of his generation, such as the poet Camille Mauclair, were revolted by the execution of idealists like Vaillant and Henry. They did not know exactly what they wanted, but they wanted it passionately, and they knew what they did not want. A future secretary of the socialist René Viviani recalled: "Convictions? I had tastes and, above all, a taste for insurrection." Nor was betterment, however radical, of the lives of the poor the major goal. "It wasn't so much that we wanted the miserable to be happy," Mauclair recalled, "as that we wanted the happy to be miserable . . . We were anarchists because it seemed grand and romantic . . . and the label covered all the grounds of our discontent . . . I hated indiscriminately deputies, policemen, judges, officers, all the supporters of the social order, as much as I hated philistines, and I believed mystically in catastrophic revolution [*le grand soir*] and the red dawn [*l'aube rouge*]."[42]

> Kings, gods, are dead, and we don't care.
> Tomorrow, we'll live free as air,
> No faith, no laws, no slaves, no past.
> We are the iconoclasts.[43]

It was young men like Mauclair who supported Paul Fort when he founded the Théatre d'Art in 1890, to stage Symbolist plays by authors like Maeterlinck and adaptations of poems by the likes of Rimbaud and

Mallarmé, while Gauguin, Bonnard, and Vuillard painted the scenery and illustrated the programs; and who then followed Lugné-Poë when, in 1893, he renamed it Théatre de l'Oeuvre, introducing the French to Ibsen, and Strindberg, and Oscar Wilde's *Salomé,* which had been banned in England. "We all took Ibsen's *An Enemy of the People,* and Stockman [its hero], and Ibsen, as models of anarchism."

Emile Zola's novel *Paris,* originally published in installments in the daily *Le Journal* in 1897 and 1898 at the height of the Dreyfus Affair, is much clearer about anarchism. In Zola's story, while Paris resounds to the explosions of anarchist bombs, we meet Hyacinthe Duvillard, the twenty-year-old son of a wealthy financier. We learn that he had been "collectivist, individualist, anarchist, pessimist, symbolist, and even sodomist—without ceasing to be Catholic as a matter of good form. In fact, he was simply empty and a bit stupid." Over a dish of paté de foie gras, Hyacinthe declares that in these days of universal ignominy a man of distinction can only be an anarchist, and everyone at table finds him absolutely delicious. A more respectable character, the unemployed and idealistic workman Salvat, throws a bomb into the entrance of a banker's house but succeeds only in killing a milliner delivering a hat. Arrested and placed on trial, Salvat evokes the sympathy of a gormless princess ("He has tender eyes . . . You know that I'm an anarchist at heart") but also of the novel's hero, the brilliant chemist Guillaume Froment ("A madman, certainly! But a madman who has so many excuses, who is simply a martyr who has gone astray!").[44]

Froment should know, since, in order to demonstrate the power of his "ultimate weapon," he plans to blow up the basilica of the Sacré Coeur when it is most crowded with pilgrims. Bombs are all very well, but "think of the relief . . . armies annihilated . . . cities swept away . . . war impossible . . . the nations forced into general disarmament." Froment is finally persuaded to apply his "formidable invention" to a new motor, "of incalculable social and human effect," which will return fraternity to mankind at last.[45] One puts down this black comedy persuaded that men will believe anything.

✳

General Legrand-Girarde left Paris for Senegal in October 1897, just as the first installments of Zola's *Paris* began to appear in *Le Journal*; he returned in mid-November. On November 27 he noted in his diary that, since his return, "a single matter troubles and fascinates everyone, the question of Dreyfus . . . Is there something rotten in France?"[46]

The matter of Dreyfus had taken some time to catch the public attention. Just three years before, in November 1894, a certain Captain Dreyfus of the Army General Staff had been arrested for passing information to the Germans. The French had long been alert to spies and spying: since 1887 a major newspaper, *Le Petit Parisien,* had run a regular rubric on "German Spies"; and one historian has described the French of those years as suffering from *espionnitis.* So, when the Alsatian officer was tried and condemned, the strongest reaction came from those who complained that the court-martial which sentenced him to deportation for life (on Devil's Island) had not condemned him to death, while other courts-martial inflicted death sentences on common soldiers for lesser crimes, such as desertion or striking a corporal.[47]

The case would have been forgotten if the traitor's family had not persisted in arguing that Dreyfus was innocent and that the verdict against him had been obtained by illegal means. By 1896 the efforts of Dreyfus's defenders were beginning to attract attention, but they remained quite restricted for another year. It was only as 1897 drew to a close that the matter became public and that, just before Legrand-Girarde, the middle-class lawyer Henry Dabot noted in his diary on two successive days (November 20 and 21): "the affair of Captain Dreyfus is surfacing."[48]

It was no use for the prime minister to affirm, as Jules Méline did in December 1897, that there was no Dreyfus Affair. If there had been none, Emile Zola's letter published in *l'Aurore,* January 13, 1898, would have created one, with its allegations that Dreyfus had been railroaded by the court-martial acting on orders from above. Zola's subsequent trials lasting into July kept opinion agog and rioters in the streets, only to be followed by news of the suicide of an officer, Major Henry of the General Staff, who had forged documents intended to prove Dreyfus guilty.

So Paris seethed and raged through 1898. There was much talk—and fear—of coups d'état, with part of the press denouncing conspiracies and *l'esprit de coup d'état,* and another part calling for them. Ministers of War waltzed in and out of office; generals yearned privately for some Boulanger to deliver them from the taunts of the

Dreyfusards; and cabinet members quaked in expectation of being kidnaped or arrested.[49]

Passions ran deep, dividing Pissarro and Sisley from Renoir and Cézanne, driving Degas to fire his favorite model because she was Protestant "and all Protestants are for Dreyfus," bringing Monet— who had broken with Zola after the latter criticized his painting at the Salon of 1896—to write him from Giverny: "Bravo! et Bravo encore!" Social life became impossible because, as Legrand-Girarde pointed out: "The Dreyfus Affair becomes a dangerous subject for friends or people who respect each other." Paul Cambon confirmed this: "Whatever you say or do, you're categorized as friend or enemy." Thus, the editorial board of the major sports paper *Le Vélo* divided, and the anti-Dreyfusards left to bring out, in 1900, a paper of their own, *l'Auto-Vélo,* soon to become *l'Auto.* The University, really the whole teaching profession, split down the middle to such an extent that even the annual banquet of the Saint Charlemagne, which brought students and teachers together, had to be temporarily discontinued. Families broke up in quarrels: as between Proust's Duke and Prince de Guermantes, so in real life between Paul Poiret, the future couturier, and his draper father.[50]

What were the issues? The Affair has been described as a settling of accounts between old Boulangists seeking revenge and old Panamists seeking rehabilitation. But it involved larger issues. The memory of past miscarriages of justice—Calas, Sirven—which had revolted Voltaire, now stirred an ex-Boulangist skeptic like Anatole France to join the League of the Rights of Man, founded at the height of Zola's trial to defend the principles of 1789, "civilization and progress" versus arbitrary action and intolerance.

While progressives legitimately questioned whether the authorities were above criticism or the rule of law, others asked just as legitimately if the prestige and self-confidence of an army that *was* France should be weakened in order to remedy a hypothetical injustice. As long as the fight was between the Rights of Man and the Rights of Generals, most French, especially those who had done their military service in the conscript army, knew where they stood: against the generals. But Dreyfus was not the only victim, and his were not the only rights to suffer: France, its order, safety, welfare at stake, was a victim too; and neither party would yield France to the other. Both Dreyfusards and anti-Dreyfusards fought for France—her honor, greatness, and glory, as Zola had put it in a public letter dated just one week before *J'Accuse*. But one party saw these as resting on Justice and Truth, the other on Order and Authority; and their fervent appeals to divergent traditions underscored the enduring division between two nations, two Frances.

The year 1899 was no better. In February the President of the Republic, Félix Faure, died suddenly: poisoned by his enemies, the Dreyfusards, some muttered, but actually in his mistress' arms, of a heart attack after a large lunch and some vigorous exercise. None were to know and few would have believed that Faure's successor, Emile Loubet, would be the first President of the Republic to serve out his term. The past record was hardly encouraging: of Loubet's six predecessors, four had resigned, one had been murdered, the last had died.[51] Worse, the prognosis for the country's health looked bad. Within five days of Loubet's election, on the occasion of Félix Faure's funeral, a coup d'état was attempted and fizzled out.[52] The new president, who had served in the government that liquidated the Panama scandal, was accused of having participated in the rackets he had helped to clear and fiercely attacked as "Panama the First." The anti-Dreyfusards raged against him because the process of revision had begun.[53]

On June 3 the High Court of Appeals quashed the 1894 judgment against Dreyfus and returned the case to be retried in another court-martial. On June 4 Loubet, attending the horseraces at Auteuil, was attacked by a small crowd of patriots and had his top hat smashed in by the cane of a Baron Christiani, who had lunched too well and bet a bellicose lady friend that he would thrash the odious Dreyfusard. On June 22 the long period of governmental instability came to an end (but who was to know this, then?) with the appointment of a cabinet (under Waldeck-Rousseau) that was to last three years—longer than any other in the history of the Republic. In August, while the court-martial began its sitting at Rennes, in Brittany, serious riots in Paris left over one hundred wounded and twice as many jailed. In September, Dreyfus's retrial ended with a limp verdict of guilty returned by a divided court. Cambon found the judgment indefensible; even Legrand-Girarde felt that one could not convict on the evidence. Maurice Barrès, who had fought valiantly against justice, summed up: "We had everything to win. What did we lack? A guilty party." The presidential pardon of Dreyfus satisfied few. "We were prepared to die for Dreyfus," complained Charles Péguy, who had battled hard on the Left Bank, "but Dreyfus wasn't." Yet one suspects that many agreed with Henry de Bruchard, when he observed, "All the same, you can't stop the life of a whole country for a Jew who's had troubles."[54]

So life went on. *Espionnitis* continued to rage, though not always uselessly, as when in January 1900 a man arrested for taking photographs in the environs of Nancy turned out to be, not a spy, but a thief long wanted by the police. In December 1900 Parliament voted to amnesty offenses related to the Dreyfus Affair. This was at once invoked by M. Pistoul, a manufacturer of packing cases, being prosecuted for assault and battery. It was a family evening, he explained, the children weren't there, so one could discuss politics. Unfortunately his mother-in-law, Madame Renouillat, was a violent revisionist. He called her an *intellectuelle,* she called him an executioner and a forger, he slapped her, she took him to court, and her daughter sued for divorce. In court the parties were reconciled and the lawsuits withdrawn.[55]

As late as 1906, only a few months before the High Court of Appeals finally rehabilitated Dreyfus, a cattle-dealer would be condemned at Château-Thierry (Aisne) to pay 500 francs damages to another whom he had called "Dreyfus"—which, the Court said, constitutes a terrible insult.[56]

But cattle-dealers presumably read the papers, and most of their neighbors did not. So the question remains, How far beyond Paris was the Dreyfus Affair heeded?[57] On April 14, 1900, President Loubet opened the new Universal Exhibition, "a symbol of harmony and peace," which turned out a great success despite disorder, congestion, and crowds. He went on to open the new bridge over the Seine, named after the country's chief ally, Tsar Alexander III, where the press noted Loubet's long conversation with the Russian Ambassador, Prince Ouroussow—without ever knowing that the two men mostly exchanged views about the virtues and dangers of Vichy water. This dedication ceremony was followed by a banquet at the Hôtel de Ville, hosted by the president of the municipal council, Lucipia, an old Communard delighted by his new circumstances. It was not attended by the Russians, for the Right-wing press had convinced them that the Republican regime had not long to live.[58]

Loubet knew better. After a journey through Burgundy in Spring

1899, he had noted that the Paris political press had not touched the provinces. By 1900 he had concluded that, to the extent that they spread beyond the boulevards, the politics of Parisian extremism lost in intensity what they gained in scope. Most of the echoes of the Affair appear to have been confined to those provincial towns big enough to have a faculty of Letters, Medicine, Law, or, as in Rouen, Fine Arts, whose students enjoyed an occasional riot; to Protestant communities; or to regions with a large proportion of emigrants working in big towns and sending home letters and newspapers. Small towns and the countryside had little reason to lend an ear. At Oloron, in the Pyrenees, for example, Louis Barthou, otherwise very diligent in keeping his electors up to date, mentioned Dreyfus for the first time in April 1899, after the Auteuil affray.[59] Which is not to say that no Bearnese had heard of the affair before, but that it just did not matter that much to them.

*

The Dreyfus Affair is but one incident, albeit a major one, in the history of a restless, anxious, uneasy time during which, at least on the political stage, there seems to have been little respite between one crisis and another. One could even describe the Dreyfus years, 1897–1899, as a "political" interlude in a longer tale of social conflict. We left this last subject as anarchist violence fell back under the combined impact of legal repression and popular disfavor. One might have thought that its ebb would leave the field to parliamentary socialism, and, as a matter of fact, when the Dreyfus Affair ended, a Socialist, Alexandre Millerand, was Minister of Public Works in the Waldeck-Rousseau government of 1899–1902. But, terrifying though they might be to the property-owning classes, true revolutionaries had always denounced parliamentary socialists as lambs in wolves' clothing. Like operatic armies, they sang "We March!" while standing fast in place. The threat and the reality of violence, once anarchism had waned, would come from other quarters.

In 1895 Paul Adam published a novel about Boulangism, in which he had dabbled, that begins with the description of a gang of masons disporting themselves on top of a Paris horse-tram.[60] They smoke evil-smelling pipes; spittle dribbles down their bristly chins; the smell of cheap tobacco mingles with the stink of plonk and garlic; their speech is incoherent and sluggish. "The sentences came slowly, and didn't manage to reflect the ill-hatched images formed in brains hardened by the stupefaction of monotonous labor. Amputated gestures tried to help the muddled utterance . . . minds labored to produce the simplest word, the mark that sets us apart from animals." Adam writes badly, but he makes his point. These workmen are beasts, or at least brutes, a herd ruminating its tobacco and indulging in hamfisted fun. When the tram is held up in a traffic jam, they begin to taunt and abuse the driver: "The consciousness of their triumphant injustice delighted them." A middle-class socialist who has watched the scene reflects: "To think that this is the people for which we give up our inner peace." It is clear that he despises "the people," and that in turn they hate and deride him.

Adam's is a cameo of relations between the industrial working classes, beginning to feel their oats, and their "betters"—including those who thought themselves sympathetic to the workers' cause. But the diffuse threat from below sensed by men like Paul Adam was taking concrete shape in labor unions, their activity legalized since 1884, and in the CGT (General Confederation of Labor) set up the very year of Adam's novel: 1895.

French labor unions remained small and, *pace* the CGT, dispersed throughout the nineteenth century—and, compared to other countries, throughout much of the twentieth century as well. Their very weakness encouraged them, as it had the anarchists, toward direct action: strikes, sabotage, and work badly executed as a form of social obstruction and protest. The most notorious instance of this last-named occurred when barbershop employees were advised to inflict nonfatal cuts on the clients of their capitalist masters. The best known articulation appeared in 1906, with the publication of Georges Sorel's *Reflections on Violence,* where the running warfare of contending classes was presented in epic terms and the general strike tendered as a final solution of bourgeois decadence. Between these two extremes, however, much room remained for industrial action that was the more terrifying for being relatively unfamiliar. It was viewed, not as it is today, as part of a bargaining process between employers and employed, but rather as a preamble to revolution.

Any strike could grow into a rebellious assembly, into a riot, even into the beginning of an insurrection. Why not, when participants and organizers, imbued with the revolutionary tradition, held this out as promise and as threat? Historical expectations could prove self-fulfilling. Police were too few and inadequate to contain serious agitation. Whenever an industrial dispute grew, or a demonstration washed over the streets, government troops had to be called in. The army's presence gave the confrontation greater prominence, while the inexperience of the soldiers made for trouble. It was during a great strike at Decazeville (Aveyron) in 1886 that Boulanger, then War Minister, made headlines when he suggested that his troops were probably sharing the food in their mess tins with the hungry miners. But a few years later, at Fourmies in the Nord on May 1, 1891, the soldiers fired and left twelve dead and thirty wounded on the cobblestones. The memory of Fourmies was still fresh in Autumn 1898, when first the navvies, then the building workers, then the railroad workers struck, at the very time the Dreyfus Affair was reaching a crescendo. In October, in expectation of the railway strike, Paris railroad stations had been occupied by troops, apparently encouraging Dreyfusard fears of a military conspiracy. In May 1899 the postmen struck in their turn, corroborating the Right's misgivings concerning authority, discipline, and "everything that makes a nation strong."[61]

In November of that same year, Dalou's great bronze statue of the Triumph of the Republic was inaugurated on the place du Trône, since 1880 place de la Nation. Dabot, the diarist, on his way to the Père Lachaise to visit his wife's tomb, ran into the tumultuous flow of red-flagged unionists marching to the monument's inauguration, singing the "Carmagnole," and "Ça ira":

> Ça ira, ça ira, ça ira
> les bourgeois à la lanterne
> les bourgeois on les pendra
>
> Et si pendr'on ne peut pas
> On leur foutra la gueule en bas.
>
> It's gonna be okay, be okay, be okay!
> To the lamp-post with the bourgeois,
> The bourgeois, let's string 'em up!
>
> And if we don't get to hang 'em,
> We'll flatten the bastards out.

The sinister rhythm, the cries, the flags, left Dabot with a frightening impression. Friendlier observers appear to have shared these feelings. Daniel Halévy and his populist friends, still in their twenties, spent hours watching the marching crowd, "masses possessed by the spirit of the Revolution." They read the banners and the slogans which they knew well from their own discussions—Justice, Equality, Liberty, Emancipation—and one of them observed: "It would be good to know just what these words mean to these men."[62]

This was the social atmosphere of the fin de siècle, at least in those urban centers where the politics of confrontation were being played out. By 1901 the respectable *Revue des Deux Mondes* reported: "all one talked about was the General Strike . . . which would turn into Revolution . . . violence . . . pillage." By 1903 even a prominent member of the establishment like Théophile Delcassé, Minister of Foreign Affairs from 1898 to 1905, did not bother to hide his disgust with parliament and with the cabinet in which he served: "The regime is lost, and perhaps France with it. What we need is a violent change, legal or not, shutting down the talking shops" in Chamber and Senate.[63]

Some of the most spectacular disorders were still to come, for the economic recovery that began in the late 1890s brought not only more employment but higher prices, and strikes became more frequent, even while trades unfamiliar with violence learned to express their grievances by the rituals of industrial action. When women cannery workers struck in Brittany, or vintners in Champagne, or poor folk rioted against *la vie chère,* red and black flags mingled with tricolors, the strains of the "International" (sometimes played by a parish band) and those of the "Marseillaise," with hymns and canticles.[64] Whatever else it was, the Belle Epoque was a fine time for ferments, flare-ups, disorders, rampages, riots, turbulence, tumults, barricades, and bloodshed. But the most dashing figure was cut by the electricians of Paris, who plunged the capital into darkness in 1907, providing a dramatic demonstration that modern power lay at the mercy of the hands that held its switches. In 1909 the leaders of the strike, Pataud and Pouget, published a work that reads like political-science fiction, entitled *How We Shall Make the Revolution* (by walkouts, boycotts, sabotage, and subversion culminating in a general strike). Pataud also wrote a play, "Tomorrow," in which a France, all of whose motor force has been centralized in the Paris works of the trust "Power and Light," is brought to its knees in one giant short circuit.[65]

No wonder that, even when things were quiet, the government continued to live in fear of a coup d'état. Or that, in 1910, no one in the little southern town of Uzès was very surprised to hear the paper-seller announcing the day's news cry out, "La Révolution au Pont-du-Gard," nearby, instead of the correct headline: "La Révolution au Portugal."[66]

6

A Wolf to All

❋

Women and men maturing in the 1880s and 1890s were the first generation in a hundred years to see no risings and no revolutions, no barricades and no serious bloodshed in the streets. They had to spin their anxieties and alarms from less dramatic stuff, and the last chapter demonstrates that they managed this quite spectacularly. But fans of political quandaries may reflect that the array of troublous topics dealt with there did not include the burning issue of anti-Semitism, and that a treatment of the Dreyfus Affair which omits this aspect is a little like a staging of *Hamlet* without a prince—or, more correctly, without the prince's hang-ups.

It could be argued that the Dreyfus Affair was an institutional faux pas blown out of proportion by the unwanted publicity which prevented the Army's washing its dirty linen in private. It has also been argued quite plausibly that the Affair belongs in the history of French xenophobia as much as French racism.[1] "Race," an equivocal term at best, was a word much bandied about in the nineteenth century and frequently used to denote "nation," "people," "birth," social or professional group, family, or even psychological type. I prefer to place French anti-Semitism in another, wider, context.

Anti-Semitism in nineteenth-century France was as French as croissants. Its roots lay deep in memories of Christ's passion and of the Synagogue's obstinate refusal to see the Christian light; in the apparent reluctance of Jews to merge fully in a nation and culture that expected the complete Frenchification of all its citizens; and in the association of Jews with usury, hence finance and banking, with trade, tricky and fraudulent, and with the discomforts of modernity. It was further complicated by what Tocqueville, writing about the condition of American blacks, described as the "natural prejudice that leads men to despise those who have been their inferiors, long after they have become their equals."

Jews were scarce and, except for a few cities, widely scattered. Between seventy and eighty thousand in a nation of thirty-nine million, about 0.18 percent of the population, the Jewish community in fin de siècle France was the smallest in any major European country: less than half that of England, much smaller than the Dutch. Yet some 60 percent of this number was concentrated in Paris and, like so much at this time, French anti-Semitism of the modern kind was a Parisian phenomenon. It was in Paris that Jewish shopkeepers, peddlers, and small entrepreneurs competed with other petty traders, trying to survive and to improve their lot. It was there that the strong Jewish position in banking, but even more in the media—theater, publishing, and the press—raised the hackles of less successful rivals. The stage allegedly was dominated by Jewish managers to such an extent that Christians adopted Jewish names the better to compete.[2] Jewish financiers supported the foundation of Meissonier's Société Nationale des Beaux-Arts (1890), briefly the rival of the old-fashioned Salon. Newspapers, from the conservative *Gaulois* to Drumont's *Libre Parole* and the socialist *l'Humanité,* not forgetting the mass-circulation *Petit Parisien,* had been founded or kept alive with the money of Jewish backers. At the same time, the Jews' appearance in fashionable circles indisposed the genteel. "Today," in 1885, "the barons of Israel represent luxury . . . charity . . . the arts . . . the smart set . . . fashion's latest style." And the fashionable poet Pierre Louÿs, attending a banquet in 1893, noted appreciatively that not one Jew was there.[3]

It was in Paris, above all, that in the 1880s and 1890s a rising tide of Jewish immigrants from Eastern Europe reminded Jews, and not only Jews, that they were not quite or altogether like other French. A young Jewish writer, Bernard Lazare, complained that French Jews were being identified with these Eastern hordes: a lot of gross, predatory, churlish *tartars,* who made people forget that Jews had lived in France for nearly two thousand years. But the tartars could not be halted, and their invasion came at a particularly awkward moment: on the one hand, because the economic depression of the fin de siècle made questions of competition very acute; on the other, because national and international politics after 1871 stressed the foreignness of Jews and their apparent kinship to Germans, hence their presumed sympathies for the national enemy.

The fact is that by now, especially in Paris, a very large proportion of the Jews came either from Alsace-Lorraine (which many of them had patriotically left to get away from the occupying Germans), or from German and Austrian lands. Many others spoke Yiddish, which sounded like a Germanic dialect. This sharpened suspicion and hostility in a period when xenophobia was riding high, as it always does in times of economic crisis.

Catholics, also, raw from their losing conflict with anticlerical Republicans, blamed their troubles on Protestants and Jews. In 1882 a major Catholic bank, the Union Générale, had collapsed under the weight of its imprudent speculations; and the ruin of thousands of Catholic investors, small and great, was blamed on the Rothschilds. Ten years later the Panama Company collapsed; this time the role played by certain shady Jewish figures was evident. Between these two dates an obscure man of letters, Edouard Drumont, had published *La France Juive* (1886), a farrago of nonsense that purported to demonstrate the Jewish hold on France and its destructive effects. In 1892 Drumont started the daily *La Libre Parole*, which thrived on firmly maintained lies such as a sensational interview with Prime Minister Henri Brisson five years after his death, and whose unflagging denunciations were to force the Army's premature announcement of Dreyfus's arrest.

Anti-Semitism appealed to established prejudices and flourished on them. It surged ahead out of the wreck of Boulangism, out of the dregs of Panama, out of the agonies of the anarchist years, with many of the same names turning up in connection with all or some of these tribulations.[4] Yet the first press reports of Dreyfus, in November 1894, failed to mention that the Captain was a Jew.[5] If one discounts the anti-Semitic press, which may be hard to do, his Jewishness was almost frosting on the cake of his treason—until it became expedient for explaining the success of the revisionist campaign. It was the publicity that the Affair afforded which really awakened and sharpened latent antipathies. For example, in September 1899, following the anti-Semitic riots that had shaken Paris and the verdict of the court-martial of Rennes, we find the attractive young Julia Manet, daughter of the painter's brother and of Berthe Morisot, whose thinking on the Affair two years before was that a miscarriage of justice would be awful, noting in her diary that she and her girl friends had just sent 6 francs to the *Libre Parole* for the anti-Semitic rioters and "for shipping the Jews back to Jerusalem."[6]

But prejudice, latent or overt, does not necessarily lead to open hostility. The Army hierarchy was not particularly sympathetic to Jews (many senior officers had learned anti-Semitism while serving in North Africa), but that does not seem to have prevented Jews from joining the regular Army in significant numbers, nor from rising in its ranks. Hundreds of regular officers and ten generals were Jewish. One student has found a constant 3 percent of Jews among regular Army officers in 1867, 1887, and 1907; this does not compare badly with the 5 percent of Corsican officers, who represented a more numerous population. Even the widespread notion that Dreyfus was the first Jew in the General Staff was wrong; it reflects Drumont's success in persuading his audience, and even some later historians. Colonel Abraham Samuel, a graduate of Saint-Cyr, who had worked in the intelligence branch of the Staff since 1871, was heading the *service de statistique* itself when he retired in 1880.[7]

Jewish army officers were not exceptional; and Jewish officers in the General Staff, although exceptional, had existed before. The problem in the 1890s was not that Jews were extraordinary, even if they were not much liked, but that they were competitors in a lot of markets, including the Army. At a time when opportunities seemed limited and too many candidates pursued too few jobs, arguments based on traditional prejudice and enduring differences came in useful. This does not make anti-Semitism less repugnant nor injustice less revolting, but it reminds us that what worked—or was meant to work—against Jews applied to others too.

✳

All societies harbor some suspicion against outsiders; it usually flares into resentment and hatred when things go badly. The French were, and continue to be, a hospitable nation. But in times of penury or war they are as ready as any other to turn first against the aliens who compete with them for scarce goods or jobs, or who appear to threaten national cohesion. Jews, designated by history as resident aliens par excellence, often bore the brunt of such reversals. But Jews were some-what scarce, so folk in search of scapegoats or, more seriously, eager to eliminate potentially dangerous rivals for limited resources, had to turn elsewhere.

Through most of the nineteenth century, "racial" prejudice focused primarily on poor French immigrants from the countryside. These savage yokels, rough-hewn, unpolished, condemned to menial and demeaning tasks, were treated by city folk of all conditions as an in-ferior race, until they adapted to city ways and were themselves ready to inflict the same treatment on new arrivals.[8] If we remember that, like all large centers, Paris is a city of immigrants, most of whom, irrespec-tive of social class, have had to struggle hard against their fellows and their fellows' scorn, and that such experience left them with bitter hearts, sharp tongues, and sharper elbows, it goes a long way to ex-plain the asperities of Paris life.

Among poor immigrants the bitterest competition, hence the bitter-est rancor, often reigned. In the spring of 1848, when Paris throbbed with demonstrations of sympathy for foreign nations struggling to be free, the Auvergnats, immigrants from the poor, arid, south-central plateaus, demonstrated against Savoyards and Piedmontese who de-prived them of work, demanded that they be expelled from France, and, rumor had it, sought to massacre them. In the 1880s and 1890s, although the economic depression was not as bad as it had been at midcentury, reactions were much the same. In 1888 the hotel workers' union denounced the "Prussians," who could well have been Alsatians, too numerous in the hotel business; in 1897 the *Auvergnat de Paris* attacked those caterers and café owners who cut musicians' salaries by hiring German or Italian trumpet or accordion players, bound to be spies of the Triple Alliance. Shortly before the war, a syndicalist stu-dent of labor competition described the northern French distrust of the "poor, dreary," Flemish laborers who sought work in France, cit-ing their "redoubtable sobriety," to justify the "muffled resentment" such "invaders" evoked.[9]

The trickle of evidence suggests that from the early 1880s, long-standing friction between French and foreign workmen—Belgian, British, Italian, and also Alsatian—began to lead to violence. But the worst treated among foreigners, as probably the most numerous, were the Italians: nearly 300,000 strong in 1891, accounting for just about

a quarter of all aliens in France.[10] The history of the fin de siècle, which
records little physical violence against Jews, is one long litany of out-
bursts against Italians, rising at times to what could be described as
pogroms. A superficial survey reveals "minor" incidents, involving
bloodshed and often death: in Var (1884), Meuse and Aube (1885),
Isère (1886), Aisne (1888), Haute-Marne (1889), rising to the level
of great battles fought in 1893 against foreign workers at Liévin
and Carmaux, and specifically against Italians around the saltworks at
Aigues-Mortes, which left eight Italian dead and more than fifty
wounded. The litany continues with more fights and more trials in
Savoy during the 1890s, in Lorraine (1895), and again in Isère, where
in 1901 Italian miners encountered the hostility of Dauphinois ones
"who fear competition and unemployment." That year at La Mure and
at La Motte d'Aveillans over five hundred Italian families fled their
pillaged homes.[11]

The comments such incidents evoked are revealing. The Italians, we
are told, are violent, dirty, and uncouth; they "behave as in a conquered country"; the hatred directed against them is "unfortunately
justified," for there are too many of them and they take the bread out
of French workers' mouths. Furthermore, they bring disorder in their
wake. A doctoral dissertation written in 1900 explains why: they take
what work they can find, accept less than the going wage, live "stin-
gily," saving money out of their meager earnings to take something
home. In other words, "more sober and thrifty than the French . . .
they attract the hatred of French workers." Drumont knew what he
was doing when, in the preface of his *France Juive,* he denounced
Gambetta as an Italian's son.[12]

Unpleasant as they may strike us, such reactions must be viewed in
perspective. More than Flemings or Jews, the Italians in France were
the "wetbacks" of the fin de siècle, hired to lower wages, to discourage
labor claims, or even to break strikes, hence resented by their French
fellows as a very real threat. Furthermore, they came from a country
which stood with the Germans in the Triple Alliance. Like most migrants they kept to themselves. Strange in their speech, their alien
ways, and their thrifty failure to socialize, provoking in their unfair
competitiveness, they could at least be despised as inferiors. Yet, if they
were different, they were also proud, quick to take offense and to
return a blow for a buffet. In the clash of mutual incomprehensions

and resentments, each party felt that right was on its side. And so it was.

As anti-Semitism was only one aspect of a broader xenophobia, xenophobia itself was a part of a more significant phenomenon. There is, says Bodley, "a nation to the members of which Frenchmen are more revengeful than to Germans, more irascible than to Italians, more unjust than to English. It is to the French that Frenchmen display animosity more savage, more incessant, and more inequitable than to people of any other race."[13]

Two hundred years before Jesus Christ, Plautus had pointed out that, while beasts prey on other beasts, man alone preys on his own kind: man is a wolf to men. Bodley coined a new version of the old aphorism: the French, he said, were wolves to the French: *Gallus Gallo Lupus*. He ascribed this peculiar harshness of Frenchman to Frenchman to the inheritance of the Revolution, which added new asperities to those of the Old Regime it replaced. The occasional clerical intolerance, the oppressive privileges, the monarchic despotism of those days, were evils found in other countries too. For these, the new order substituted intolerance, despotism, and even privileges new in kind and in degree because inspired, justified, and reinforced by the conquering principles of national democracy: Liberty, Equality, and Fraternity. And principles, especially when they are fresh, enhance the natural ferocity of mankind.

Many of those who believe in Liberty, mean liberty for ideas that accord with their own. After 1793 this attitude was engraved in French tradition, when Terror designed to force the unenlightened to be free became part of the governing process. For Bodley, the chief domestic occupation of the first Republic seems to have been the slaughter of Republicans. Actually, proscription and carnage enjoyed a much wider scope. As Jean-Baptiste Carrier, who drowned suspect subversives by the hundreds in the Loire before losing his own head to the guillotine, declared: "We shall make a cemetery of France, rather than not regenerate it after our own fashion." The revolutionary terror lasted less than two years, before being ended by a rival terror. Since then the world has known horrors far bloodier and longer lasting. But that first exercise in public regeneration left its mark on French history; the more so because Republicans chose to perpetuate the memory of internal strife by celebrating the days on which the blood of compatriots had been shed. When the Third Republic came to choose a national holiday, it did not pick August 20, date of the Declaration of the Rights of Man, but July 14, when French had slaughtered French around the Bastille. It was fortunate that things went no further. In the summer of 1892 the government successfully resisted pressure to celebrate the sack of the Tuileries (August 10); and the Paris Municipal Council's celebration of the September Massacres of 1792 did not become an annual affair, although nostalgia buffs could praise the Council's vote to build a statue to Danton a few hundred yards from the Abbey where the September butchery had begun.

Such attitudes are to be expected when political conflict turns to religious war and high principles justify the basest actions. But clash of faiths was also clash of interests, of individuals and social groups grappling over power, status, jobs, and material gains; and changes of regime were incidents in a running combat with no end in sight. In 1880 a diarist thought he saw "two Frances taking shape, two castes, two nations, almost two races, which will have different mores, ideas, principles, and feelings. If this goes on . . . they will look upon one another with hostile eyes and will end by going for each other's throats."[14] Fidus was right, but what he described was not exactly new.

If the principle of Liberty contributed to turning political controversy into a desperate struggle between irreconcilable elements, the bitterest feelings of the French for other French—and sometimes for themselves—should perhaps be ascribed to the idea of Equality as a natural right, when it is a natural improbability. Discrepancies between social myth and social practice are not limited to France—American currency bears the inscription "In God We Trust"! But the myth of equality, never quite realized, could lead to frustration, acerbity, and spite—especially when what it really meant, as Camille Desmoulins put it in 1789, was "to bring down to my level those whom fortune has set above me."[15]

If I am as good as you, you are no better than I and will not be allowed to be if you are. The guillotine was the perfect symbol of this kind of leveling. While the guillotine as a leveling agent was soon abandoned, it left behind that peculiarly French disease variously described as envy, jealousy, covetousness, or begrudging that which others have. As the Tenth Commandment testifies, this too was scarcely limited to France, let alone to modern times. In the days of

Louis XIV, Nicolas Boileau admitted to a friend that he had "never heard anyone being praised, even a cobbler, without feeling a little jealous."[16] But where envy once had been recognized as one of the Seven Deadly Sins, it could now be taught as a social virtue. The spite it generated could be regarded as a national virtue; Pierre Dupont, a popular midcentury songwriter, composed a piece called "Ma Vigne" (My Vineyard), in which he explained how much more he enjoyed drinking his glass of wine when he reflected that the English hadn't any.

Balzac has testified to the way in which envy filled everyday life with fervor in those provincial towns where the locals "use their wits to grudge everything." A generation later, in the 1860s, a student of the French working classes noted that envy had become their ruling passion. And when Charles-Louis Philippe described fin de siècle life in "A Little Town," he listed among its frustrations and its small defeats the case of Alice Lartigaud, who died of jealousy at the age of seven, as revenge for the affection shown by their mother to her little brother.[17] Deprivation was everywhere, and far from mere material indigence, so survival meant hardness and dissimulation. Disparaging what one coveted turned life into a vast game of sour grapes. Conformity, respect for convention, resentment of the unorthodox, the glorification of reassuring mediocrity, the oppressive mediocracy of public and private opinions ready to excommunicate the nonconforming, provoked the reactions of bohemians and aesthetes eager to bait the "bourgeois." Even more it spurred the search for protective coteries where one could affirm one's identity by conforming with those of like mind and despising those who were not.

Another effect of equalitarian passion was a conviction that service was demeaning. Victor Schoelcher, the man most responsible for the abolition of slavery in French colonies, who died in 1893 as a senator of the Third Republic, in his youth served as a salesman in his father's store on the rue Drouot. If a customer complained about the price or quality of his wares, Schoelcher challenged him to duel. Although a plague in practice, the once aristocratic practice of dueling to resolve differences of opinion or affairs of honor was one of the equalitarian conquests of the Revolution. Even a nonaristocrat henceforth had a personal honor that he was entitled—indeed, sometimes uncomfortably required—to defend. But in extreme form, Schoelcher's pride and his refusal to admit another's point of view, although they may have affirmed his ego, were not an advantage in business. In 1894 *l'Economiste français* attributed the inferiority of French commerce to the French businessman's lack of business sense, his refusal ever to admit the superiority of others and to learn from them, or to make the efforts necessary for effective competition. A few years earlier, a critical Swiss banker had noted the reluctance of French businessmen to look for trade: solicitation was demeaning. He described them as cosily installed behind their desks or counters, indifferent to rival products or to their clients' tastes, then surprised when fewer and fewer customers sought them out. Rommel attributed this to idleness and decadence. It could more fairly be ascribed to the aristocratic sense that there was something ignoble about trade, and that, whether behind a counter, a desk, or a *guichet,* one's ego had to be affirmed against and asserted over the person being dealt with.[18]

That sense of equality, which dispensed one from acknowledging a superior, did not diminish the expectation of deference from inferiors. Those on top looked down upon inferiors; those below scorned masters denounced as no way better for being better-off. The deferential structures of society had been cracking ever since midcentury. Now they were toppling under the impact of equalitarian propaganda and institutional discredit. In 1901 a well-known lawyer would note the wind that blew in gusts of irreverence: "Contempt is the voluptuousness of the moment . . . Never has authority managed better without respect."[19]

One might add: and without self-respect. What Bodley described as the middle-class anarchy calling itself popular government,[20] helped to precipitate the disillusion of those who had believed that the Republic would be better; it was beginning to affect even the doctrinaires of Revolution. No modern nation had sacrificed so much to social theories and political ideals; none henceforth numbered so many embittered by the failure of reality to live up to their theories and ideals. The general public, which wanted only to be left to live its life in peace, made do on a reasonable diet of credulity and cynicism. But intellectuals and others who had been brought up on higher principles lived with a sense of failure, hence of guilt, that often ended in mysanthropy or sullen selfishness.

The last of the revolutionary trinity—Fraternity—is a topic that could be dealt with as expeditiously as Niels Horrebow dealt with that of snakes in his *Natural History of Iceland* (1758), chapter lxxii, "*Concerning Snakes*": "No snakes of any kind are to be met with throughout the island."[21] Prince Metternich once observed: "Fraternity as it is practiced in France had led me to the conclusion that if I had a brother I should call him cousin." The interesting thing is that 1789 had been about Liberty and Equality, inherited from the Enlightenment (and from England). Fraternity seems to have been added to the motto in 1792, the year before the Terror, perhaps as a palliative of the more direct assertion of the terrorists: "Liberty, Equality, or Death."[22]

The true cohesion of national brotherhood was reflected in the widespread propensity to execrate the bourgeois, especially when, like Flaubert or Cambon or Huysmans or Proust or so many other French, one was a bourgeois. And even more in the tendency to attribute all failure to betrayal, as well as the prevalence of terms like betrayed, deceived, sold out, tricked, trapped, led astray, ensnared, beguiled, and duped, which continue rife in the vocabulary of politics as in that of affairs, or intimate relations. In France a defeated army is an army betrayed; the worker is perpetually sold out by his leaders, the citizens by their government, the government by its members, the monarchist or republican by other monarchists and republicans.

Most often, though, one is betrayed by those closest, and by oneself; among the first lessons that we learn is to give nothing away. In both senses of the term. That may have been why an American tourist in the capital enjoyed and appreciated Paris and the Parisians, yet could not help questioning "whether they possess . . . that true politeness which comes from the heart." And when Hilaire Belloc, born in France of a French father, listed the four powers that govern men—avarice, lust, fear, and snobbishness—he placed avarice first. Many corroborate this view, including Elisabeth de Clermont-Tonnerre, who remarks of her millionaire grandfather, the Duc de Gramont, "though rich, he practiced *l'avarice française*."[23]

The thrift of modest people seeking to make ends meet or save a little something, the poverty of underpaid employees forced to live up to a social status beyond their means, first praised as a social virtue, could easily become a canker of privation of self and meanness toward others. This meshed with the puritan restrictions of Jansenist Catholicism, with the protective coloring of defensive mediocrity, with the sour satisfactions of denigrating the satisfactions of others as consolation for lack of one's own. A 1912 study of the middle classes commented wryly—and unfairly—that everything among the middle-classes is mediocre and mean, to begin with, the heart.[24]

The love of mankind is easy, said Jacques Chardonne. People have to get really close in order to hate each other.[25]

7

The Old Arts
and the New

---　❋　---

The great positive message of the nineteenth century was one of human capacity, self-sufficiency, and progress. History appeared to be the story of man's increasing control over his environment and over himself. The world was seen as a finite place with infinite possibilities, and this vision was translated into the politics, the economics, the literature, and the education of the time.

The advocates of reason and science thought it possible to explain and rule the world. But a reaction soon developed, one that stressed irrational factors such as the unknown, the mysterious, and the wonderful. Largely ignored at first, this reaction persisted and grew throughout the 1870s, parallel to the then dominant Naturalism and Positivism, keeping up a running fire of dissent from the dominant view.

The great white hope of rationalism had been that mystery could be destroyed and the unknown, source of superstition and its attendant ills, be driven out—or at least back. Yet even in its heyday of the 1870s the strongholds of the unknown held fast; mystery began to reaffirm itself, partly because science had not kept the overweening promises made on its behalf, and partly because men, and women even more, are seldom content with merely material explanations. English and German influences seeped in, suggesting the notion of an Unknowable power behind the visible world (Herbert Spencer), and an Unconscious, intractable spirit that lay behind and was the prime mover of worldly reality (Eduard von Hartmann). A final ingredient was contributed by the pessimism of Schopenhauer, whose thought was not intentionally antiscientific, but whose despair before the findings of science helped supplement the growing disillusion over its "failures." Meanwhile, the internal disagreements and rival theories of the scientists themselves aggravated doubt about the possibility of arriving at unique positive truths and persuaded many that the wisest attitude would be an eclectic one, pursuing experience for its own sake, rather than a certainty of knowledge that was unattainable.

Ever since the Romantics had presented reality and experience as manifold, it had seemed wise to sample as many facets of them, to drink from as many different sources, as possible. If there are many truths and many sources of pleasure, it is important to try them all. What mattered was no longer the single philosophy, work of art, or situation encountered—it is but one of many—but our experience of them, which is unique and hence invested with a supreme value of its own. In the absence of an ultimate objective reality, the subjective experience becomes the important thing. From this point of view, art for art's sake meant little more than experience for experience's sake. But the knowledge that no experience is ultimate, that everything deceives in the end, could lead to the refusal of experience; to a falling back upon imagination, which alone cannot let us down; to the decision, since illusion fulfilled must end in disillusion, to avoid fulfillment and concentrate on the safer realms of illusion. As to life, says Villiers de l'Isle Adam's *Axel* (1890): "Our servants will see to that for us."

Pessimism, eclecticism, a taste for mystery, disbelief in the value of effective action—which had resulted in the rise of such "decadent" movements as the Hydropaths, the Hirsutes, the Zutistes (Phooeyists), and Jemenfoutistes (Couldn'tcarelessers)—all these tendencies came together in a strong current of metaphysical idealism. The dominant preoccupation of the Realists had been the inventory and investigation of human society; the new men wanted to pierce this superficial shell to locate the secrets of life. The former were interested only in objective reality; the latter were not the least interested in surface reality and inclined to deny the very possibility of being objective. "Objectivity," according to the *Symbolist* review, "is nothing but vain appearance, that I may vary or transform as I wish." This was the belief of many Symbolists: reality, whether present or past, either is subjective or is not at all.

If that is true, if scientist and sociologist clamber precariously over an insignificant exposed part of the iceberg of reality, then our true interpreters and guides must be the poets and artists who dive beneath the surface of the unknown and bring back snatches of a more profound truth unattainable by "positive" methods. Because these new discoveries, these new experiences, are in the domain of the senses, the emotions, that realm in which we approach closer to truth than through surface experience, the question of communication has to be reconsidered. Poets, profoundly influenced by Wagner's operas, found reason to think that their statements might borrow from song a suite of words chosen for the sake of their tone, their sonority, their evocative possibilities, and their capacity through some mysterious connection (*correspondance,* or analogy, Baudelaire called it) to evoke the desired reaction by some apparently irrelevant allusion. "The most perfect creation of the poet," Wagner had written in 1860, "must be that which in its final conclusion would be perfect music." Wagner's influence was limited by the anti-German reaction of 1870–71 and affected only narrow avant-garde circles for the next decade or two.[1] After 1885, however, and especially in the 1890s, Wagner became the inspiration and touchstone of everything that was bold and new. The *Revue Wagnérienne,* devoted to his gospel, became one of the advance posts of decadence and symbolism.

By that time nationalist reaction in music had revived great forgotten composers of the seventeenth century, like Lully and Rameau, and stimulated original and more confident native musical enterprises. The new generation had worked out its relation with German music, as with the poets of symbolism, whose refinements, preciousness, and allusiveness they sought to reproduce. In 1893 Chausson set Maeterlinck's *Serres chaudes* (Hothouses) to music; and Fauré, Verlaine's *la Bonne Chanson.* Debussy did the same for Mallarmé's *Après-midi d'un faune,* then, in 1898, for Pierre Louÿs's *Chansons de Bilitis,* and, in 1902, Maeterlinck's *Pelléas et Mélisande.*

The introduction of such composers, and of Wagner himself, to a broader public owed a great deal to two musical entrepreneurs of genius: Jules Pasdeloup and Jules-Edouard-Juda Colonne. The former started his Sunday "popular concerts" in 1861. The latter, once conductor for Pasdeloup, founded his own series in 1873. Here, for the first time, music lovers could actually listen to the great orchestral works so seldom heard by those who lived before the age of the phonograph.[2] And though, in the wake of the Franco-Prussian War,

Pasdeloup had promised to play no more German music, he soon broke his promise, as did Colonne. When Wagner died, in February 1883, *Le Figaro* noted in passing that fragments of his operas were "now accepted in France and played at the *concert Pasdeloup*."[3] After 1890 Wagner's works seem to have figured in every Sunday program.[4] Along with those of Berlioz, Beethoven, and Brahms, and of the new composers in France and the rest of Europe, they contributed to the musical education and delectation of a fairly broad public, to the fin de siècle's tendency to cultism, but also to the fashioning of new concert-hall standards: punctuality, silence, and applause restricted to ritual instances.[5]

It is tempting to consider the literary and musical expressions of "decadence" as a neo-Romantic reaction against the over-bold and boastful positive Realism that preceded it. Yet the break between the two is not clear: just as Realism had grown out of certain tendencies in the Romantic quest for reality, so what we might, for simplicity's sake, call Symbolism grew out of the positive investigations of Realists and Naturalists. Man had set out to grasp the mechanism of the world and discover what made it tick. He started to take everything apart and soon realized that his powers of observation, be they as controlled as you like, were not sufficient for the task. He started, then, to take apart his problems and the various objects of his research, the better to examine and depict them in detail. Having gone as far as he thought he could in examining the objects of his sensations, he turned back upon himself and began to examine these sensations for their own sake, as well as the possibility of communicating them in suitable terms—that is, in a language of their own.

If reality is a collection of sensations—our own feelings about the things we see—what can evoke it better, offer a readier access to its hidden worlds, than music? Thus it was that this vague and suggestive art form triumphed over every other—musicians putting verses to music, poets wanting their verses to be nothing but music, and painters trying to do the same with their works. As early as 1849, one of Murger's Bohemians had worked on a great symphony on the influence of blue on the arts. Puccini's *La Bohème* was staged in 1898, when such ideas had come into their own. Only now the tables were turned, and painters like Whistler, Gauguin, Cézanne, or Odilon Redon, fascinated by the influence and the possibilities of music, adopted its terminology and tried to adapt its techniques. Redon called himself a symphonist painter; Gauguin spoke of harmonies of line and color which he called the music of painting; Cézanne painted an *Overture to Tannhäuser*; and Whistler, when his *Young Woman in White* was refused by the Salon, accepted the suggestion that "Symphony in White" would be a better name for it and henceforth composed symphonies, nocturnes, and variations, all possessing the evocative quality of the music he so much admired.

The scale of apprehension also changed with the approach: notes, syllables, vowels, dots of color, acquired a significance they never had had before. Whereas the Renaissance and Enlightenment had sought to see the world in perspective, as a whole, modern man tried to discover its secrets in details. Art need no longer imitate nature but delve into its recesses to discover the hidden meaning of things, which are to the artist signs, symbols, of a deeper reality. The artist-explorer inquires into the hidden aspects of reality, then tries to reveal them to others. (So, incidentally, did those paramount revolutionists of modern thought: Marx and Freud.) He can no longer do this by objective presentation. Before he can communicate the ideas and sensations he has discerned, they must be transposed into terms that will reach the public's inner ear or eye, its heart rather than its head. The artist must, in the words of Delacroix, seek to build a bridge between his heart and that of his listeners or beholders. Mallarmé told Alphonse Daudet that he regarded his poems as mysteries, whose key the reader had to discover.[6]

Such ideas spread throughout Germany, England, and France during the nineteenth century. By 1886, when *Le Figaro* published the Manifesto of Jean Moréas, explaining decadence as the perception that reality was best apprehended by intuition and best expressed by allusion,[7] poets like Baudelaire, Verlaine, and Rimbaud, painters like Puvis de Chavannes, Gustave Moreau, and Odilon Redon, had produced all, or much, of their work. To the would-be objective and scientific theories of Naturalism, these men opposed a subjective and poetic point of view in which the artist played the part of a magician, delving into and exalting the importance of the unconscious that French and German scientists like Hartmann and Charcot were exploring at about the same time.

✳

What this could mean for the plastic arts became apparent in 1888, when Emile Bernard, whose ideas would seriously influence Gauguin—and through Gauguin the whole of modern art—decided that because the idea is the real form of things, the painter should paint not things but the idea of a thing in the imagination—and this idea itself simplified to its essentials and divested of all insignificant details. Memory, Bernard said, does not retain everything, but only that which it finds striking. Thus, if you paint from memory instead of from objects before your eyes, or, at least, if you let those objects filter through your imagination and then paint the result, you can rid yourself of the useless complication of shapes and shades. All you will get is a schematic presentation: "all lines back to their geometric architecture, all shades back to the primary colors of the prismatic palette." In search of simplification, it is necessary to seek the origins of everything, in pure color, and in geometry which provided "the typical form of all objective forms."

In this way line and color become the means of poetic allusion that enabled a Gauguin to suggest ideas and feelings pictorially and, as he put it, "clothe the idea in a form perceptible to the senses." In Germany, Wagner had long since revived the leitmotif as a constant and significant reminder, the musical representation and symbol, of a person or theme. In France, both Baudelaire and Rimbaud had long explored the same territory, and Rimbaud had endowed vowels with color: "A black, E white, I red, O blue, U green. —I regulated the form and movement of every consonant and, with instinctive rhythms, flattered myself that I had invented a poetical language accessible, sooner or later, to every sense." Soon after Moréas's Symbolist Manifesto, the relation between the ends of decadent poets and musicians and Postimpressionistic painters became clear. They all sought a language that could express and suggest feelings which they held to be as real as, and more significant than, the objective surface realities that had concerned their predecessors. "Drop a syllable into a state of pure consciousness," Herbert Read wrote, "and listen for the reverberations."

But once an artist abandons an accessible idiom for symbols whose first meaning is clear to himself alone, he no longer addresses himself to a general public but to a chosen few. Nor is there anything to prevent passage from one symbol to another in search of further and more effective simplification or evocation, anything to prevent stretching the association between origin and effect, experience and its end-product, to the breaking point. Finally, there is no telling how close our perceptions, let alone the symbols we use to communicate them, come to the core of things. Reality is somewhere else, authenticity is something else, the core of experience was accessible in other times or is accessible in other places where nature was (or still is) natural: but not here, not now. André Gide's *Prodigal Son* describes the fruit he found to quench his thirst in far-off places: "The same as in our garden, but wild." Above all, different. So the modern style, unsure of its authenticity, goes with instability, self-doubt, and dissatisfaction. All that would become evident in modern art. And this is the time when modern art, in that particular sense, was born.

One of the most forceful expressions of this point of view sprang, fully armed, from the pen of a converted Naturalist as early as 1884. Joris-Karl Huysmans, when he wrote *A Rebours*, was a high civil servant, deputy head of that branch of the Sûreté which kept an eye on anarchist and other subversive activities. The book's conclusion was not that everything was decaying; it was already hopelessly rotten. The aristocracy had been despoiled and cast aside, the clergy was at a low ebb, the bourgeoisie was vile, the people crushed, the crowd turpid and servile, the arts silly at best. "Collapse society: die, old world!" Des Esseintes cries as the book ends and the tide of human mediocrity surges to the heavens.

The disgust with humanity, already striking in the writings of the Naturalists, erupts among the aesthetes of the fin de siècle. Huysmans in his private letters is no more tender than in his published books: "Society . . . disgusts me . . . The ruling classes are repugnant, the ruled exasperate me." Leconte de Lisle hated "the carnivorous plebs," as did many others. He thought the bourgeoisie was worse. So did Mallarmé: "trade is shady . . . I don't like the workers . . . the bourgeois are hideous."[8] Conclusion: avoid getting involved, avoid politics, avoid gain, insofar as possible avoid work. Money, like politics, was gross. Gide has reported that "the very idea that literature could bring returns shamed us . . . Getting paid, for us, was selling oneself." This was a conventional upper-class view, not unrelated to the existence of some income for which one did not have to work. When Lucie Delarue-Mardrus, then in her twenties, had an article published, she was shocked to be paid for it: "I was scandalized . . . Earning money seemed a sort of dishonor . . . I didn't dare to tell my father."[9]

On the other hand, few scrupled to ask for money. Pierre Louÿs, having dissipated a substantial legacy, asked his brother, explaining that he had spent 12,000 francs in the past year but might just manage on 500 francs a month ("it's the minimum that permits a frock coat made to measure").[10] Such elegancies, reserved to a few, expressed distaste for creeping social slackness and vulgarity, asserted prodigality against petty meanness and distinction against mediocrity. Decadence was, or was also, about revolution against unsatisfactory society, about rebellion against unsatisfactory elders. Revolutionary criticisms of bourgeois society, most of them formulated by bourgeois, were plausible enough to convince some of the bourgeois or, at least, their offspring. Between 1888 and 1891 Maurice Barrès, in his twenties, published three novels affirming the cult of the ego (*Le Culte du Moi*), a skeptical aestheticism in search of new sensations. Many found him inspiring, though surely their egotism had not needed his books.

Decadence was a phenomenon of youth. In its search for novelty, its hostility to repetition, its rejection of specialization for dilettantism, its quest for new relations, new experiences, new ideas, and the constant escalation of its stimulants, in its pursuit of whims and fads, even in its nostalgia for certain traditions that were meant to provide not structure but color, the new ideology was a creation of idleness. Yet, however trivial, frivolous, and sometimes shallow, it was responsive to its times, and just as capable of stimulation and seduction as certain eighteenth-century arts.

Fortunately such innocent gratifications as it offered were not always without a sense of humor. In 1885 two young men published a slender work, *Les Déliquescences,* which they attributed to Adoré Floupette who, though hampered by sturdy health, was determined to become a decadent poet. Floupette sets out to learn how in a café whose clientele cultivates sensations, neologisms, rare flowers, and perfumes, while neuroses, macabre sensuality, mysticism, satanism, and drugs whet their spirits and their sensibility. He even takes a girl home, pleading with her to be perverse: "Promise me you'll be perverse," then insists that she tread softly while going up the stairs, so as not to wake the neighbors.[11]

The same ambiguous commitment to perversity could be found in *Le Décadent* (1886–1889), one of whose editors was an anarchist and another a police employee. In its three years of life this journal published works by Verlaine and Rimbaud, Rachilde, Mallarmé, Paul Adam, and other luminaries—a kind of yellow pages of the avant-garde. Anything and everything, its editor proclaimed, except the banal. A ballad contributed by Verlaine intimated

> We're few in the Paris crowd,
> We live pinched and proud,
> And though drink we oughter,
> It's usually water.[12]

Nevertheless, by 1888 *Le Décadent* was printing 9500 copies—not bad for a review that emphasized elitism and interest in "enlightened spirits" only.[13]

One of the *Décadent*'s most revealing editorials advocated "Mystification," arguing that everyone in France was to some extent a fraud, impostor, humbug, or charlatan engaged in hoodwinking others ("one of the most irrefutable proofs of progress").[14] Mystification remains to this day a characteristic form of French humor, one for which, fortunately, little humor is required, since most humans find an easy satisfaction in the dismay of their fellows. It was in this spirit presumably that *Le Décadent* printed a poem about a young man who poisoned his father and cut his mother into little pieces:

> Then, having raped his sister, also hit her,
> Because he found an orphan's life was bitter.
> . . . .
> He was ill-mannered, Boulangiste, and lewd,
> Cheated and smoked, wrote verses when he could.
> . . . .
> One morning, after he'd caroused a lot,
> Upon his head there fell a flower pot.
> The Lord admitted him to Paradise
> Because, though naughty, he was rather nice.[15]

All of this should remind us to take a great deal of decadence and symbolism (the terms were used interchangeably) with more than a pinch of salt.[16] And, above all, to remember how *confidential,* how widely ignored, their actual words remained even while their legend grew. An academic critic like René Doumic is unfair when he refers to Mallarmé as having achieved notoriety by publishing nothing. He is not far wrong when he adds that now (1894), when everyone could read "The Afternoon of a Faun," which Mallarmé had rashly published, no one could make it out.[17] What Doumic ignored was that we do not need to understand a message to be influenced by it, that a work of art need not be clear to be effective. The decadent/symbolist style prospered because of its obscurity rather than despite it. That too was a novelty in its time. As was the apparent cacophony of voices, which persuaded critics that the symbolists did not know what they wanted, nor how to say it. In fact, they wanted many things, because symbolism was less a school than a coalition, a *salon des refusés* who were also *refusants,* and who therefore ran through a whole spectrum of denials, which they found far more inspiriting than their affirmations.

This brings to mind the thought that, if life imitates art—which Oscar Wilde was probably first to say (in 1889) and his French admirers to repeat—art sometimes imitates life. The incoherencies and contradictions found in French politics were mirrored in the contemporary arts. Answering an influential survey of literary trends (published in *L'Echo de Paris* in 1891), Mallarmé pointed out that no stable or definitive art could exist in a society without unity or stability.[18] As we have seen, stability and unity did appear to be lacking around 1890, if not in French society, at least in that society of Paris which counted, or counted itself, as being equivalent to France.

Social barriers were breaking down, altered patterns of life were showing the first signs of standardization, human relations became more complicated as they broadened, accelerated change picked away at stabilities, the progress of the press reduced the gap between the tastes of fashionable elites and those of the masses, placing a premium on being with it, ahead of the crowd. As exclusive society gave way to the mass public, fashion replaced style, distinction replaced originality. The press was becoming a crucial adjunct of fashionable society, "confessional of their scandals and cinematograph of their little glories." "Cultural" activities became an avenue or badge of social promotion. The cult of "culture," so characteristic of modern times, would not have occurred when the upper classes either had it or did not need it, and the lower did not have it (they had their own) and did not care. A *fashionable* now (the English word was widely, and incorrectly, used) need not be born but made, and had to be remade every other day—hence all the name-dropping that we find in Proust. It was a heady but nerve-racking life style, self-absorbed, other-directed, and calling (again, as with Proust) more for nerves than for muscle.

In *Le Temps* (March 31, 1889) Anatole France asked "Why Are We Sad?" His answer: we know too much, we fight too hard, we have lost Faith, Hope, and Charity. That, in a way, takes us back to the Revolution.

The Revolution had been and remained a project for the future. It had also become a tradition, and a hallowed one. Most French intellectuals, while looking to the future, were never able quite to reject the past. Triumphant yet repeatedly aborted, the myth and the memory of revolution lived on, as promise and as threat. There was no looking forward without looking back, no hope without frustration, no exaltation without an undercurrent of fear—fear not only of failure but also of success. For revolution, as none could help remember, meant not only freedom but destruction; the life-giving force expressed itself in violence, in blood, in terror, and in mindless devastation. Revolution was about the people, but the people, exalted in the name of revolution (as revolution was exalted in the name of the people) was feared in the name of experience. The ideal of the people was undermined by the reality of the rabble. It was the duty and the privilege of creative intellect to civilize the brutish mob. But Victor Brombert has pointed out that if the people "had to be constructed," it was because it had remained that unreconstructed rabble whose terrifying surge continued to strike terror in many a heart.[19]

Intellectuals viewed their role with ambivalence, even when they saw it in a positive light. Go to the people by all means. But will the brutes listen? Emancipate the people: will that mean unshackling its destructive force? Is it possible to reconcile progress and the past, or does commitment to one imply rejection of the other—and of the present too? And if existing culture, and perhaps ourselves, are placed at risk by "revolution," what will become of the social mission of art? André Chénier's "indignant muse" had to face a rival, more detached figure, aloof from civil storms and the demeaning militancies of "conscript art."[20] Brombert has shown how such a conflict was fought out and never quite resolved within the giant frame of Victor Hugo. If the "immense old man" could not resolve his conflict, why should others? French intellectuals were caught in the grip of irreconcilable contradictions, their private obsessions increasingly intertwined and confused with political ones. This grew worse as the lower classes became more militant, as the emancipation of "the people" grew more likely, and the purely literary resolution of one's conflicts less so.

Long before the fin de siècle the literate had learned how to substitute words for deeds and even how to pretend (for it sometimes proved true) that words were deeds. It may be, though, that at the fin de siècle the semantic revolt of the symbolists, the tonal revolt of some painters and composers, were taken as counterparts of social and political revolt. This helped confirm what would become a national tradition: that of the intellectual uneasily committed to, or just as uneasily detached from, causes that he recognized as half good but did not dare denounce as half bad.

And of another tradition too: that in the end the avant-garde is always right. Hence those failing to join, or at least recognize it, in time ran serious risk of drowning beneath the tide of history. In a society increasingly devoid of stable, dominant standards of taste, one had to look to others for confirmation, while constantly ensuring against error. Lacking standards and remembering history, the *fashionable* few feared they might ignore beauty, misjudge greatness. Uncertain in their taste, they accepted all tastes, their judgments oscillating between sneers and admiration, their enthusiasms as fragile as they were facile.[21] Aesthetic detachment became an attempt to avoid saying the wrong thing, eclecticism an attempt to avoid missing the right thing. So one was credulous and one was skeptical. Since anything might turn out to be the thing of the future, the easiest way to judge was by two criteria: against the vulgar herd; and for the latest, hence best—that is, the avant-garde.

But an avant-garde, by definition, is small and recognized by few. Only when the large body of the public has caught up with it does it represent more than eccentricity, and then its style is no longer avant-garde but a commonplace. The danger is that, looking back, we may treat the eccentrics of a time as representative, regard impressionists or aesthetes or other political or cultural rebels as typical, when they were exceptional.

Painting furnishes an object-lesson of this risk. Even more than print, nineteenth-century painting was a social art. Its products, meant for viewing by as wide a public as possible, sought to present those scenes that were approved for contemplation, recommended for vicarious experience, and in most general demand.

Appropriate to the nineteenth-century triumph of mass, scale, and improvement, the most successful paintings appealed to the developing taste for didactic effect, sentimental melodrama, sensationalism, and spectacle. Historical reference furnished opportunities to combine all of these, and the nineteenth century was the great age of historical painting, drawing on an inexhaustible fund of literature, legend, and antiquarian scholarship, as well as on dramatic current events (Géricault's *Raft of the Medusa,* Delacroix's *Massacre of Chio*). Much of it was sentimental or melodramatic, but much also was a serious attempt to recreate the historical past, especially the national past, or a response to widespread interest in contemporary reality.

An art historian recently described the Beaux-Arts as an institution which for rigid didacticism, bureaucratic inflexibility, and sheer hidebound conservatism can have had few rivals in the history of the arts.[22] That is as may be. But critics of academic painting (the painting taught and approved by the Academy of Fine Arts) forget its solid virtues: the research that went into getting detail right, the deliberate didactic intention in times when the public had a lot to learn, the moral message and practical information their narrative conveyed, and the scrupulous workmanship. This was just what their critics would criticize them for by the century's end, when their virtues had worn thin and cheap. We now deride the academic criticism that was directed against the new schools of painting. True to their age, the new men regarded spontaneity, lightness of touch, swiftness in execution and effect, as vital. The old pointed out that their canvases looked unfinished and, above all, unstudied. Most of the public agreed.

We do not know how many people catered to these tastes. But in 1891 France counted 22,976 "artists, musicians, sculptors, painters, engravers, etc.," and there were probably four to five thousand working artists in Paris alone.[23] The annual Salon, which one could visit without charge on Sundays (sometimes on Thursdays too) counted as many as fifty thousand visitors on days when admission was free. Fashionable painters were public figures of consequence (Bonnat and Bouguereau painted in their morning coats), and famous paintings received wide publicity. They were exhibited in special shows and provincial tours, restaged in theaters as *tableaux vivants,* reproduced in illustrated papers and engravings that sold in vast numbers. The style and subjects of the Salon seeped into common life by way of chocolate boxes, calendars, picture postcards, and the covers of illustrated supplements. The inventions of the avant-garde made themselves felt by other means.

One of the chief criticisms of Impressionist and Postimpressionist painting, with its preference for land- and cityscapes and scenes from private or leisure life, was that it carried no inspirational message. Another form of art, equally criticized by pundits, was dedicated to conveying the most explicit message possible: poster art. Publicity was nothing new, theaters and politicians had long advertised their wares in print and poster form, but with little recourse to illustration, less still to color. The law of 1881, establishing liberty of the press, changed the aspect of the street in France and made the illustrated placard first a commonplace and then a major craft. Its products, reported as "pullulating" into villages and hamlets, were soon denounced as "mural madness," visible proof of ambient decadence, as one grumpy moralist would claim. It was also the typical "art of our time."[24]

Though colored posters had flowered on city walls and billboards since the 1830s, they had begun to be recognized as an art form only about the time when the Second Empire gave way to the Third Republic. With the century's end, illustrated advertising proliferated, recruiting among the best professionals: Jules Chéret, Willette, Steinlen, Mucha, Toulouse-Lautrec. Whereas the Impressionists had wanted to catch the moment on the wing, advertising artists had to capture attention at a glance. They did it by marrying bright colors and stylized forms to images of the shows, stores, sewing machines, or bicycles that they sought to sell. Their placards flashed out not from walls alone, but from special pavement columns (*colonnes Morris,* still to be seen in Paris), sandwich boards, public lavatories, and omnibuses. Whenever possible, the product advertised was combined with the erotic appeal of a feminine image. "Wherever the crowd stops, wherever it passes, the poster follows."[25]

By now, indeed, amateurs were pursuing posters: sneaking down armed with a razor, knife, or a wet sponge to remove what postermen had just stuck up in the dawn. Or simply buying. Advertisers, Sarah

Bernhardt among them, began to use only a portion of their poster orders for publicity, keeping the rest for sale.[26]

When the Director of Primary Education for the Paris region lamented "the abominable imagery deployed on walls and shopfronts" as corrupting, he admitted that he was singing a tune already old.[27] What he failed to realize was that he spoke better than he knew: this imagery was training the public eye to fresh perceptions and to tastes he would deplore. The swift allusions of Steinlen and Toulouse-Lautrec provided vulgarization in the best sense of that much misused word. Post Office calendars and the illustrated advertisements of insurance or fertilizer companies that hung in many a home and office continued to reflect majority, that is, traditional, taste.[28] But posters held out an invitation to share the visual language and perceptions of the educated elites, an offer that no one, in the long term, could refuse.

By the last quarter of the century the more refined had begun to sag under the bombardment of pictorial stimuli and to denounce the currently dominant style of narrative and spectacular painting as emollient and vulgar. Joséphin Péladan was one of the most eloquent of those denouncing The Esthetic Decadence, which was the title of a series of art criticisms that he published between 1888 and 1898. In 1882 Péladan had berated "Monsieur Manet and his gang" for their barbarous style. In 1883 he noted the passionless eclecticism ("without passion, no art, no poetry"), deplored the meanness and banality of works in the Salon. "Its epitaph: *decadence*." Only a few found grace in Péladan's eyes, among them Gustave Moreau ("the bourgeois can't make anything of his works, which are hermetic and painting for initiates only") and Félicien Rops ("unknown to the public").[29] Moreau, who was also one of Huysman's favorites—Rops was another—was actually successful in his lifetime and highly appreciated for the morbid opulence of his works. He would be elected to the Academy in 1888, appointed to teach there a few years later, and some of the great names of the modern movement sharpened their brushes under him: Rouault, Matisse, and Marquet, not to mention one of the cinema's great innovators, Georges Méliès.

Other painters, more highly regarded today, did not do as well. The Impressionists were not of course a fin de siècle school, but the fin de siècle found them still on the fringes of the art market.[30] After Manet's death in 1883, his *Olympia* had been withdrawn from his atelier sale because it failed to reach even 10,000 francs. In 1890 a private subscription led by Monet and the American painter John Singer Sargent raised 20,000 francs to buy and present it to the Museum of Contemporary Art at the Luxembourg. There it remained, half-hidden, until Monet's friend Clemenceau, prime minister in 1907, used his influence to have it transferred to the Louvre. He had to exert further influence in 1917, to get it displayed.

In 1894 a member of the Impressionist circle, Gustave Caillebotte, died and left sixty-seven paintings to the state. Renoir, his executor, had to negotiate for three years in order to obtain partial acceptance of the bequest. Twenty-five paintings, including eleven Pissarros and eight Monets, were refused and went to enrich German and American collections. Gérome, one of the favorite painters of the time, threatened to resign his chair at the Beaux-Arts: "filth . . . moral disgrace"; and the Academy officially protested the acceptance of such "a collection of horrors" into the Luxembourg Museum.[31] But when, in 1908, Baron Isaac de Camondo presented the Louvre with his collection of 450 Japanese prints and 135 works by contemporaries who had been influenced by Japanese art (among them Manet, Degas, Sisley, Monet, and Toulouse-Lautrec), innocent eyes were shielded from their sight. Sylvain Bonmariage, then private secretary of the Minister of Labor, had to obtain a special order to visit them in the room where they were kept under lock and key.[32]

The Impressionists, as all decent people knew, were hardly respectable and not to be hung in upright homes where there were marriageable daughters. Nor were their luminous canvases portentous enough to please tormented aesthetes. The Impressionists' successors seemed still worse. In the *Figaro,* the pointillism of Seurat and Signac was derided as a technical jest, Gauguin's paintings as colonial art, Toulouse-Lautrec's as pictorial gangsterism, Cézanne's as a memorable joke, and, finally, in 1905, the Fauvists as *art boche.*[33] When, in 1891, Octave Mirbeau, who liked and defended Gauguin and Van Gogh, bought two of the latter's canvases (the *Irises* and the *Sunflowers*) for 250 francs each, he asked the dealer to deliver them with a note explaining that they came as a gift, lest his wife scold him for wasting his money.[34]

Yet the Impressionists were not as persistently ignored as it might seem. Camondo had bought them from an early date, as had enlightened businessmen like Ernest Hoschedé and Emile Rouart. Ernest Cognaq and Louise Jay, of the Samaritaine, began their great collection in the 1870s with Impressionist paintings, though they later sold most of these to concentrate on the eighteenth century. On the other hand, the director of another department store, Bader of the Galeries Lafayette, shifted his interest from the Barbizon school to the Impressionists. By 1900 Camondo was paying 43,000 francs to acquire Alfred Sisley's *Flood at Port-Marly*; and *La Nouvelle Mode*, a fashionable review, was ready to recognize the "melancholy and imbalance" of the modern style as truly contemporary: "Symbol of a tormented, refined, skeptical epoch, thirsting for an uncertain ideal, documented by incomplete science, elaborating exasperated and indecisive dreams."[35] By 1910 a series of great sales would put the stamp of commercial success, not just on Impressionists (with a Degas reaching the sort of price that only the greatest academic masters had fetched in the 1880s), but on Picassos, Van Goghs, Vuillards, Bonnards, and Derains.[36]

The general public still appreciated the painters of the Academy, the boulevards, and the Salon. But eclecticism triumphant permitted, or rather demanded, new brushstrokes and new tastes. Paul Valéry (who courted Mallarmé's daughter) drew the conclusions of this. A surfeit of innovations can leave the senses drooping, the imagination jaded. The essence of modern art no longer lay in a particular style, but in change itself, the quest for the unexpected novelty that startles and astounds. "A good study of modern art should point out the solutions found every five years to the problem of how to shock."[37]

8

Theater

---------------------------------✳---------------------------------

Just as a history of twentieth-century taste would be incomplete without reference to the movies and television, so a discussion of the later nineteenth century would be deficient unless it cast more than a glance at the most popular and pervasive of the arts: the theater. In the 1880s and 1890s half a million Parisians went to the theater once a week, more than twice as many once a month. "The population of Paris," a journalist observed, "lives in the theater, for the theater, by the theater." So, it seems, did many enthusiasts who flocked to join them in their passion from outside the capital and outside France itself. The stage, a fin de siècle publicist tells us, provided the primordial subject of conversation in society. And, as with today's motion pictures, a stage success was the surest road to fame and fortune in the letters.[1]

We have already come across those stages—Lugné-Poe's Théâtre de l'Oeuvre, Antoine's Théâtre Libre, Paul Fort's Théâtre d'Art—which in the late 1880s and the 1890s held high the banners of the avant-garde and introduced their audiences to Ibsen, Strindberg, Gerhart Hauptmann, and Maeterlinck, as well as the more daring of French authors, from Courteline and Brieux to Alfred Jarry. Antoine himself admitted that his theater, like the others, caught on only with "a small elite." Even these did not always take his offerings seriously: when he produced Ibsen's *Wild Duck,* the public showed an unfortunate tendency to quack at the wrong moments.[2] Many a first—and only—night ended in chaos. Nevertheless, the effect of the new ideas and stage business such works conveyed became evident. The taste of the elites was being insensibly altered; as were, to an extent, staging techniques, which crept closer to realism as the century ended: settings simplified, dialogue approximating contemporary speech more closely, more current themes being adopted, and stage behavior becoming more natural, so that an actor's back could be turned away from the audience.

Although fringe theaters of the 1890s were recognized, as they are in retrospect, as crucial to the cultural interests of a few, they remained very much on the fringe. Until the later 1890s such theaters offered their subscribers one or two shows a month. Their productions never had a regular run but were mounted once, perhaps twice, as matinees or otherwise exceptional performances in houses that offered more mundane regular fare. Maeterlinck's stage version of *Pelléas et Mélisande* was performed once (May 22, 1883) as a matinée on the stage of the Bouffes-Parisiens, which thrived on operettas. The following year the Théatre de la Gaieté, which also specialized in musical comedy and operetta, rented its stage for a matinee of Villiers de l'Isle-Adam's *Axel*. Both performances were subsidized by Princess Metch-tcherskaia, Swinburne's translator, who attended *Axel* in a loge sur-rounded by the three husbands she had divorced.[3] Such sporadic offerings could not progress very far. Paul Valéry has remarked that the theater is like the Mass: to feel its effects, you have to return to it often. The fringe status made such returns both difficult and unlikely.

Even less exotic fare took time to catch on. When in 1895 a regular theater, the Ambigu-Comique, staged Courteline's *Les Gaietés de l'esca-dron,* now regarded as a model of period verve, the Ambigu's public, accustomed to more patriotic treatment of the army, stayed away, and the show had to be withdrawn. Antoine had to abandon his Théatre Libre in 1894, for lack of support. When he started it up again three years later, it offered real plays with nightly performances, ones that had been toned down to suit a more general taste. The first play staged by the new Théatre Antoine was Eugène Brieux's *Blanchette*. In 1892 the heroine, a country girl educated above her station, becomes a prostitute. In 1897 the ending was revised to have her marry a decent man, and presumably, live miserably ever after.[4]

Unrevised pathfinders did not get very far. It has been claimed that the one-time production of Alfred Jarry's *Ubu-Roi* (December 10, 1896) at the Théatre de l'Oeuvre was the forerunner of avant-garde symbolist theater. If so, neither Jarry nor the public knew it. A histo-rian of French theater, not unsympathetic to the new movements,

declares that the failure of the single show was notorious; even Antoine could not summon up much enthusiasm for it.[5] By 1902, when
the Opéra-Comique, with great courage, put on Debussy's version of
Maeterlinck's then almost forgotten *Pelléas et Mélisande,* the public
remained indifferent or hostile. In this case, however, persistence (possible in a state-subsidized theater) and snobbery won out over the
philistines. An admirer of the work admits, however, that it would take
thirty years before the novel harmonies of Mallarmé and Debussy came
to be appreciated by others than "snobs."[6]

The greatest success of the fin de siècle was left to a novelty of quite a
different kind. On December 28, 1897, a play in verse was greeted
with prodigious and quite unexpected enthusiasm and at once became
one of the classics of modern theater. Yet Edmond Rostand's *Cyrano de
Bergerac* was a return to an earlier romantic tradition; its recreation
of a real historical figure of the seventeenth century, the "libertine"
(freethinker) philosopher-swashbuckler of the title role, was as unreal-
istic as could be. Poet and swordsman, paragon of honor and courage,
Cyrano challenges authority and accepted ideas in the name of integ-
rity and free thought. He composes rhymed couplets while fighting a
deadly duel and hides his timid, tender heart under a bushel of wit and
his high principles behind a barrage of pungent jest, none of which
helps him to win his love (whom he woos on behalf of another) until it
is too late. Denis Diderot had observed that cynicism, unpleasant in
society, does excellently on the stage. Allied with sentimental pessimism in magnificent verse, it touched a contemporary nerve.[7]

Antoine, who worried over *Cyrano*'s romanticism, as five years later
he did over the symbolism of Debussy's *Pelléas,* found in it "an element
of literary reaction." That was precisely what pleased Jules Renard,
who had had enough of social and socialist theatricals. "At last we shall
be able to talk about another love than the love of humanity!"[8] So
Cyrano's triumph must bear witness to the moment's taste, and mood;
but it remained sterile—a champion without heirs. Meanwhile, the
theater of social significance that Antoine championed, and that is still
with us today, won its greatest victory not in the theater but on the
political stage. In 1901 two plays with social content gave rise to
particularly violent debate. In February the anti-Semitic overtones of
Albert Guinon's *Décadence* led to its being indefinitely "adjourned" by
the Ministry of the Interior. In November a Brieux play, *Les Avariés*

(Damaged Goods), about the effects of venereal disease, was prohibited by the censor's office. The public debate that followed led to the abolition of censorship in the theater, and both plays were produced in 1904—with indifferent success.[9]

The fact is that, when attending a serious play, the man and the woman in the street generally expected to see a reproduction of the life and problems they knew—above all, money problems. A dissertation on the French bourgeois theater between 1887 and 1914 declares its chief topic to have been love.[10] Yet, if we do not confuse love with 'sex, theater was more about romantic exploits, historical feats, social conflict and ambition, and domestic crises most often connected with money. Marriage, above all, was not about love but about money. In *L'Enchantement* (1900), a play by the spurious and widely popular Henry Bataille, when husband and wife fall in love, he has to pretend she is his mistress. When not concerned with money, relations between men and women were concerned with sex. This could be dealt with more directly in the light comedy of the vaudevilles, and in a still lighter genre inaugurated in 1894 by the success of a non-play entitled *Le Coucher d'Yvette*. This new species of "cubicular" plays, so-called because the bed (Latin: *cubiculum*) played the central role, turned around the actions of a young woman undressing to go to bed or else rising from bed to dress, and grasped at any pretext to offer a degree of striptease on the stage: *Le Bain de...*, *La Toilette de...*, *Le Coucher de...*, *Le Réveil de...*, *Le Lever de...*, *Le Déshabillé de...*, or simply *La puce*. They seem to have done vastly better than the pale or tweedy progeny of the fringe.[11]

But the truly popular theater of the fin de siècle, as of the generation or two preceding, was to be found elsewhere. In the 1880s Villiers de l'Isle-Adam, enthusiastic participant in all the fashionable isms and perpetrator, among other works, of the spectacularly unsuccessful *Axel*, expressed the hope that lots of theaters might offer lots of plays where lots of people could experience everyday events far better than they could be experienced in reality.[12] Villiers's wish could easily be fulfilled, for a few francs, in many a theater offering a few hours of vicarious enjoyment—not of reality as it really was but as fantasy could dress up and enrich it.

"The theater is a place of luxury," a theater architect explained in 1893, "and its job is to reflect this. The public loves lavish displays."[13]

In tune with the tenor of the times, the public loved shows that offered it mass, color, grandeur, and elaborate ornaments. The grand spectacle of contemporary urban architecture had counterparts in the public arts. In the Victorian cult of the spectacular, a highly theatrical kind of painting went along with a highly picturesque kind of theater. As in painting, the sort of scenic treatment that gave an audience its money's worth was supposed to be elaborate, beautiful, costly, and opulent. This was encouraged by the widespread practice of "realizing" famous paintings on the stage, by combining actors and scenery to imitate pictures in what was significantly entitled a "tableau" or "tableau-vivant." This practice accustomed audiences to viewing the stage as if it were a painting, and stage designers to trying to make scenery deliberately resemble some pictorial composition familiar to the public. Almost inevitably, theater came to share the interest in authenticity that colored academic art and made for its historical realism, archaeological accuracy, and pictorial veracity. A theatrical writer of the 1870s pointed out that the sciences, the arts, archaeology, and ethnography could tell authors, directors, and producers about the "true monuments, costumes, and landscapes of every land."[14] The technical means at their command permitted lavish staging. But if realism was good, fantasy was better.

Since the eighteenth century, melodrama had allied sensationalism and music to depict violent incident and exaggerated sentiment. With new techniques to draw on, it now set out to reproduce events on a scale appropriate to the conflict between good and evil that it depicted in high colors, and to the emotions it wanted to evoke. Short on language, long on pathos and on terror, great stage effects were the meat and potatoes of melodrama: strong incidents, striking effect, stirring sensations, villainy, fire, flood, shipwreck, volcanic eruptions, avalanches, provided cut-rate catharsis for all. Grand opera was no more than romantic melodrama in disguise.

Romanticism had inspired a revival of interest in the supernatural, especially in fairies. The search for older, simpler values had been bolstered by the folktales revived by the disciples of the Brothers Grimm and the admirers of Hans Christian Andersen. Yards of fairy painting, sprites, nymphs, mermaids, and angels adorned the walls of salons and of the Salon. Stories from folk, from legend, and from that great Romantic favorite, Shakespeare, inspired great fairy ballets—*La*

Sylphide, Giselle, A Midsummer Night's Dream—and operas (Wagner himself had committed *Die Feen* in 1834) that sketched brave fairy worlds of light and color, rich costumes, songs, and bowers of bliss and whisked the viewer from bustling streets to exotic locations to celestial harmonies.

To these delights the fin de siècle added a special contribution, with its interest in spiritualism, levitation, spirit photography, and such. Nineteenth-century progress contributed the material means to fulfill almost the wildest dreams: real ships, live horses, acrobats and railway carriages, gas-filled balloons, real cannon and real fumes, acres of glass and mirrors, cremation, levitation, rain, snow, waterfalls, raging seas, thunder, lightning, optical effects of every sort, from ghosts, dismembered bodies, or dissolving visions to gigantic fires with charred ruins crashing in so lifelike a manner that the terrified public fled. The Deluge, the Valkyries riding through Wagnerian skies, Saint-Saens's Sampson making Dagon's temple crash, or Herculanaeum sinking through quaking boards—nothing was beyond the ingeniosity of stage engineers.[15]

Some of the greatest triumphs of the Châtelet and the Gaieté theaters, an English expert tells us, were associated with nautical plays: the decks of great vessels rolling, whole ships blowing up or sinking into stormy seas in which their men float until picked up by boats. Of many spectacular plays, none did better than those based on Jules Verne's novels, especially *Around the World in Eighty Days,* launched in 1874 and celebrating its 1550th appearance in 1898. Its staging included the paneled smoking room of a London club, moving panorama views of Suez and India, balloons, burning pyres, a railway train with a steam whistle, a steamer (to blow up in raging seas), eight hundred costumes, eighty mechanical serpents, and an army of eighteen hundred stagehands, machinists, musicians, extras, and actors to put it all on.[16]

Spectacular productions required large houses. Stage machinery and scenic effects could mobilize hundreds of operatives, supernumeraries in spectacular scenes could number as many as five or six hundred, not counting the figures painted on scenery or scores of costumed dummies at stage back. Labor was cheap and not unionized, and in some large theaters there might be more personnel than public. On the other hand, as Henry James commented in 1889, it was much easier to get good scenery than good actors, easier to build up a situation or site to look real than to suggest them in dialogue.[17]

Most of these special effects, connected with movement and light, resulted from the harnessing of steam, gas, and electricity, and from a development standardized in the century's second half. When quick-lime (calcium oxide) is heated to incandescence, it emits a dazzling light: limelight. This method of illumination, originally devised for lighthouses, became, after midcentury, focused on theatrical uses. There were electric carbon-arc lamps and magnesium lamps; the incandescent carbon-filament electric lamp appeared in the 1880s. But limelight remained the standard of the stage. As Percy Fitzgerald put it: "All the great triumphs of modern stage effects date from the introduction of a strong light . . . [Limelight] really threw open the realms of glittering fairyland," begetting a whole series of shows (*féeries,* burlesques, *pièces à femmes*) whose attraction "consisted in making the bodies of nude or seminude women do duty as scenery."[18]

There was more to light than lasciviousness. In 1900 few homes had electric light, plate glass was associated primarily with the poshest stores, and large mirrors were reserved for the wealthy. The effect of electric light on glass—twinkling, reflecting, bejeweling—was fascinating to a public starved of light and hungry for vicarious lavishness. Ostentatious show was box-office attraction. Tinsel, gilt foil, sequins, spangles, and crystal mirrors to reflect and refract light became common, along with a dazzling armory of breastplates and shields. So did the use of bright satins, brocades, silks, and other shiny materials that showed up well. All in all, research into the relations of light to color seems to have been as active in stage design as in painting and may have been pursued there from an earlier date.[19]

The century had seen a series of revolutions in theater lighting, not only onstage but off. Oil replaced candles, then gas replaced oil lamps. But oil, especially that of indifferent quality, could be suffocating and dirty, stinking up and defiling the public's clothes. The murky smoke of oil lamps rose to the galleries, its smuts fell on the boxes and the pit. Gas did away with those discomforts (though oil lamps continued to supplement gas ones, as in turn gas would supplement electric light), but its peculiar ventilation problems meant that auditorium doors had to be kept open, which made for drafts and sometimes high winds. If one dressed for the opera, one sometimes dressed for warmth—with muffs, fur pieces, and even foot-warmers.[20] The Paris Opéra, which had experimented with electric light as early as 1846, installed it in 1887. By the twentieth century most major houses boasted electricity.

But electricity was subject to frequent failures, and other lamps had to be kept in reserve. Whatever its tendency to break down, however, electricity had one crucial advantage: it was less prone to catastrophe than its predecessors. Scenery or gauze transparencies, dresses, tutus, wigs, or garlands, were easily set afire by candles, oil lights, and gaslights. In Europe and in the United States eighteenth- and nineteenth-century theaters averaged twenty-two or twenty-three years before burning down, and one-fifth of them lasted less than ten years. In May 1887 a gaslight set a piece of scenery on fire at the Paris Opéra-Comique. The almost fifty dead left in its wake may have had something to do with the Grand Opera's installing electricity that year.[21]

Another revolution followed. Until now the stage had been only a more intensely lit extension of the auditorium. The coming of gas permitted some theaters to dim the houselights during the performance, but none could carry this very far as long as much of the show (the best part, some would say) was in the auditorium, where the spectators looked at each other as much as they did at the stage. Percy Fitzgerald ruled that "a theatre should be lit soberly enough to see faces and features and to read a play . . . utter darkness is unnatural." Many wanted to follow the play or, more to the point, the libretto, on paper. Many more wanted to see their neighbors or be seen by them. In 1892 the composer Paul Dukas, in London for Wagner's *Rheingold*, reported that all lights in the hall went out (as they did at Bayreuth), but that there was enough light from the stage to read the libretto. A fashionable lawyer at the Opera to hear a revival of Halévy's *La Juive* was pleased to note: "In the Hall, the chandelier, superb, shone like a sun . . . [upon] resplendent bodices [and] people busily chatting."[22] Gradually the new realism and call for audience discipline taught stage managers to dim the houselights or extinguish them altogether. More slowly, the horseshoe-shaped hall, where people looked at each other more than at the stage, gave way to the stage-oriented design which we have grown used to.

For the wealthy and the less wealthy, operas and operettas, féeries, and "spectacles" continued to provide the chief attractions of the stage until the century's end. So did equally spectacular melodramas which, in 1897, spawned a new form of thriller: the Grand Guignol, dedicated to horror plays, whose chief purveyors, like André de Lorde, despised or ignored by intellectuals, became as popular as Eugène Sue had been.[23]

Intellectuals denounced the increasingly mindless féeries, as George Bernard Shaw denounced their English counterpart, the pantomime, as a "glittering, noisy void," with no appeal for the intellect. But that was not why it waned. As the spectacular show had grown more spectacular, the public became used to one prodigy after another, and the producers were running out of special effects. They were also running out of new plays to produce—witness the endless revivals, especially of Jules Verne; and they were not averse to heeding the criticism of overdone effects and turning back to simpler, hence more economical, productions. The public, however, continued to yearn for *grands spectacles* and was delighted to return to them in a new guise when, in 1908, Franz Lehár's *The Merry Widow* introduced the lasting vogue of Viennese operettas.[24]

"The public" is a vague and general term. To whom does it apply? In the first place of course to the better-off, those with the means and leisure to appreciate art and consume it. In 1855 the younger Dumas had declared "simply absurd" a proposal to establish a prize for a play that proved most edifying to the working classes. "Doesn't art address itself above all to the intelligence, the passions, the senses of the delicate, refined classes rather than to the working classes? Do they go to see [plays] when they are shown?"[25] They certainly did not go to the posh Paris theaters, where a seat in the 1880s might cost 26 francs, or to the Opera, where a box rented for as much as 25,000 francs a year and a seat cost 16 or 20 francs, the equivalent of several days' wages.[26] But a concert of wails deplores the unfortunate popular taste for the theater: "every suburb has its own, not just for farce or musical comedy, but for drama and melodrama."[27] Just as in the 1960s and 1970s local movie houses continued offering double features, while first-run houses shifted to the swifter turnover of single films at a high price, so to the end of the century local theaters in lower-middle-class and working-class quarters went on giving melodramas in five or six acts and eight or ten scenes, whose length required an early start and a picnic meal during an intermission. Lucien Descaves noted the long lines to get in at Belleville, just as at Nîmes an artisan remembers that working-class culture, "what there was of it," depended largely on what could be picked up, and often was picked up with enthusiasm, at theater or opera—from melodrama to *Cyrano*.[28]

Jules Chéret was the Watteau of poster art. Here, a young woman clashes her cymbals to announce the opening of the Olympia Music Hall in April 1893; it is still there today.

The first version of Chéret's Olympia poster was part of a
quartet celebrating the arts. This represents Music.

After the Dreyfus Affair, populist intellectuals attempted to create a "popular theater." This proved quite successful with intellectuals and the middle class, even though a Popular Opera founded in 1901 foundered miserably after a few performances of Armand Silvestre's *Charlotte Corday*. But the people had its popular theater: that of the *mélos,* the operas, and the classics. Poor small repertory companies carried this into the provinces and even into village barns.[29]

The best example of such popular interest, or at least the best known, is provided by Marcellin Albert, who became famous in 1907 as leader of the winegrowers' rebellion in Languedoc. Son of a small vineyard owner, educated in the village school and then, until sixteen, in a Catholic institution, Albert returned home to earn a meager living tending his vines. But he brought back with him an interest in the theater which Catholic schools long favored, in the French language, which was rare in his region, and in the arts. His village, Argeliers, close to Béziers and Narbonne, had a hall in which strolling players could play on occasion, and Albert began to act there. He opened a café to make ends meet, and founded a company of neighbors, fellow-amateurs, with whom he toured nearby villages, putting on plays like *Ruy Blas,* and *Marceau, or the Children of the Republic.* That was how he developed the rhetorical talents, the gift for leadership, and the local reputation that stood him in good stead when he decided to rouse his neighbors to political action.[30]

There may have been other thespian ventures in places just as small as Argeliers, whose population barely exceeded 1200 souls. But almost all larger urban centers of nineteenth-century France had their theater, or had acquired one by the century's end. Some functioned in a disaffected church or chapel, some in a barn, the back room of a café, or even an apartment in a larger house. Bigger towns, like Toulon or Agen, had proper theater buildings with resident companies; those in prosperous centers like Bordeaux were handsome eighteenth-century structures. But even minor centers like Guéret (Creuse), where through the 1890s the young Marcel Jouhandeau regularly attended the Municipal Theater, enjoyed their own repertoire of operas and dramas or that of touring companies.[31] Municipal theaters were subsidized more or less richly, but by the century's end every small town—Alençon, Mamers, Vesoul, Die, Bar-sur-Seine—wanted its own, even if it could rely only on the occasional tour from Paris. In far-off Brittany a local poet found reason to exult:

Henceforth, thanks to the care
Of a most zealous mayor,
The absence of a resident company at Quimper
Will be made up from Paris . . .[32]

Testimony to the popular taste not just for vaudeville but for more substantial fare to which nearly all could accede a few years after Paris.

Meanwhile, provincial theater was becoming less of a fashionable pastime. As railroads made access to the capital easier, the better-off got into the habit of traveling up to Paris to enjoy its entertainment and its shopping. That was where the best acting and the most spectacular productions were to be found, and one could be assured of dinner invitations for a long time by recounting the experience once one was back home. The trend that started under the Second Empire accelerated through the 1880s and 1890s, when provincial theaters gradually lost the most demanding and high-paying portion of their audience. Meanwhile Parisian houses, once condemned to change their offerings with greater frequency to cater to a rather limited audience, learned to rely on a constant influx of provincials whose interest permitted much longer runs.[33] By then, the new invention of the Lumière brothers (first shown in 1895) had begun to supplement the declining small town theater trade, before supplanting it altogether.

Motion pictures both borrowed the themes and tricks of the popular féerie (catastrophes, illusions, supernatural activities, voyages through skies or undersea) and contributed to stage action by the projection of celestial rides and other extraordinary doings.* When the Lumière brothers explored the possibility of public shows for their first films, their earliest discussions were with the waxwork Musée Grévin and

---

* In the first half of the century, Jacques Daguerre (1787–1851), the painter responsible for inventing the phenomenally successful *diorama,* had been a well-known designer of stage sets—notably one for the Opera's production of "Aladdin." Searching for more spectacular stage effects, he worked with a physicist, Nicéphore Niepce, and with Niepce's chemist nephew, to discover the principles of photography—hence the daguerreotype. A generation later, Léon Gaumont (1864–1946), a manufacturer of incandescent lamps used in stage effects before he turned to photography, would perfect the bioscope, designed to project moving images more effectively than magic lanterns could. For him the cinema would be one more step in the art of optical illusions that fascinated the century. The public agreed. Kinescopes and bioscopes offered one more scientific curiosity, on a par with Dr. Roentgen's new machine. *La Revue Encyclopédique* (March 28, 1896, p. 50) mocked the boulevard cafes whose shows of cinema and radiography were turning them into branches of the Faculty of Sciences.

This poster of 1891, by an unknown artist, advertises one of Georges Méliès's favorite magic tricks, whose fame apparently attracted even the public executioner, Mr. Deibler, and his assistant. Within a few years, Méliès, who sometimes designed his own posters, would reproduce this "fantastic pantomime" on film.

with the Folies-Bergère, always looking for new acts. Their great competitor of the 1890s was Georges Méliès, director of the Théatre Robert Houdin, built by the illustrious magician and dedicated to magic and prestidigitation, whose films for years simply amplified the magic shows of his playhouse. Méliès saw no difference between the tricks made possible by his kinescope and those of his make-believe. The film studio he built at Montreuil in 1897 was designed as a theater stage, with all the traps, flies, and springboards needed to have infernal or divine beings appear and disappear, swing through the air, or swim through the waves: "on a smaller scale, a pretty faithful reproduction of a théatre de féerie." One of his best-known films, *A Voyage to the Moon*, made in 1902, was going to reproduce a standard stage illusion act developed in 1891.

Another pioneer, now forgotten, Raoul Grimoin-Samson, was also a professional conjurer who began by developing tricks useful to his trade. In 1900 he went up in a balloon to film the great Exhibition, then used ten synchronized cameras to project his hand-colored 70-mm film in the first wide-screen *cinéorama* show. By that time images could speak or sing, though adequate amplifiers for sound pictures would not be developed until a generation later. But even silent films attracted a growing public. The first permanent movie theater opened in 1897. Soon their increasing numbers inspired Charles Pathé (followed by Léon Gaumont) to create the first weekly newsreels. The most popular form of stage entertainment had spawned the most popular form of twentieth-century entertainment—truly, the invention of the century.

Few provincial playhouses had been able to match the spectacular resources of the Paris Opéra or Châtelet. The moving pictures promised to do so at a very small price. As a magazine commented, the combination of photograph and phonograph now provided the absolute illusion of life.[34] By 1908 Nice had five cinematographs, by 1914 it had ten. Avignon, which entered the twentieth century with four theaters, built its first cinematograph in 1908, by which year France counted nearly 1000, many of them housed in remodeled theaters.

Of course, the provinces had other sources of entertainment beside the theater. Trials often "turned the courtroom into a theater," as a Minister of Justice complained; and public executions (abolished in 1939) attracted large and lively crowds.[35] Musical societies, choirs, and brass bands (one per political persuasion) thrived; and there were

In 1896 or 1897 a waxworks show advertises not only the latest novelty, the Lumière brothers' cinematograph, but an equally curious invention, Roentgen's X-rays.

traveling circuses and public fairs. But the most accessible entertainment for the lower and middle classes was to be found in music-halls and café-concerts, which could be enjoyed in the smallest towns, and where even working-class families or peasants who had made a profit on market day had access to the musical hits of a few years past for the price of a beer or a cup of coffee, that is, 10 cents—25 cents with a shot of alcohol (the sugar was free).

Caf'concs or *café-chantants* were just what their name suggests: places where drink was accompanied by entertainment that could range from the warbling of an unaccompanied singer to an orchestra, dancers, comedians, and other acts. The average was probably represented by the two caf'concs of Chateauroux, one of which boasted three singers and a comic, the other a pianist, a comic, and two singers. Bigger establishments with something of a stage offered a *corbeille* of young— and less young—ladies seated in a semicircle facing the public, who might join in the chorus and would circulate among the audience between the acts. This practice, abandoned in Paris in the last quarter of the century, continued in the provinces until the First World War, in the guise of *poseuses,* from half a dozen to a dozen unpaid supernumeraries at the back of the stage, "to give the illusion of a drawing-room." Such ladies enjoyed a dubious status. But a policeman's report that refers to their reputation for lax morals distinguishes between them and the prostitutes who lacked the regular income that allowed artistes to "give themselves only as they please." Not all who started as poseuses in the corbeille came from the lower classes: Gabrielle Chanel and Yvette Guilbert had been schooled beyond the average; Jane Avril had been the private secretary of an Academician; Grille d'Egout, her companion at the Moulin Rouge, a schoolteacher.[36]

The public varied widely. One bitter critic has left a description of a "popular" establishment on a weekday afternoon: "no less than four or five hundred persons, small shopkeepers, workmen and working girls, mothers with their children, fathers and grandparents with their small boys on their knees." It sounds like a family atmosphere. More elegant establishments varied from those that catered to a family clientele, like the Eden-Concert in Paris, where sketches and songs "were fit for young girls' ears," to the Moulin Rouge, which shifted from low farce in the early evening to the notorious quadrilles and can-cans that attracted the "public chic" after 9:30 or 10.[37]

The most splendid café-concerts were found in Paris, which is where the stars were made, like Yvette Guilbert who moved from the licentious Eldorado to the family-oriented Eden, then to the Moulin Rouge, carrying with her the long black gloves that she had copied from a teacher whom she had had at school. Large prefectures and garrison towns could boast splendors of their own, like the Café de l'Univers at Limoges, which advertised itself in 1900 as "the richest, most sumptuous of France" and boasted 200 electric light bulbs ("one of the sights of town and worth a visit"), a ladies' lavatory, and even a telephone at a time when the whole of Limoges counted sixty-eight subscribers. More modest establishments provided fair entertainment, and perhaps a springboard to fame. Thus, at the Rotonde of Moulins, opened in 1860 as a café and reading cabinet but soon turned into a café-chantant that catered to the garrison even more than to locals, one could hear debutantes like Gabrielle Chanel, who literally made her name there in 1905 by singing one of the successes of 1889: "Who saw Coco in Trocadero?"[38]

The growth of a specialized entertainment industry awaits its chronicler. The history of French music halls remains to be written, as does that of the caf'conc', of the mélo, the Grand Guignol, and the spectacular féeries, all of them vulgar in the best sense of the term—that is, accessible and attractive to ordinary people—which means that they have been dismissed as too vulgar for serious attention. It has not been clearly demonstrated that more pretentious enterprises contained more substance or more intelligence. But even when their fare was vapid, facile, or superficial, it conveyed the values and the tastes of the metropolis. Popular entertainment can be decried as a wardrobe of hand-me-downs or appreciated as a painless form of cultural integration. The value of the cultural product itself remains as subject to debate today as it did then.

9

Curists and Tourists

---------------------------------❋---------------------------------

In the nineteenth century holy days turned into holidays: weeks or months of nothing but Sundays. More and more people acceded to the leisure and leisure activities hitherto reserved for a tiny minority, and the quarter-century preceding 1914 saw an acceleration of this process. It was the high point, in human history so far, of curism and tourism.

Tourism, like so many words connected with leisure activities, adapted from the English, began to be used in France under the Restoration. It described, a dictionary of 1876 explained, the perambulations and other activities of persons traveling out of idleness, curiosity, or, simply, for the pleasure of travel.[1] You could add: and for the pleasure of saying they had traveled. For even as the century advanced, traveling remained an exceptional accomplishment and those who sampled its charms exceptional themselves. Even those who could afford to travel, did not do so often, or go very far. Pauline de Broglie, daughter of one of the richest men in France, spent summers in the family villa at Dieppe and in her father's chateau in Normandy. In 1903, when she was fifteen years old, she marveled at the experience of a girl her own age who had actually been abroad. That same year she saw the mountains for the first time, when visiting the chateau of family friends in the Massif Central.

The advent and improvement of modern transport during the last half of the century had wrought great innovations. It used to take one hundred hours to cover the three hundred miles (463 km.) from Paris to Lyons. With the railway it took ten. What this meant was stated clearly in an 1877 lecture: "Until recently no one left his native town . . . Today no one stays put. Until recently we stayed in Paris all year round. Now, in 1880 . . . how can we stay in Paris during summer? We have to go to the country . . . We have to take the waters. If we don't take the waters, we go to the seaside. If we don't go to the seaside, we go to Italy." Alfred de Foville, who quoted these lines in a work on the economic and social consequences of the new means of transport, added that, of late, every summer Sunday found Paris abandoned for the countryside.[2]

The rise of urban living standards after midcentury had included better facilities for escaping urban pressures. Idyllic riverside villages, like Argenteuil on the Oise or Bougival on the Seine, could henceforth be reached in a twenty-minute train journey from the capital. The forest and rocks of Fontainebleau, half an hour by train, inspired poets and painters as much as courting couples and picnickers. Go a little farther, forty-five minutes or an hour away, and you could be in Pontoise or in Rambouillet, which, thirty-three miles from Paris, at the end of the century was still considered an unspoiled, "rural, distant, provincial nook."[3]

We recognize here the curiosity of the Romantics and their quest for unfamiliar places, their penchant for the exotic, for nature, for the bucolic life. But here too was a longing to imitate lifestyles once reserved for those privileged (usually noble) classes that owned country estates and lived on them part of the year, mimicry that drove those who could afford it to acquire a country residence or at least to spend weekends in the country. Fashionable references to nervous disorders and other medical problems attributed to city living linked the hankering after socially prestigious activities with a respectable solicitude for health.

It was not just relief from the congestion and pollution of urban living that people sought. They wanted the advantages of the latter, without its pressures.[4] To have, as Gérard de Nerval observed of Bougival, the resources of the city and to be almost completely in the country. Recall the living conditions that we have seen obtain in provincial towns, where there was nothing to do, nowhere to go, and little welcome for strangers—let alone in villages. Nerval's appears a tall order to fulfill. Only one category of urban (or semiurban) centers provided the exception to the almost general rule that condemned locals to dreariness and outsiders to isolation: the spas and holiday resorts which developed at an incredible rate throughout the century.

A normal town, however small, had specific functions. Trade, exchange, administration, justice, attracted the urban crowd, however sporadic or relative. Resorts, on the other hand, were centers where people came together in pursuit of interests that had little or nothing to do with business, but with leisure and pleasure: concerts and shows, promenades, excursions, dancing, gambling, meeting each other and, especially, the opposite sex. Once they abandoned their walls (and remember that, more than a figure of speech, city walls were a stifling nuisance into the last third of the century!) townsfolk also abandoned many restrictions and constraints that the walls represented. What was exceptional in everyday life became the rule on holiday. The ease with which people removed from the rigidities of life at home struck up new friendships, flirted, courted, was a special attraction of resorts. So too were the gargantuan meals and the gambling—above all, the gambling in casinos one could not find elsewhere and whence a large part of a resort's revenue was drawn.

Freed of their routines, of local constraints, of a society where everybody moved under the perpetual surveillance of everybody else, the tourist or the curist were free—if not to do exactly what they liked, at least to do things differently. To act out a certain urban ideal where the social order was less rigid, relations were easier, mobility was greater; where standing was determined on the basis of display rather than on that of a well-defined situation; and where everybody was busy doing nothing in particular.

These resorts, divorced from the industry and productivity that made their existence possible, these centers, increasingly dedicated to consumption in times when production was still the order of the day, tended to develop in places whose nature stressed their artificiality: isolated, ill-accessible regions like the Alps, the Vosges, the Pyrenees, the Massif Central, and, in due course, the seashore. They existed in the first place because of the medicinal virtues attributed to waters that justified the trip and the cure: that is, a stay of several weeks. But they were also, or soon became, leisure centers: pleasure resorts whose chief, sometimes sole, industry was to provide accommodation, services, and entertainment to a growing clientele for whom the traditional day of rest had expanded from a single feast day to a longer period—*les vacances,* the holidays or vacation. So what began as rural resorts eventually turned into showcases of specifically urban lifestyles, propagating a consumer economy long before more normal towns had one.

Railways brought fresh air and natural beauties within easier reach. First of course in the immediate rural environs of large cities, but very soon at the seashore too; especially on the Channel Coast, so conveniently close to Paris. The cool summers of the Norman Coast were much praised as offering a respite from sweltering summer heat—particularly discomforting for the heavily garbed bourgeois of those days. The hydrotherapy provided by the sea could help sterility or coughs or constipation, and discourage the pernicious solitary practices too many adolescents allegedly indulged in. But what salt water and sea air cured, above all, were the ills occasioning the characteristic urban flight from strain, stress, and pollution, which ranged from depression, chlorotic languor, and hypochondria to neuroses, delirium, and assorted nervous strains.

The sea's invigorating action was so powerful that exposure had to be carefully measured. Few men are so vigorous as to prolong a plunge beyond a quarter of an hour, warned a midcentury travel writer. And a fin de siècle schoolbook put it in a nutshell: salt water fortified, provided one did not stay in it more than five or ten minutes.[5] Since this held good of sea air too, many expensive villas were built well away from the sea, looking inland, in order to avoid the humidity.

Such considerations did not deter Parisian businessmen and financiers who appreciated the coast's convenient closeness to the capital, or the artists and writers who liked the moderate prices there. Their approval was matched by that of speculators who discovered that, with a little judicious publicity, they could multiply their investment seven—even twenty—times in a couple of years. They were bolstered by the railway companies, which recognized the possibilities of tourist traffic and built special lines designed to orient it toward resorts they wanted to develop. Trouville and Deauville did not have railway stations until 1863, but Arcachon near Bordeaux had the third line in France in 1841, Dieppe had one in 1848, Les Sables d'Olonne in the far Vendée in 1850. Railway construction from Marseilles (which had just got its railhead) as far as the Italian border on the Var was authorized in August 1859, three weeks after the treaty of Villafranca. Cannes had a railway station in 1863, Nice in 1864.

The small southwestern fishing village of Biarritz, launched by the

Empress Eugénie in 1850, got its own railway station in 1860 and enjoyed great prosperity in the decade that followed. Perhaps because it specialized in the treatment of apathy, languor, languidness, weariness, and other *maladies de femmes*, it became a fashionable meeting place for an international society that stayed either in the Palace Hotel (built in the shape of an E in honor of the Empress), or in the luxury villas that sprouted all around. Yet in 1872 half the population of the commune was still described as agricultural (by 1911 that would be 5 percent), and Biarritz did not become the seaside resort that we know until after 1875. That was when a real estate company began to sell off the seafront property acquired by the Bonapartes, and when a narrow-gauge railway line linked Biarritz to nearby Bayonne, allowing the Bayonnais to visit it cheaply and easily for weekend or day excursions.[6]

Seaside resorts were only one category of holiday centers, and for some time they were not nearly as well-known as spas. The Romans had appreciated the virtues of a spring or fountain of healing waters, and the earliest spas of France boast Roman origins, as their names often related to *aquae* (Aix or Aigues) attest. In 1603 Henry IV opened the modern thermal era when he reserved the waters of Aix-en-Provence for officers wounded in his service. In 1605 he created a Superintendent of Mineral Waters for his realm, decreeing that the function should be exercised by the King's Physician.[7]

What was good for soldiers was good for civilians too. During the centuries that followed others learned about the marvels of mineral muds or waters supposed to cure a variety of ills. The local population were not unaware of this and often had recourse to "good springs" or fountains with reputedly magic qualities. Provincial burghers also did so, visiting local watering spots for a day's outing or a longer cure. So eventually did the nobility, which could afford the costly journey from Paris or Versailles (though Paris had its own mineral springs at Auteuil, Passy, Batignolles, and elsewhere). By the eighteenth century the vogue of taking the waters was well established.

Although the number of tourists and curists grew, it was so limited by the costs and difficulties of travel that their presence did little to change conditions in the small towns and villages to which they journeyed. Wealthy visitors appreciated the exoticism of rustic living; but rural resorts remained primitive, uncomfortable, and shabby, their natives as underemployed as ever. At Aix-les-Bains in Savoy, in 1785, the best houses in town collapsed, presumably under the weight of their distinguished boarders. When the future empress, Josephine, visited Plombières in 1798, a wooden balcony collapsed under her feet, and several of the company were injured.[8] Aix, Plombières, and most of their counterparts continued semirural and underdeveloped into the 1850s and 1860s, sometimes later still. The carriages of the great rubbed wheels with peasant carts and cattle; hygiene and facilities were often primitive even by contemporary standards.[9]

This was only moderately disturbing or not disturbing at all. What mattered more was the availability of facilities for diversion, and these improved throughout the century. Roads were traced and others mended, sidewalks built, streets were lighted, parks and promenades laid out, trees planted for decoration and for shade, assembly rooms, dance halls, theaters, and casinos were put up to make life pleasanter for cure-seekers—and for the more numerous visitors for whom health was less important than amusement.

One of the amenities that resorts were expected to provide was protection from the harassing activities and the discomforting sight of the miserable. Beggars, who swarmed in most city streets, were regulated or banned. Poorer patients were discouraged, or relegated away from the fashionable center. In place after place, facilities that once had been free or very inexpensive came to cost more, until serious treatment became too expensive for the really poor. Needy patients, now admitted as indigents, were limited in numbers and restricted to special hours, special places of residence, and often separate thermal buildings. As early as 1806 at Mont-Dore, or 1811 at Plombières, the poor who had used the baths free of charge were excluded. Small hospices for indigent patients, mostly peasants from the neighborhood, eventually opened. At Aix-les-Bains, where indigents were *reglemented* in 1825, a *bain des pauvres* opened in 1836: the reservoir, hitherto reserved for dunking horses, had been made over for the poor. Within a few years the director of Aix's thermal center noted "the great reduction of bathers belonging to the working class . . . especially remarkable in the last three or four years," as well as the income loss this meant for those inhabitants who had made money by renting modest quarters for modest curists.[10]

The loss that some incurred was nothing beside the gains of others.

Wealthy visitors built villas, or rented them from locals who built to suit the seasonal renters. Inns grew in number and in scale. Local entrepreneurs opened stalls and stores to cater to idle shoppers, carriage services, stables with horses or mules to rent for excursions. Centerpiece of all, the thermal establishment grew, built, and rebuilt, employing scores of bathing personnel, chair carriers, masseurs, sweepers, and laundry workers. French establishments, which developed tourist attractions relatively late compared to those of their neighbors, were not as large as English ones nor as fashionable as their well-established central European competitors. After 1871, however, "thermal nationalism" reoriented patriotic curists toward home establishments, which grew in consequence. An official report in 1884 rejoiced over the massive shift in patronage and the resulting expansion and improvement of French resorts.[11] By the beginning of the twentieth century half a million people made all or part of their living from the thermal industry.[12]

During the season, and for some out of it, there was employment for building workers, carpenters, joiners, gardeners, street-cleaners, road-menders, mule-drivers, and guides. At Vichy, whose population quadrupled in the course of the Second Empire, the Compagnie Fermière that managed the enterprise employed better than 10 percent of the local population: a work force ranging from masons and carters and printers to the people who made cardboard boxes for effervescent lozenges. As this last item suggests, mineral water could be enjoyed away from its source. In the 1890s a small station like Vals-les-Bains in Auvergne exported several million bottles a year, Vichy eight or nine million. An official survey of 1910 counted 115 million bottles shipped every year for an annual revenue of 45 million francs.[13] The market for neighborhood produce also expanded: eggs and fowl, milk and fresh vegetables.

Found a spa and make a profit. Not always. Not, for example, at Besançon, which tried and failed around 1890 to launch Besançon-les-Bains because the local watchmaking industry was doing badly.[14] The weather in the Jura is not significantly worse than on the Atlantic Coast, but Paris is farther away, and the investment foundered. Nevertheless, beach (and other) resorts saved many a small port from decline; the more so since sailors and fishermen, who traditionally refused demeaning manual labor, did not mind renting rooms, functioning as bathing attendants, or rowing tourists around at exorbitant prices.[15]

At Nice and Cannes, Chamonix and Sables d'Olonne, the effect of tourism on a lagging economy were not to be gainsaid. "A major resource," rejoiced one historian of Nice; "salvation" for the Sables when its fishing flagged; aid to the unemployed—as when the English colony of Nice put them to work building the Promenade des Anglais; metamorphosis for Cannes after Lord Brougham and his fashionable neighbors persuaded the government to build sidewalks along the dangerous coast highway. Where resorts arose, "the barren fields are touched as by a magic wand, turned into villas, casinos, terraces . . . streets," and of course income. At Nice, where municipal tax revenues rose 160 percent between 1877 and 1881, revenue from the door-and-window tax tripled in the twoscore years preceding 1904; the number of doors and windows per inhabitant (hence light, air, and a certain comfort) was almost double the French average.[16]

The rate of growth might vary, but its nature seldom did; and it contrasted with the sluggish performance of most other towns, especially in this period. The spa acted as an *agent provocateur:* affording an opening for a variety of products and services, it suggested their creation and their more efficient production. And it did this in regions that were particularly poor and isolated, where economic activity was generally feeble. It went on doing so, at a reduced rate perhaps but faster by far than other urban areas, even when times were hard. The continued expansion of resorts during the economically depressed 1880s and 1890s suggests that if the rising leisure industry did not operate countercyclically, it found enough grist for its mills to continue to turn when most other industries flagged.

One illustration of this can be seen in the annals of Vittel, founded in the 1850s by a wealthy outsider called Louis Bouloumié, who discovered that the waters of the local spring helped his otherwise incurable liver and kidney and stomach troubles.[17] At the time, Vittel was a small village that had just lost 8 percent of its population of some 1,300 souls to the cholera of 1854. It was so poor that it could not even afford to build a bridge across the stream that divided the village; so isolated that only a path led to it from the neighboring spa of Contrexéville, four miles away; its lanes were the usual mess of dung and liquid manure. Under Bouloumié's patronage all this would change. Before the 1850s ended there would be a real bridge in lieu of a ford, a proper road between Vittel and Contrexéville; and several hundred visitors were using the local inn, now much improved, or, more likely, Bouloumié's new hotel, complete with casino, ballroom, concert hall, great wooded park, and other amenities. The lost little village in the Vosges became a prosperous small town with numerous inns and shops and even, in 1881, its own branch railway line.

The wretched 1880s, followed by the slow 1890s, were precisely when the real development of Vittel began, with a new casino designed by Charles Garnier (architect not only of the Paris Opéra but also of the casino at Monte Carlo). There would be a shooting range, a pigeon shoot, a gym, a boxing ring, a fencing room, and so on. The hotel and the thermal pavilions were rebuilt and enlarged. There followed in fairly quick succession a velodrome, a racecourse, a golf course, tennis courts, a football field, a polo ground—all rarities in normal towns and all affording seasonal employment for the local population and spectacular incentives for intensive market gardening in the surrounding countryside.

Spas provided significant opportunities for a relatively new industry: advertising. When Bouloumié inaugurated the first of his posh hotels in 1863, he invited forty Paris doctors and assorted representatives of the Paris press, paid their travel expenses, and entertained them royally. Publicity and public relations remained a major item in the budget of resorts, most of which were launched by articles in the Paris press. They made themselves known by pamphlets of subsidized puffery like *Fifteen Days at Mont-Dore, A Season at Salins, A Summer at Aix,* and guidebooks like the *Guide aux stations minérales des Vosges,* published in 1879 by Bouloumié's eldest son, Ambroise. Guides were sometimes presented in verse, or as novels, like the tale of *Jean Bonnet at Luchon,* whose eponymous hero meets a wealthy American family on the train to the Pyrenean spa, guides it around Luchon's surrounding beauties, its casino, its grottoes, and the laxative fountain of Barbazan, and ends by marrying the daughter.[18] By 1890, when Jean Bonnet was pursuing his courtship of Miss Rickson, life in the spas was being treated in a number of uncommissioned novels and plays and operettas. Still the public relations budget grew. Vittel, for example, had spent some 150,000 francs on it before 1882. It paid ten times as much to keep itself in the public eye during the following decade.[19]

Investments on this scale, however, cost much more money than a single entrepreneur could find. Typically, the 1880s were the time when Vittel, fully funded by the Bouloumiés until then, had to turn itself into a joint-stock company, as other resorts were doing, because the standards of holidaymakers, the costs of equipment and publicity, the growing competition between rival resorts, all began to involve sums beyond the means of a family enterprise.

✳

The very rich who traveled with their own establishments were being joined by growing numbers of vacationers from the upper and middle ranges of the bourgeoisie, who expected standards of comfort not to be found in ordinary inns. The very notion of comfort was a foreign novelty. For the wealthy, luxury had preceded comfort. For the poor, the image of other people's luxury long concealed any concept of comfort. Few French of any class came close to comfort as we conceive it today. The equipment of public establishments would eventually suggest comforts for the home as well. For a long time, though, the discomforts of private life were multiplied in public places. Fin de siècle Paris counted few good hotels, even fewer of the middling sort, nothing but fleabags for the modest purse. In the provinces hostelry standards were abysmal. Most were dirty, ill-furnished, and ill-served, offering poor facilities for ablution or purgation. Karl Baedeker, in 1892, found latrines repulsively dirty, even in pretended grand hotels. The hotels Proust frequented boasted elevators, but only one water closet per floor. Their condition may be deduced from the misadventure of the man who, in 1897, sued for damages from the Casino des Fleurs at Cannes. The seat of the toilet had broken while he used it and he had fallen off and fractured his arm. When the Defense pointed out that this happened because, instead of sitting on the seat, he had stood upon it, the plaintiff retorted that he had done like everybody else, given the rotten state of the facility.[20]

Here was the sort of vicious circle often encountered when standards change, rather like "coal in the bathtub." Those who in the twentieth century warned that bathtubs in working-class dwellings would be used for storage, often proved right. Cleanliness, like manners, or a taste for oysters, is an acquired habit that can take a generation or more to assimilate. The shift from squatting to sitting to defecate was surely as difficult to negotiate as the shift from coins to paper money. So indeed was the more or less contemporary change from the washstand with its pitcher of hot water and basin to the "American comfort" of running water from a tap. In 1895 Goncourt objected to hot and cold water that flowed out of taps that could not be moved, and whose presence made washing very awkward.[21] Old habits die hard.

Nevertheless, standards altered and expectations with them. Few until now had traveled for pleasure, few had stayed in public hostelries. When away from home, most folk were put up by family or friends. Not many thought to use a hostelry, or that relatively new facility, the restaurant, whose quality, therefore, they never thought about. But now the doctors and lawyers and prosperous businessmen who began to frequent holiday resorts in greater numbers, expected "modern" conveniences and service. They found them in the new hotels that started to go up at the turn of the century: "palaces" that offered free electric light, and lavatories, bathrooms (not free) on all floors, elevators, telephone booths, sumptuous restaurants and public rooms, courteous service. While outer show continued to be more important than private ease, and while the palaces were never numerous, their presence set standards, at least of convenience and of cleanliness, that the public learned—as did, eventually, some of the landlords.

This was especially true of health resorts which by the turn of the century acted and perceived themselves as models: not just of modernization and industry in a rural context, but of urbanization as it should be, providing unpolluted water, clear light, fresh air, public sanitation, and hygiene in the home. Spas pioneered in planning and developing landscapes and streetscapes. Their architecture led the way, outside of Paris, in the use of new materials: cast iron, ceramics, stucco, and plate glass. The design of their rooms and their public areas eliminated dust traps—moldings, hangings, tapestries, heavy upholstery—and introduced white as a fashionable color. Transport kept up with the times. Vittel was among the first centers to introduce motor coaches for its guests. By 1914 a plane service linked Deauville to Dieppe (for the races); by 1919 Cabourg offered *avions de promenade*—that also flew to Paris in two hours—before most French towns had seen an airfield. Resorts continually brought themselves up to date, pulling down the old, putting up the new, models of conspicuous consumption and of consumption *tout court,* long before society as a whole was ready to accept such values. Thus, having introduced remote provinces to city rhythms and ways, they also revealed new standards to their clientele.

The clientele of the "palaces" remained restricted, even though more modest souls slipped in to glance around or take tea in the public rooms. By the end of the century, however, with three hundred fifty thermal establishments and more than one hundred other resorts, the leisure industry was catering to a variety of purses. A furnished villa at Biarritz might cost around 3,000 francs for the season, from mid-July to mid-September.[22] Luxury villas, there or at Deauville, could cost ten times as much. At Cabourg, the Balbec of Marcel Proust, which an 1888 guide declared to be beyond the reach of middling purses, the Grand Hotel charged about 20 francs a day for room and board for one. But there were supplements—for service, candles, electricity, and whatever else fertile imaginations summoned up—and these could add another 20 percent to the bill, not counting the accommodation and board of accompanying servants, stable or garage charges, and the tips that caused Proust so much concern. (At Evian, in 1899, he finally gave everyone 10 francs, which must have amounted to a tidy sum!) At the other extreme, what the French described as *petits trous pas chers,* offered houses for rent for as little as 50 francs a month, though even these soared in the decade before 1914, testimony not only to the higher prices brought by economic recovery but also to rising demand.[23]

Board and lodging were hardly the extent of holiday expense. Train fares were high, and they changed very little during the fifty years before 1914. A one-way first-class ticket from Paris to Vichy cost 40.20 francs in 1864, 40.90 francs in 1914 (third class fell from 22.55 to 18 francs).[24] Whatever the class, for a family of four or five, and perhaps a nurse, the outlay was significant. Shows, excursions, bathing, or therapy, an *abonnement* to the casino (between 60 and 100 francs per person per season, 1 and 3 francs a day for trippers), not counting gambling and other assorted expenses, made holidays expensive. In these circumstances, it is the more noteworthy that summer migration became a habit for so many, "a passion as general as that of racing." Vichy, which welcomed 20,000 visitors in 1860, was entertaining 100,000 in 1890, out of a total of about 800,000 attending spas. As many again traveled elsewhere—to the mountains, to a country house, or to those "popular beaches" welcomed by Grand-Carteret in 1883 as a gift of the Republic, "where a very modest public can in its turn enjoy the pleasures hitherto reserved for the rich alone."[25]

The numbers such developments concerned, though highly significant in contemporary terms, were not large from today's perspective. Tourists and campers pressed on, but popular tourism also grew, became more truly popular, and again the railroads' role was crucial. It is worth recalling that tourism had existed before tourism: it was called "going on pilgrimage," an activity that provided an ideal combination of adventure, therapy, and trade. Certain nineteenth-century pilgrimage shrines, some associated with a healing spring, expanded even faster than watering places. Pilgrimages, like thermalism, not only were a quest for healing but also provided relaxation, diversion, adventure. Popular speech in many parts of France affirms the relation between pilgrimage and travel by using the same term for both: *vias, viages, visages*. For modest folk, and especially for women, going on pilgrimage probably long remained about the only opportunity to travel. This became easier and more current in the last quarter of the nineteenth century, which was the golden age of large-scale popular pilgrimages, when the same special trains and special fares that railroads devised or conceded to encourage holiday travel were enlisted to take hundreds of thousands to shrines like La Salette in the southeast, Lisieux in Normandy, and especially Lourdes in the Pyrenees, where crowds and the business that they generated seemed almost as much of a miracle as the apparitions of 1858.

By the beginning of the twentieth century, the special trains alone were carrying between 300,000 and 400,000 pilgrims to Lourdes every year. In 1908 the fiftieth anniversary of Bernadette's vision brought a million and a half visitors and 22 million francs for the season: seven times the seasonal revenue of Vittel. In an ecstatic report the prefect noted that the local bailiff charged with recovering bad debts had had to fire his only clerk because there were no recoveries to be made in the Lourdes area. Prosperity on this scale spread throughout the Pyrenean region as a whole, as travelers to Lourdes used the occasion to visit nearby spas or beauty spots. It also affected Lourdes's hinterland, which shipped increasing quantities of foodstuffs, wines, and liquors, as well as novelties, to satisfy the soaring consumption of pilgrims on the spree.[26] The personal effects were just as remarkable. Marcel Jouhandeau's grandmother, who had never left her native village of the Creuse except when she married and moved to nearby Guéret, went on a pilgrimage to Lourdes. That was when, her grandson tells us, "she discovered the world of which she was a part, and whose extent she had never suspected."[27]

Here was the advent of the *nouvelles couches sociales,* those new social strata hailed by Gambetta in the 1870s, with the middle and even the lower middle classes, promoted to social as well as political significance by the Republic, aspiring to imitate their betters and to share their fun. In 1880 the subprefect of Dieppe noted that bathers were more numerous but less select. Ten years later we hear that Trouville has exchanged its wealthy clientele for a more modest one: professional men, tradesmen, clerks. Another few years and *tout se démocratise,* the fashionable few founder in the throng and become lost in the anonymous crowd.[28]

These are exaggerations of course. The fashionable few certainly did resent the appearance of a humbler public poaching on their well-kempt preserves: first parvenus of finance and industry, then professionals, finally shopkeepers and *fonctionnaires.* They shifted their favors from one resort to another (Dieppe to Trouville, Trouville to Deauville) as each became overrun by vulgar crowds. Yet even if their privacy ebbed, which not all regretted, they managed to maintain a high degree of exclusivity.

The vulgar crowd was not yet a truly popular one. We can glimpse this when an article of 1902, discussing "Holidays and Health," refers to men who "go to the office at nine or ten, leave at noon, return at two, to close shop at five" as those who need to rest from overwork yet don't know how to relax.[29] Such objects of solicitude may well have qualified as vulgar, but hardly as poor. This should be borne in mind when reading the massive testimony to a Paris deserted during the summer months; the well-attested stories of bourgeois families' tightly closing their shutters from mid-July to mid-September to make it appear that they are out of town even when they are not; the observation of such a serious witness as Vidal de La Blache that many Paris cab-drivers returned to their native Limousin in summer because their rich clientele had disappeared.[30] A hard look shows that all these tales, some true, refer to particular social groups and particular parts of town.

The best intelligence in this respect comes from the *Fin de Siècle* (August 8, 1897), which declares, "There remain in Paris only those who cannot leave." That category was large, though probably not among the readers of *Fin-de-siècle*. It included the cocottes who, the magazine explains, remain behind because so many of their clients spend the week in Paris, joining their families only for weekends, and also the employees of those businessmen who have stayed behind. At the fin de siècle a few enterprises had begun to offer vacations without pay to members of their staff, and a very few (the Bon Marché, for example) some days of holiday with pay. For most working folk, though, free time meant not leisure but dreaded unemployment. The idea of a vacation did not yet exist for them.[31]

True, some of the workers' young, again a very few, were getting a taste of it. Beginning in the 1880s, church and secular charities began to found *colonies de vacances,* summer camps, in mountains or at the seaside. The Comité parisien des colonies de vacances dates from 1887, the Oeuvre des enfants à la montagne, in Saint-Etienne, from 1891. Paris led, but all big cities followed until, by 1905, almost as many poor children spent summer in camps as there had been idle tourists in France half a century earlier. That same year the mass-circulation *Petit Journal* unveiled a scheme to send young Paris seamstresses to a beach resort.[32] Such recognition of the publicity use of charitably funded vacations suggested that the exceptional privilege was turning into a desirable norm. Another half-century would pass before aspiration became a civic right. But the groundwork was laid during the fin de siècle.

One story may help to place this in perspective. Born in Nîmes (Gard) in 1886, Paul Marcelin, the son of a small artisan, was a tinplate worker like his father. When he wrote his memoirs as an old man, he mentioned that until 1890 people of their condition never left home, except perhaps to visit a nearby village where a relative or an old nurse might live. Then, around 1900, "we went, my mother and I, to the Grau-du-Roi," a tiny fishing town on the Mediterranean Coast, some thirty miles south of Nîmes. "Life wasn't easy, there was no water, you had to buy it by the barrel, and of course no lavatory. All the same, the stay was for my mother a luxury she wouldn't have dared hope for in her youth."[33] This helps remind us that if the nineteenth century evokes the discomforts of the Industrial Revolution, it deserves to evoke also its benefits: the expanding notion of vacation; the spread of travel, rest and restoration from a few to many, before that actually became a mass enterprise; the affirmation of the right to idleness not just for a favored few but for everybody.

❊

Meanwhile tourism had shifted from leisure activities rationalized by some useful function such as medical need—a sort of ludo-therapy—to activities that were frankly oriented to sheer consumption: looking at views or monuments, lounging about, or consuming energy in new sports like cycling, motoring, or mountaineering. The earliest kind of mountaineering, fallout of Rousseau and Romanticism, had produced voyagers like M. Perrichon, the hero of Eugène Labiche's famous play, who takes his first trip from home in order to be photographed in front of a glacier. A more serious kind of mountaineering, inspired by English practice, developed after 1870. The Club Alpin Français was founded in 1874, the Société des Touristes du Dauphiné in 1875, and the Pyrenees prompted several climbing clubs of their own.[34]

The patriotic atmosphere of the 1870s, the new interest in fresh air, gymnastics, and "physical regeneration," suggested the use of mountains as a sort of superior gym on whose slopes and peaks fitter generations could train for the *revanche* to come. More direct considerations intervened: alpine warfare, and the training for it that mountaineering could provide. Consequently, the new alpine clubs were not limited to climbers, on the English model, but were open to all, in Adolphe Joanne's words, "who had not committed murder and could pay 20 francs a year" (10 francs for the Touristes du Dauphiné). A second generation followed at the turn of the century, stimulated by the new literature of sport, fitness, and muscle-power that encouraged not only exercise but exploits. Still, just as the curists had preceded and attracted tourists, so the vogue of climbing encouraged more modest trippers too. Mountain stations were the first to set up *syndicats d'initiative* (tourist information bureaus). Group excursions began to cater to less expert mountain lovers, and the later 1880s witnessed an "invasion" of eager trampers, alternately encouraged by eulogies of "the mysterious and savage beauties" of Pyrenees and Alps, and deplored by those who regretted the loss of their solitary preserves. An enthusiast like Henry Beraldi recorded the Pyrenees' majestic peaks vulgarized, besmirched, behotelled, serving aperitifs and *biftecs,* where terror and exaltation once reigned. The mountains of the 1890s, he lamented, placed a café next to every natural marvel, matched pints of beer with torrents, cascades and lemonades, glorious vistas and apéritifs. Worse, the new generation, heedless of past glories, *liked* the new comforts, decent roads, mountain railways, hostelries. The splendid mountainside was turning into another tawdry suburb. There, commented Beraldi, was the havoc that vulgarity and utilitarianism had wrought: "*A nous les Pyrénées,* let's make a profit from them!"[35]

Once again the exaggeration is evident, especially since Beraldi writes with brio. But the principle reflected in his sarcasm deserves attention. Should beauty spots have been preserved for their own sake and for the enjoyment of "pure" devotees willing to rough it? The modern state or capitalist enterprise that improved access roads or laid down narrow-gauge lines also built hotels and lemonade stands that blemished pristine sites. More visitors to enjoy the beauty, the air, the exercise, meant more defilement, garbage on the greensward, the rustic glade besmirched. More visitors also meant a greater diversity of people with access to good things hitherto reserved for the very few. A phrase that Beraldi used to express the acme of gracelessness, "*on commence à saussiçonner,*"[36] anticipates what dismayed holidaymakers said about the workers invading their beaches in the 1930s. The petty bourgeois of the 1890s, with sausages and bread and liters of red wine in their picnic baskets, anticipated the proletarian weekenders who benefited from the Popular Front: a shock to some, a model to many. The sight of their vulgarity where more distinguished feet had trod— apart from the native smugglers, sheep, and goats—was also an earnest of emancipation. And if the emancipated expected and got some lemonade with their beauty spots, this meant that someone, probably a local peasant, was prepared to sell it. The employment and unfamiliar cash that spas had brought to regions short of both, tourism contributed to others.

In 1890 a lover of the Cévennes, a region long ignored as backward and inaccessible, describes the tourist development of the Causse Noire in Aveyron. "Only a few years ago, the natives couldn't understand our finding it beautiful. 'It is bad country,' they would say in their rude patois, 'all rocks, no houses.' But in 1885 they were saying, 'It's true, this place is not so bad: all these posh visitors have already paid our taxes for the year.' And they were setting up shops, and building rooms to rent, and training their mules to carry the tourists. They are beginning not to fear the Devil's Canyon, now that they see its cliffs producing not evil spirits, but bright new coins left behind by curious tourists."[37] The horrors and vulgarities of modernity are felt most keenly by those who, enjoying its comforts, can treat them with contempt.

Many French, rich and poor, began to discover France during these years—the very country they or their children were at this very time learning about in schools, beholding in newly available engravings and illustrations, contemplating in another contemporary novelty: maps. The Touring Club de France boasted 20,000 members in 1895, the year it was founded, 100,000 by 1905. Both the Automobile Club de France (also founded in 1895) and Michelin, the tire manufacturer, brought out their first road guides in 1900. These and the publications of the Touring Club played a great part in spurring the improvement of roads, of hostelries, and of restaurants, all of which began to abandon mediocrity (and worse) in response to their criticism.

By then, some hundred thousand *automobiles de tourisme* were chugging on French roads, and railway statistics had begun to reflect significant rises during the summer months. The nature of the clientele that swelled the statistics was changing visibly, helped by the special holiday fares increasingly available for "the season." In August 1900 *La Nouvelle Mode* recognized that the mass departure of Parisians was largely compensated for by the influx of provincial visitors, "the small bourgeois of small towns, peasants from the villages." Their description of these clodhoppers reads like a litany of contempt: halting speech, diverse patois, shambling bodies, floundering arms, dim eyes, dull faces, closed countenances, no sense of refinement, nothing but the "dreary ennui born of obtuse brains." Where, asked *La Nouvelle Mode,* were "the slim straight silhouettes of the Parisians?"[38] Presumably the Parisians they had in mind were on holiday. But so, for once, were their provincial counterparts, able at last to sample the hitherto inaccessible delights of exotic Paris.

Some had not waited that long. But few middle-range folk had looked on pleasure travel as a serious possibility until the fin de siècle. At that time most spas and resorts abandoned their exclusive aspirations and set out to attract anyone who had leisure and money to spend. Biarritz, for example, set up a tourist information bureau to compete with neighboring resorts along the Basque Coast, in the Pyrenees, and elsewhere.[39] Biarritz was not alone. In 1910 a National Tourist Office would be set up to coordinate the efforts of local syndicats, with a new residence tax to fund its activities and those of tourist bureaus. The sausagification that Beraldi feared was on its way.

10

La Petite Reine

❋

An emblem of Progress and one of its agents at the fin de siècle was the bicycle. "Run, *vélo,* run in your bright light," sang an *Ode au véloce,* "Progress rides upon you."[1] The exalted tone had changed little since the 1860s, when the rather unwieldy machines sporting one, two, three, or four wheels of varying dimensions had become a familiar sight and print had begun to exalt cycling, symbol of "moral and material progress," means of regenerating man by physical exercise. By 1898, in Zola's *Paris,* we hear that riding a bicycle is "a continuous apprenticeship of the will, an admirable lesson in steering and defense."[2] Though intellectuals have always been prone to give ponderous treatment to simple matters of convenience or pleasure, this sort of encomium was neither exceptional nor undeserved. It becomes more comprehensible not only in the context of the contemporary obsession with physical and moral decadence but also in the context of a world where the sort of mobility permitted by the bike was scarce, rare, and exciting.

For a long time cycling remained an expensive pastime for the rich and idle. The bicycle itself was likely to cost 500 francs or more, equivalent to two months of a lieutenant's pay or three of a schoolteacher's. Regarded as a luxury, it was first subjected to a direct tax; then, after 1900, taxed indirectly through the requiring of a license plate. Characteristically the first prophets, champions, and practitioners of the new sport were *fils de famille:* heirs of wholesale grocers like Frédéric Charron, of wholesale wine merchants like Paul Ruinart, both great racers of the 1880s. Tristan Bernard, the wit who undertook the management of the Vélodrome Buffalo (built on the site of Buffalo

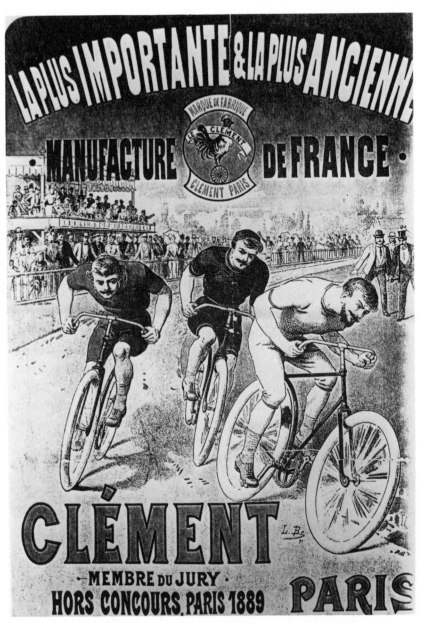

This ad for Clément Bicycles, one of the earliest French cycle firms, shows a highly idealized picture of a velodrome. The 1890s proved the golden age of these newfangled structures, devoted to cycle racing and to the commercialization of sporting exploits. Note the absence of brakes. Riders braked by inserting their foot between wheel and fork.

Bill's Circus) in 1892, was the son of a builder and real estate man. Henri Desgrange, who took over the new velodrome at the Parc des Princes in 1897 and launched *l'Auto*, destined to become France's major sporting daily, was a notary's clerk, representing another social group. His humbler origins reflect the relegation of the bicycle from luxury object, one with which an arch-aesthete like Robert de Montesquiou did not disdain to be photographed, to solid investment accessible to middle- and lower-middle-class budgets. The change came swiftly.

In the middle 1880s a century of experiment with wooden models, boneshakers, and bi-, tri-, and quadricycles culminated in the Rover safety bicycle, which, allowing riders to fall from lesser heights and hurt themselves less, quickly replaced the precarious penny-farthing. The dominant tricycle ("instrument de père de famille") weighed 40 to 60 kilos, the new bikes 20 kilos, the first Rover racer about 16.[3] One could go faster and farther; and, a veteran of those days recalled, "the feeling of liberation was inconceivable."[4] Between 1889 and 1891, John Boyd Dunlop's pneumatic tires began to replace solid rubber ones, inner tubes permitted André and Edouard Michelin to develop detachable tires, cycle prices began to fall, and cycle racing was attracting more public attention. After 1891, cherished and publicized by the press, cycling became the most popular of sports. The winner of the Paris-Brest race (on *pneus Michelin*), national champion Charles Terront, had a place of honor reserved for him at the Opera.

In 1898 Maurice Le Blanc, son of a wealthy textile manufacturer, published one of France's first sporting novels. *Voici des ailes* glorified "the new friend that destiny has granted man," the bicycle that gives us wings to rise above the vileness of the world.[5] The new steed facilitated other ascensions: first, above our limited condition as bipeds, especially for those unable to afford the expense of a horse; then, not least, above a fixed social condition.

Competing manufacturers of bicycles, tires, and cycling accessories needed a stage to exhibit the superior virtues of their rival products.[6] They found it in competitive racing, first on roads (the Paris–Clermont race of 1892 was organized by Michelin to prove that its tires were better than Dunlop's), then in specially built velodromes. In this realm what began as an upper-class fad was quickly taken up by more modest fans. The first large indoor bicycle track in Paris, the

Illustrations reproduced from Pierre Giffard, *La Reine Bicyclette*
(Paris, 1891).

Let us honor the
village tricycle

Marital tricycle

MARS

The firemen

In breeches
and blouse

Vélodrome d'Hiver, was set up in 1893 on the Champ de Mars, in a fashionable quarter, but facilities were soon extended to serve a younger and poorer public on the east side of town. In contrast to horseracing, long a preserve of the better-off, cycle races were the first popular sporting entertainment of modern times and the first to offer numerous professionals an avenue of economic, hence social, promotion.

When in 1904 the teenage Pauline de Broglie watched the endurance races at the Vel' d'Hiv, from the box of Madame de Rochetaillée, a son of the Comte de Vogüé was among the riders; but most of the contestants, like the mass of the public of what struck her as a "brutal, smelly, and barbarous sport," came from the lower classes.[7] The champions of the fin de siècle were delivery boys like Terront, bakers' apprentices like Constant Huret or Edmond Jacquelin, butcher boys like Louis Pothier, chimney sweeps like Maurice Garin, winner of the first Tour de France, and of 6,125 gold francs with it.[8] Successful riders could earn five, six, seven thousand francs a year, and many an apprentice inspired by their example yearned for an iron steed of his own, while lining the roads or filling the stands of the tracks that sprang up all over France by the century's end.

By 1897 H. de Graffigny's *Manuel pratique du constructeur et du conducteur de cycles et d'automobiles* estimated the number of cyclists in France at 300,000, not far from the taxation figures which indicate over 375,000 bicycles in 1898. By 1914 they would be three and a half million. What a Paris paper had once sneered at as *imbéciles à roulettes* had become part of the landscape. General Robineau, "the elegant sportsman," made his tricycle tour of the Champs Elysées every day in morning coat and top hat. The Comtesse de Mercy-Argenteau decreed that a woman of the world would be wise to arrange for her chambermaid to follow her, when on wheels. She went unheeded.[9] In April 1897 *Fin de Siècle* introduced a regular cycling column.

There were those who repined. In 1893 the Nantes Medical Society debated whether the new manner of locomotion, besides being undignified, was not dangerous for the spinal column.[10] In 1894 the Congress of the French Association for the Advancement of Science reflected on the breathing problems facing a man moving at forty miles an hour, albeit for only a few hundred yards. Dr. Ludovic O'Followell marked the danger of jumping into the saddle too soon after sexual intercourse.[11] The government, more impressed by the growing number of traffic accidents, regulated the circulation of velocipedes, which would henceforth have to be equipped with an *avertisseur sonore*—hooter, horn, or bell—audible 50 meters away. The reviewers of a useful manual, *The Bicycle Before the Law,* aware that every citizen committed at least one minor offense a day, expressed their conviction that no cyclist could possibly avoid them.[12]

If infractions were likely, fractures were even more so. Auguste Renoir, the painter, who had fallen off his bicycle while going down a hill too fast and broken his arm, hated the dread machines. "M. Renoir," Julie Manet noted in September 1897, "attacks all *mécaniques,* saying that we're in decadence . . . What's the point of going so fast?"[13] Julie, who was learning to ride a bike, agreed with M. Renoir that all these mechanical contrivances were tiresome and invasive; nevertheless, she wanted to ride one. Like her, those who could afford it grumbled but pedaled. Octave Uzanne, who found the cycling fashion too new in 1894 to predict its eventual effects, expected ways and manners to be seriously unsettled by it. We have already seen that none were more unsettled than those involving women. Even commentators who appreciated "the new wheels of the chariot of progress" could not help noting that, in their velvet breeches, women were beginning to look like men. Uzanne himself soon recorded that, "with the bicycle, the last appearance of feminine modesty disappeared."[14]

Uzanne may have been premature, but worse dangers lay in wait. Dr. O'Followell quoted a newspaper article that compared the effects of the bicycle with those of the sewing machine, which, as was well known, fated seamstresses "to nymphomania and characterized hysteria." Cyclomania was alleged to bring about "the same lubricious overexcitement, the same accesses of sensual madness." O'Followell took issue with such views. Cycling could indeed "procure genital satisfactions, voluptuous sensations," and a kind of "sportive masturbation." One fifteen-year-old, "an assiduous cyclist," had as a result become faded, pale, emaciated. Even so, the bicycle could not be compared to the sewing machine, whose mechanism and effects were altogether different. Although women were advised not to ride a bicycle without a previous medical examination, velocipedic exercise carried no danger to childbearing; it cut into the ravages of alcoholism and was generally good for women—not least because it

T.-A. Steinlen, *Motorcycles Comiot,* 1899. By the end of the century women cyclists were no longer extraordinary, even in the countryside. Bicycles, for those who could afford them, might well be equipped with a small petrol engine, loud enough to disturb the geese. The crossbar suggests that the rider wears an unobtrusive trouser-skirt. The road behind shows traces of stone paving, a novelty that may have resulted from pressure by cycling clubs.

discouraged corsets.[15] Another medical enthusiast agreed: for Dr. Lucas-Championnière, the bicycle was a revelation to women and an occasion for them to prove themselves. It developed their shoulder muscles, their thighs, their sense of balance—and, another commentator added, their sense of independence.[16] No wonder that at the banquet which followed the feminist congress of 1896, the president, Maria Pognon, raised her glass in a toast to the "equalitarian and leveling bicycle" that was about to liberate her sex.[17]

The velocipede's liberating effects were not limited to women. Both sexes could explore the countryside on it, and they were doing so in growing numbers. On Sundays and in summer railway stations bulged with cyclists, and observers noted the new "frenzy for speeding in the open air, for physical exercise, for movement by one's own muscles" (not those of a horse).[18] The vogue of "excursionism" was opening up France, carrying wheeled explorers off the beaten track into parts of the country long unvisited, inspiring innkeepers to improve their primitive facilities and their unsavory food, and prompting those who tried them to sour comments. Guides catered to the new tourism, as did advertising. The railroad companies provided special trains and special facilities for cyclists. By the 1890s Jules Bertot had published twelve volumes of the *Guide du cycliste en France,* small red books full of maps and information that one could slip into a pocket or a sack. The Touring Club de France was founded in 1890 by cyclists, with untold effects upon the quality of hostelries and of roads. A turn-of-the-century chronicler of trips through the French countryside referred to their "democratization" by the bicycle and to the work of the Touring Club in providing "a description of landscapes and of monuments to fit this rapid means of locomotion": maps. Maps too were rare and unfamiliar, even more so than bicycles. Now anyone who did not know how to read one was condemned "to travel fumblingly like a one-eyed snail."[19] The first *Guides Michelin* date from 1900.

Roads took longer to improve. Muddy in winter, dusty in summer, rutted or cobbled, and generally full of potholes, they were no joy to frequent. Their hazards were enhanced by dogs (velocipedists were advised to use riding whips against attacking dogs, not a revolver!) and hostile natives, more dangerous than dogs.[20] But growing numbers brought growing acceptance. By 1894 there was even talk of cycle paths.[21] And, since one touchstone of success is theft, that same year the *Gazette des Tribunaux* recorded that never had so many bicycles been stolen. Soon new buildings would include "garages" for bicycles, and older ones build special shelters for them, away from the pilfering grasp of predators. Meanwhile the Académie Française admitted the term to its dictionary, along with its derivatives: *cycliste, cyclable,* and so on.[22]

No wonder that a devotee like Baudry de Saunier could find only two reasons now "to refuse to taste velocipedic delights: poverty and hemorrhoids"![23] And the negative effect of the former waned with the century. A young schoolteacher in the Normandy countryside remembered seeing his first cyclist in 1890 and yearning for the machine that would put the surrounding world within easier reach than walking. But "in 1895 bicycles were still very rare; in 1897 their price was still too high for me." Finally, in 1898, help from his farmer father, a loan from an uncle who was a village mason, and 50 francs in savings enabled him to buy a secondhand bicycle. It took him five years to repay the loan, but the bike was worth it. "Henceforth I was king of the road, since I was faster than a horse." He considered himself one of the privileged few, "perhaps the only one of my class on an iron steed."[24]

It is a characteristic of our modern times that, while privileged and unprivileged subsist, the number of the former grows, that of the latter shrinks apace. Thus it was in the matter of bicycles. By the latter 1890s, though good bicycles and cheap ones still stood in steady contradiction, the latter could be bought for something between 100 and 150 francs—even on credit, with a five-year guarantee.[25] We hear about a small village entrepreneur (he sold contraband matches) in 1905 who bought a bicycle for his business and rented it out at 10 sous an hour (50 centimes) to neighbors who wanted to try it.[26] Soon miners and workingmen were acquiring the new steed; young men of the laboring classes were observed training on it at the day's end, "in shorts, bare arms and legs";[27] and the Socialist Party set up its Union Sportive du Parti Socialiste (1907).

The economics of purchase indicate why bicycles remained few and far between for a long time, but also how they ceased to count as objects of conspicuous consumption. The cheapest bicycle of 1893 cost the equivalent of 1,655 hours' wages of a factory hand. By 1911, with hourly wages up and bicycle prices down, a cheap model cost less than the equivalent of 357 hours—about half the price of a sewing machine, and hence accessible for working-class bachelors. By 1914 their acquisition by urban workingmen was helping, as did trolleys, the shift of population from city centers to more affordable, and generally more livable, suburbs.

The bicycle was no longer in the forefront of progress, and the evolution of cycling clubs shows what this meant. Cycling clubs of the 1880s and 1890s had gathered members of the middle and upper middle classes—professional men, professors, merchants, officials. After the middle 1890s the membership of new clubs was several notches below the middle of the middle class: shop-assistants, artisans, noncommissioned officers. We witness the appearance of clubs like the Société des Cyclistes Coiffeurs-Parfumeurs (1896) or the Union Cycliste des Postes et Télégraphes (1897); and dignified labels like Club Vélocipédique or Véloce Club are outnumbered by lightheartedly vulgar ones: Société des Cyclistes Rigolards Argentonnais, La Bécane d'Ecueillé, or Le Rasoir Sportif Montpelliérain.[28]

These associations inspired by and focused on the bicycle encouraged their members to participate in other activities. By the last quarter of the century upper- and middle-class velocipedists already were providing the backbone of other sporting clubs, and velodromes opened their grassy centers to tennis courts in summer and ice skating in winter. Less socially exalted enthusiasts were similarly drawn to related forms of exercise. In 1905 at Bordeaux the eight-year-old postmen's cycling club turns into an Association Sportive des PTT, and the hairdressers apparently followed suit.[29] So the shift from elite to popular cycling was followed by a shift from one sport to others, and, although cycling remained a spectator sport for most people, its influence upon the future of other sports in France was vast. It was the first to suggest the pursuit of sport for pleasure in social circles where this possibility was not normally envisaged; many clubs that did not appeal exclusively to the middle and upper classes were formed to promote it; finally, it led directly to a commercialization of sport, which, though much decried, made it accessible to great numbers that would have ignored it otherwise.

The better to prove the democratization of the bicycle, fashionable attention was shifting to a costlier toy. It was no coincidence that in 1897, the very year when the founding of the Cyclistes Girondins at

Bordeaux offered a haven for middle and lower-middle-class bicyclists excluded from the earlier and more expensive Club Vélocipedique de Bordeaux, the first auto club was founded in that city.[30] That was also the year when cycling publicists like Baudry de Saunier abandoned velocipedes for automobiles. In April 1898 *Fin de Siècle,* ever the weathervane, added a new feature: "Automobilisme." Whereas in 1891 the first sporting daily had forthrightly entitled itself *Vélo,* its rival ten years later hedged by setting out as *Auto-Vélo* and by 1903 had shed the second word. Those who could afford it were turning to more exclusive activities.

Like bicycles, horseless carriages operated by steam, compressed air, electricity, or a variety of fuels had been around since the eighteenth century. In 1885, however, Karl Benz, a German, invented a petrol engine that worked. In 1891 Armand Peugeot, who had turned the family hardware manufacture from farm implements, umbrella spokes, and corset stays to bicycles, built a small car in which he traveled from Montbéliard in eastern France to Paris, then followed a bicycle race to Brest and back at an average speed of ten miles per hour, before returning home—2,500 kilometers later—without a problem.[31] By 1895 Peugeot had sold two hundred vehicles—two-fifths of those then being driven on the roads of France. The cars built by Peugeot, Panhard, Levassor, and others were for the rich alone. Custom-made, they might cost 40 to 50,000 francs to build, and several thousand francs a year to run. One owner paid 1,500 francs a year (a workingman's total income) simply for new tires.[32]

The spirit and enterprise which built and raced motor cars—and airplanes not long afterward—were kin to those which launched the velocipede. Cycling enthusiasts bought and drove the first automobiles. As in the United States, where the Wright brothers and Glenn Curtis started out building bikes, many cycle manufacturers, like Adolphe Clément, turned to building cars, then airships and airplane engines. Cycle racers like the Farman brothers (great footballers too!) built and raced motor cycles and motor cars before they turned to aviation. Hélène Dutrieu, winner of the world cycling title in 1898, would go on to get her pilot's license and establish a whole series of flying records before World War I broke out. Nor was this surprising. The components of cars, cycles, and planes of those early days were often the same. So was the inspiration of those who made them and who made them run: love of danger and novelty, of speed and adventure.

The figure of Albert, Marquis de Dion (1851–1946), though generally remembered by the courtesy title of Count that he carried until his father's death, is typical of early automobile enthusiasts. In the 1880s Dion entered into an association with a mechanic, Georges Bouton, to build steam boilers, steam tricycles, and steam carriages, some of which he then drove to victory in a number of road races. In 1895 he built a petrol-driven tricycle, then a real automobile, and began to experiment with cheaper models. In this he was overtaken by Louis Renault's more innovative designs, which combined lightness with greater horsepower (Dion did not believe in multicylinder engines). Dion also found time to found the Automobile Club de France (1895) and—earnest of his adventurous nature—the Aéro Club de France (1898). The pugnacity that made him risk family disapproval and public scorn for his mechanical extravagances was reflected in his politics. An ardent anti-Dreyfusard, he was one of the group arrested at the Auteuil races in June 1899 for attacking President Loubet. This reflected the political coloring of the Automobile Club, with its fine palace on the place de la Concorde and its membership of wealthy, titled, and reactionary *automobilistes;* and the club itself was briefly closed down after this escapade as a den of conspirators against the Republic. Dion, however, whose only idea of flight was to charge forward, ran for election as a Nationalist in the Loire-Inférieure and was elected departmental councillor, then deputy, and eventually senator of this solidly Monarchist and Catholic region. Nor did that lessen his interest in building and racing autos; in 1907 he joined the newspaper *Le Matin* in organizing a spectacular International Rally from Paris to Peking.[33]

Racing was dangerous but it sold cars as it had sold bicycles before them.* Competition between manufacturers—fin de siècle France had more than any other country—made their publicity crucial. Renault, like other pioneers, raced his own cars to bring them to the public eye and prove that small, light vehicles performed as well as or better than

---

*In 1899 France exported 2 million francs' worth of automobiles and parts; in 1903, 51 million; in 1906, 140 million. The driving permit was introduced in 1899. By 1901, the socialist *Petite République* was denouncing "the sport of millionaires," and the anti-Semitic *Libre Parole,* the Jewish drivers, responsible for too many accidents.

larger ones. In 1901 he won first place in his category in the Paris–Berlin race and had to double the capacity of his works at Billancourt, near Paris. In 1902 his brother Marcel came out first overall in the Paris–Vienna run, at an average speed of 39 mph—faster than the fastest train in Europe, the Arlberg Express. Marcel would kill himself the following year, missing a dangerous curve in a cloud of dust while trying to overtake a competitor during the Paris–Madrid race; after this the government prohibited road races as being too murderous, allowing only closed-circuit ones as at Le Mans. But the Billancourt firm never looked back.[34]

Although France had the best roads in Europe, their quality was relative. Automobiles proceeded in a cloud of dust that blinded and choked other drivers or users of the road—and often, as with Marcel Renault, the conductor himself. Rudyard Kipling remembered "the soft roads that went to pieces under the tires and revenged themselves by breaking the strongest springs"—as well as the tires. He recalled that chauffeurs and passengers were not only muffled and goggled against the dust and wind, but equipped with a long-lashed whip to ward off dogs.[35] Despite such drawbacks, the automobile forged ahead, in part because it promised to reduce the noise, congestion, and pollution of city streets in process of being increasingly overwhelmed by traffic. True, cars smelled bad and made a lot of noise, but they would displace the horse which also smelled and cost a lot of money. Above all, they represented progress and "the triumph of regenerating sports which would forge a strong race."[36]

They were certainly forging an increasingly speedy one. Taxicabs were replacing horsecabs, even in provincial towns; bandits and police adopted the new means of locomotion; municipalities regulated their use.[37] In 1909 Deauville counted 2,218 cars (and 896 horse-drawn carriages) at its annual races; by 1912, 3,613 cars (no carriages) were encountering parking problems there. The hippodrome had built a special garage for bicycles in 1893. Now, the eight hundred slots of the new *vestiaire de voitures* did not suffice.[38] Courts of law began to fine imprudent drivers and to regulate their speed. But the intelligence that more French were dying from bicycle and automobile accidents than died from drinking was greeted calmly by those aware that bolting horses had frequently caused accidents and injuries.[39] In December 1901 the Fourth Salon of Bicycles and Autos, inaugurated by the

President of the Republic, welcomed 40,000 visitors a day to look over the 693 different automobiles and the 645 bicycle models on show. A ten-horsepower car still cost 8,000 francs, but Louis Renault's new chassis sold for 1,500 francs, and Dion was about to bring out his suggestively named "La Populaire." *L'Illustration* opined that automobiles could actually prove useful: more than toys for millionaires, they represented the beginning of profound economic changes that would affect everyone.[40]

Still, while cars and airplanes now led the parade of progress, the humbler bicycle did more for human comfort—and for modernity.[41] That tends to be lost from sight behind more spectacular performances. Yet a careful look at the era's newspapers indicates that, while thousands thrilled at the achievements of new petrol-powered engines, millions looked on the bike as something to admire and also to acquire.

A French sporting press, catering first to horse-racing fans then to Sunday cyclists, had risen from uncertain beginnings to 1894, when the weekly *Bicyclette* printed 20,000 copies and the daily *Vélo*, founded three years earlier, claimed sales of 80,000. By that time France boasted a lot of velocipedes, and the sporting press that catered to their owners had discovered the close relationship between a certain kind of sporting activity, publicity, and circulation. The rivalries of bicycle-manufacturers and the circulation wars of the sporting press greased the wheels of competition. Track meetings held in velodromes drew big crowds; but road races brought the bicycle closer to its public and provided even more sensational features for the press.

The tale of the Tour de France is an exemplary one. It begins with a circulation war between the well-entrenched *Vélo* and its competitor, *l'Auto,* founded because the Marquis de Dion, who had previously financed the former, had been incensed by its criticism of the incident at Auteuil. Withdrawing his support from the *Vélo,* Dion and nationalist friends like Michelin set up a rival paper whose title reflected the latest fashions in the world of "sport," and whose editor, Henri Desgrange, was himself an enthusiastic cyclist and cycle racer.

L'Auto needed a sensational publicity venture to attract new readers. It began by reviving the Paris–Brest road race, which had last been run in 1891. But although the 1901 winner knocked nearly two hours off the previous record and vast crowds gathered to follow the progress of the race on the immense map that hung on the facade of the paper's editorial offices, such limited contests provoked only limited excitement. Something more grandiose was to be found in the unheard-of notion of a bicycle race around the whole of France, "from Paris to the blue waves of the Mediterranean" and back, one highly reminiscent of the popular Tour de France par deux enfants and partly reproducing the circuit followed by its schoolboy heroes.

The distances that the new race involved were quite unheard-of, and possibly beyond the capacity of man: a good gambit to keep the public panting, even though twenty-one of the first sixty competitors actually managed to finish. The first Tour, in 1903—2,400 kilometers in nineteen days—was a great success; that of 1904 a disaster: threats from gamblers and from supporters of rival racers, pistol shots, cyclists attacked and wounded, gave it all the ingredients of drama and of rising sales.[42] By 1906 the distance to be covered had almost doubled (to 4,600 km.), the starters were more numerous by one-third. In 1914 one hundred forty-five contenders started out to cover 5,400 kilometers, and fifty-four finished: a tribute to training and improved performance, and also to Desgrange's success at persuading his riders that they could rise to ever stiffer challenges and his public that the runners' solitary struggle against natural obstacles, accidents, and weariness had an epic quality that deserved special attention. As Geoffrey Nicholson has put it, he "turned his riders into champions and his champions into heroes."[43] Not a bad thing, when other kinds of hero were relatively scarce.

During the 1913 race the very popular Eugène Christophe broke his front wheel while tooling down a Pyrenean pass, shouldered his bike and ran seven miles to the closest backsmith's shop, repaired it with his own hands as the rules required, and rode on two hours late. Unfortunately, while busily welding back his broken stem, he had allowed a little boy to work the bellows at the blacksmith's forge. For this, Christophe was penalized three minutes, and with this penalty he entered racing history: the stuff of legend.[44] Like the French genius for improvisation, the French revulsion against impersonal officialdom and its rules could find a new domain, and the human yearning for something to admire could focus on new objects: the self-made (also press-made) Giants of the Road, no less respectable, surely, than the men of sword or state held up to public acclaim by the establishment.

The Tour contributed more to France than new-model heroes. It brought life, activity, and excitement into small towns where very little happened; it introduced a festive atmosphere wherever it passed; and it acquainted provincial backwaters with the spectacular displays only the capital and big cities knew. At Cosne-sur-Loire, 174 kilometers from Paris, the Cosnois rejoiced to view at last "the spectacle of a great highway drama"; at Nevers (227 kms.), "the town, normally calm, is extraordinarily animated"—cycling clubs riding in en masse from surrounding centers. At Moulins (281 kms.), "great liveliness . . . this is a new spectacle." At Lyons, a staging point where the start took place at 2 A.M., all the regional cycling clubs rode past first carrying lanterns, while the crowd went wild.

Many towns, like Montauban, had never seen a bicycle race: "enormous enthusiasm, indescribable animation, noisy crowds." Others, however small, turned out to see the local champion pass: at Grisolles, a village halfway between Toulouse and Montauban, "everyone is on the road to see Dargassié . . . At 4 A.M. the highway is black with people."[45] Even the incidents of 1904 testified to the participation of the public, its partisanship going as far as violence and rioting, an identification as novel in direction as it was in degree.

By 1905 and 1906 the Tour had acquired a great many aspects familiar to us today: the curious streamed in by train or bicycle, horse-carriage or car; the roads were lined with sightseers; shops, offices, and factories let their employees pour out to watch. Where the Tour stopped for the night, or even at a halt or checkpoint, impromptu fairs sprang up: illuminations, local cycle races, other competitions, boxing matches, public dances, concerts, orchestras. The mayor and the municipal council came out to greet the racers, to toast and make speeches to them. Soon roads were being cleared and closed to traffic, public transport halted, children let out of school. As its inventor, the sports writer Géo Lefèvre, wrote in 1906: "the Tour is henceforth the mighty annual tam-tam which for a whole month wakes an entire nation to cycling . . . the prodigious vulgarizing cavalcade of sport."[46] The mayor of Lyons, Edouard Herriot, agreed when he toasted the racers that passed thru France's second city, *l'Auto,* and the Tour, for their mass impact and their stimulus to sport.[47] He might have added: to business. But also to public entertainment and fun and joy, at a time when all of these were still in short supply for ordinary folk.

The Tour was already being criticized for crass commercialism. Crass or not, it was, and has remained, a commercial enterprise designed to sell more papers, then more bikes, then any number of products that subsidized riders or advertised in *l'Auto*, not counting the wine and beer drunk on its passage, the booths that sprang up, the entertainment offered to the fans and to the merely curious. Without the commercial impulse there would have been no Tour, nor the excitement that went with it. There would not have been the incentive to buy more bicycles, hence the mass production that made them accessible to more buyers at modest prices; or the aspiration to imitate the champions, to become rich and famous and perhaps save enough to open one's own café or store, or buy a farm, when one reached middle age. The Tour carried modernity with it, revealed more of France to the French, if only on the maps on which so many followed its progress. The next time the French focused on their maps was in 1914. The Tour that year took off on Sunday, June 28, a few hours before the news of Archduke Franz-Ferdinand's murder at Sarajevo. By the time it returned, on Sunday, July 26, Austrians, Russians, and Serbs had begun to mobilize. Henceforth maps displayed a different progress, another kind of heroism. Was that so preferable?

11

Faster, Higher, Stronger

---❄---

One of the many books and articles published before 1914 to comment on and encourage the rising energy and activism of France's youth praised cycling, driving, and flying, each born of the other, as "great movements that had profoundly modified both souls and bodies."[1] The author ignored what others marked as characteristic of the new spirit: "above all, the taste for physical exercises and open-air games that affects young men between eighteen and twenty-five."[2]

Such physical activities, which England and Germany had known throughout the century, arrived in France late and quite sui generis. Originally they came to serve a patriotic purpose that consisted, in part at least, in locking the barn door after the horse had been stolen. And they approached the task of national revitalization from several directions. Thus, the Club Alpin Français, born in 1874 with its founders still "under the impact of their patriotic grief," sought to provide "a school of physical energy and moral vigor," training French youth to be "more virile, more apt to bear military life, more prepared to face a long conflict without losing heart." Despite relatively high dues that restricted membership, the Club Alpin counted some 7,000 members by the end of the century.[3] One of these, Henry Duhamel, founder of the CAF's Grenoble branch, discovered snowshoes and skis at the Exhibition of 1878, bought them from their Swedish manufacturer, tried them out in the mountains behind his town, and in 1896 established the first French ski club there. Within a few years, military converts to the sport had talked army authorities into training ski troops.[4]

Skis were expensive, skiing even more so. But less exalted and less expensive walking, climbing, and touring clubs subscribed to the same cause. Witness the Société des Marcheurs Touristes de France, founded in Bordeaux in 1885. Its end, its statutes proclaimed, was "both patriotic and scientific, since it favors the study of our country and since, at the opportune moment, excellent guides for our armies might be recruited from its ranks."[5]

Most specific of all these enterprises and most clearly directed to premilitary training were gymnastic societies, founded in great numbers "to restore to the French their muscles." Physical training would and should contribute to national preparedness. Shooting clubs and gymnastic societies, according to one pamphlet (1886), were the seedbeds where the young soldiers of the future could be nurtured and tested. They sported names like La Française, La Patriote, and La Vaillante, and in 1887 Bordeaux counted ten of them with titles like Patriotes Bordelais and Jeunesse Patriote de la Gironde. "Your societies," a high academic figure reminded the Association of Gymnastic Societies of the Seine in 1898, "were born, nearly, all, under the impact of our disasters . . . all imbued with the same duty."[6]

The great idea that inspired all such clubs, at least in their inception, was that of national unity and revanche. Their members practiced shooting, marching, military drill, map reading, the use of fire pumps and hoses, and lifesaving exercises. High aspirations, however, did not last long, except on the political plane where gym clubs long provided the firm base of Boulangist and Nationalist politics. Beyond this, most clubs soon degenerated into semisocial societies open to those who could afford not only their moderate dues but also the costumes they adopted, which usually consisted of body-length tights, special trousers and jacket in blue or white, sports shoes, and a peaked cap or some other suitably martial headgear. By the 1880s many who joined them did so in the hope of losing weight; or to establish connections useful in business and politics; or, simply, because they provided occasions for members to meet, wives to chat, and children to admire their fathers' prowess. Workingmen occasionally had separate societies, such as La Fraternité in Bordeaux; but men who worked, when they worked, eleven or more hours a day for six or seven days a week had little time or energy left over for self-imposed exercise.

Champions of national revival soon realized that the campaign for physical regeneration had to begin elsewhere, notably in the schools, where gymnastics appropriate to institutions dedicated to discipline and to control could be taught to large numbers of the country's youth. As usual the idea was not new. In 1793 the revolutionary Convention had approved a motion to the effect that children's time should be divided among study, manual labor, and gymnastic exercises. But nothing had come of such unimpeachable sentiments. The French Army taught gymnastics (and dancing, which was good for balance) to its recruits, but the idea of school gymnastics made its way more slowly. The revolutionaries of 1848, like those of 1793, worried about "the physical degeneration of the race" and called for an all-round education, including "rational gymnastics in schools."[7] The Second Republic actually passed a law in 1850 that placed gymnastics among the optional subjects that primary schools could teach. But schools lacked the resources, let alone the room, for such activities. Other optional subjects, such as drawing and singing, could be taught in the classroom, but physical education required space and equipment, and most schools had narrow playgrounds, if any at all, and no funds to spend on gym equipment.

When, in 1853, physical training became a compulsory part of the secondary curriculum, the new requirement remained a dead letter. So, naturally, an 1869 decree made gymnastics compulsory in primary schools, where it did no better. "The urgency and even the utility of gymnastic instruction," one local authority noted, "do not yet seem evident." Many reacted as skeptically as the Conseil Général of the Nièvre, which alleged the diminished respect that children would display toward teachers who "engaged in exercises where the dignity of the man associated to the child can suffer cruel failures." Teachers should not be asked to step off their podium onto a playing field where they could be outrun by their charges or splashed with mud. Nor did any teachers ask for it.[8]

This spirit began to change after the Franco-Prussian War. The ministries of war and public instruction discussed ways and means of avoiding a break in continuity between gymnastic training at school and in the army. An 1880 law made gym training compulsory (again!) in all public boys' schools, and a ministerial circular explained that this was being done with a patriotic goal in mind. In 1882 another decree set up *bataillons scolaires* (drill batallions) for military and gymnastic training in all teaching establishments. The civic and patriotic instruction begun in the schools was to be advanced in premilitary training units that would provide opportunity to apply the theory. The initiative, identified with the revanchard politics of men like Gambetta, was approved by patriotic republicans, coldly received in conservative circles. The time devoted to gymnastics would be lost to catechism. Besides, argued the ultra-Catholic *Univers,* even if the government taught all Frenchmen arms drill and somersaults, such methods could not forge a military force, let alone a nation. "Corporal instructors and perfect acrobats" did not an army make.

The sartorial expense involved when the bataillons sought to outfit themselves with uniforms, the cost of equipping the little warriors with approved rifles, the difficulty of finding retired soldiers capable of training them, discouraged goodwill. Then came the Boulangist crisis, and republicans who had supported them found the bataillons, like the gym clubs, a bit too Boulangist for their taste. Patriotism was shifting from Left to Right, and the Republic preferred to go easy on its symbols. The bataillons were quietly faded out: "a patriotic error," one sporting enthusiast described them in retrospect.[9]

Whether for bataillons or for straight gymnastic instruction, instructors and coaches were recruited in haphazard fashion and hired at cut-rate salaries: from 300 to 700 francs a year in collèges and 1,200 to 1,800 in lycées. Most were retired noncommissioned officers, many were ignorant of any real teaching method, and their dim figures pass unrecorded in their pupils' memoirs except for the boredom or the pranks that they aroused. Economically, most coaches were less well-off than miners (1,300 to 1,500 francs a year) or village postmen (1,100 francs a year); nor did they benefit from the local prestige of village schoolteachers, whose annual salaries after 1905 ran between 1,100 and 2,200 francs a year. Their meager wages had to be supplemented. Fireman, janitor, shopman, or petty artisan, the *professeur de gymnastique* was obviously the social inferior of his students. Whether he took this out on them or dazzled them with acrobatic exhibitions, the few hours they spent with him left little impression and less effect.[10]

Another factor mitigated enthusiasm for physical education. One aspect of the exertion involved was the unusual need of washing it created. This presented difficulties in a society where ablution was a rather exotic enterprise. Most lycées, lacking baths or showers, marched their boarders to a public establishment—once a term at

Orleans, once a month at posh Louis-le-Grand in Paris. Day-students were no better off, since few private homes were equipped with bathrooms. The soiled and sweaty heroes of playing field or gym presented a perplexing problem.

Sporting clubs tried to provide showers on the premises for a membership that often lacked such facilities at home. One reason why, in 1889, the Bordeaux Université Club agreed to merge with the Stade Bordelais was that the latter had showers and dressing rooms. But such luxuries called for financial means beyond those of most societies—and beyond the credits that municipal councils were willing or able to make available to schools. The fact that gyms had to be outfitted with showers, although it made for greater cleanliness, also restricted the number of public gymnasiums and playgrounds undertaken. The public health law of 1902 led to the appearance by about 1908 of local health services interested in setting up public bathhouses and showers. But as late as 1916 the inspector of health services in the Nièvre complained that "no playgrounds exist, no sporting institutions for adolescents, no one thinks of sports."[11] Certainly not for long, once they became aware of the costs involved. Nevertheless, in relatively remote or backward regions the patriotic efforts of the 1880s and the 1890s produced the first and for a long time the only opportunities for physical activity, and for hygiene too.

But French sport did not grow out of the bataillons scolaires. Gymnastic inspiration entered France from Germany, and the first French gymnastic societies had been founded at Guebwiller, in Alsace, before the end of the Second Empire. Sports, on the other hand, came from England. For the fin de siècle, the very word "sport" had an equivocal sound. Emile Littré's great Dictionary described it as an English word and warned: "In France one often confuses sport and turf; but turf (racing) is only one kind of sport." Nevertheless, to most people both terms remained connected with the "vulgar and unpleasant" overtones of horse racing, race courses, and betting.[12] *Le Sport,* "journal des gens du monde," first published in 1854, had been devoted chiefly to hunting and racing. The fashionable Société Sportive de Bordeaux concerned itself solely with horse racing. Until the turn of the century, a sportsman was usually a man who owned, rode, or betted on horses.

Thus, in 1894, when Léon Blum joined Tristan Bernard to launch a regular "Critique du Sport" in the fashionably avant-garde *Revue Blanche,* their first article equated "sport" and horse racing. The same confusion was to reappear (slightly mitigated) in 1897 in Blum's *Nouvelles conversations de Goethe avec Eckermann.*[13]

On a less literary or aesthetic plane, contemporary publications mirrored this prejudice. Louis Baume's *Moeurs sportives* (1895) deals with racing, betting, and the race-course public. Jacques Lozère's *Sport et sportsmen* (1896) consists of racing chronicles. That same year the only reference to sport in Henri Rochefort's *Aventures de ma vie* was a comparison between the "turf" of 1865 and that of his old age, ruined by the introduction of pari-mutuel betting. Significantly, J. E. C. Bodley thought that people who styled themselves sportsmen were more likely "vice-presidents of a bicycling club or frequenters of the race-courses."[14] When in 1899–1900 the Baron de Vaux published two large, magnificently illustrated volumes on sport in France, the first volume was devoted to shooting, fencing, and the sporting activities of royalty. As Vaux's order of priority suggests, the manly sports came first; among these, the manliest for a long time continued to be fencing, which was also one of the most practical as long as dueling continued to be an established practice of the upper classes.

This ancient manner of settling conflicts between gentlemen without recourse to vulgar brawling deserves a moment of attention, if only because it has completely dropped from sight. The nineteenth century saw it revigorated by middle-class aspirations to noble deportment, as by the prestige of military swordsmen (or pistoleers) who held honor dear and life far less so. Military discipline relied heavily on dueling; not just for officers, who could be cashiered for declining a challenge, but for enlisted men, who, if they were caught brawling, were forced to fight it out with foils—a rule that kept the average rate of duels per regiment at about fifty a year. "Without the duel," an army captain declared, "discipline and dignity would be impossible to maintain."[15]

Such views were not limited to the armed forces. A stern Protestant moralist like François Guizot refused to moderate the duel's murderous effects. When in 1845, following the dueling death of a prominent young journalist, a law was proposed to limit such encounters, Guizot opposed it: dueling was "no prejudice, but a factor in perfecting manners." Certain "feelings and interests" important to social order were protected by it.[16] The maintenance of this conceit ensured that duels would be prosecuted only if irregular conduct was alleged or death ensued.[17] The former generally occurred when one combatant grasped his opponent's sword in the heat of fighting. But juries, many of whose members knew the hazards and temptations of the sport, seem to have been indulgent. Alfred Naquet, senator from the Vaucluse, was given two months in 1887 for using his left hand in a duel; on appeal, the sentence was reduced to six days.[18] As for death, if the proceedings had been regular, trial was a mere formality, followed by acquittal.

In 1904 one law dissertation deplored the possibility that a duelist who killed his opponent and was condemned for murder—a "man whose honesty and chivalry would be above suspicion"—could thereby be barred from "the right to wear his decorations."[19] The author need not have worried. When, in 1899, two interns at the Bordeaux hospital fought with pistols and one died, the survivor and the four witnesses were speedily acquitted. In 1904, when a Toulouse jeweler fought an attorney whom he accused of "assiduities toward his wife" and was killed by him, the court found that "everything had been very correct" and acquitted everyone.[20] Only when witnesses failed to make a serious effort to reconcile the parties before fighting did the courts raise a criticism—before acquitting all the same. Around 1900 nary a week passed without the press carrying some mention of a duel. Those too unimportant to be mentioned must have been more numerous still.

Many duels were matters of form; and some never reached the field. When Claude Debussy refused to allow Maurice Maeterlinck's mistress, Georgette Leblanc, to sing the part of Mélisande, the two men quarreled and the irascible Belgian challenged Debussy. The dispute was settled eventually; before it was, Maeterlinck, desperately practicing gunmanship, used his own cat as a target and shot her dead.[21] Still, there was no knowing how a duel would end, and they might come about for the most futile reasons. When Sarah Bernhardt revived her production of *Hamlet* in 1899, the poet Catulle Mendès and another writer argued whether Hamlet should be fat or lean; a duel resulted and Mendès was gravely wounded in the stomach.[22] Most encounters at that time, however, turned about the Dreyfus Affair—as when Henry Ferrette, Nationalist and anti-Dreyfusard deputy of the Meuse, struck fifteen inches of his blade into the lungs of an old friend of republican days, leaving him dead on a tavern floor.[23] All the public professions were affected. Dion was notorious as a duelist; so was Clemenceau. Wise lawyers, playwrights, critics, and journalists kept themselves in training. Frequenting a fencing school was as common among the upper classes (and more serviceable) as joining a golf club is today. As late as 1910 Robert Sherard devoted two chapters to the vitality of the practice, the public favor it enjoyed, and the contempt evoked by those who sought to avoid challenges. It took the hecatombs of the First World War to place fencing in perspective and bring about its end.[24]

✳

Other sports, recognized leisure activities more or less athletic according to mood and circumstance, had names that proclaimed their English origins. The Rowing Club de Paris was set up in 1853. The Bordeaux Athletic Club was founded by fourteen British residents of that port. *Le yachting* and *le footing* (hiking) were not taken very seriously. For one thing, they often involved women of light virtue; for another, they seemed to go with worldly vanities and, only too often, with the idle rich. "It was the fashion in those days to scoff at sports," wrote Guillaume Apollinaire revealingly in 1907 about the mood of the 1880s.[25]

The great sporting revolution of the fin de siècle was less concerned with traditional sports than with organized open-air games of the kind associated with English public (that is, private) school education, particularly running and ball games, which continued to seem strange to most French for a long time. In his memoirs, Pierre de Coubertin remembers how, in the 1890s, the newspaper *le Gaulois* referred to "the long flat mallets" with which football was played. Another newspaper believed it was contested with racquets and small hard balls.[26] By that time football of one kind or another had been played in France for twenty years. It would remain a quasi-confidential enterprise as long as most people continued to ignore games, or to regard them as fit only for children.

The first young men to run, or kick, a ball round Paris in the later 1870s were taken for Englishmen. Their clubs did not survive long. Soon, however, a number of boys from Right-bank lycées got into the habit of running impromptu races after school in the great entrance hall of the nearby Gare Saint Lazare. Joined by some veterans of earlier groups, they founded the grandiloquently titled Racing Club de France (1882) and began to organize regular Sunday foot races in the more tranquil atmosphere of the Bois de Boulogne.[27]

First of French sporting associations, the Racing did not belie its name. Its terminology and style were borrowed from the turf. Runners were divided into stables, wore jockey costumes with colored sashes and caps, sometimes carried horsewhips to complete the pretense, idled in the "paddock," and ran under assumed horse names in races whose titles were borrowed from Longchamp and Auteuil and whose results were bet on by the assembled sportsmen and their fashionable friends. Soon Ferdinand de Lesseps himself accepted the honorary presidency. On July 6, 1884, he presented the winner of the Prix de Panama with a handsome horsewhip. The horse-racing folderol was soon abandoned, and Racing's influential connections secured the club a permanent home in the Bois, where running tracks were later joined by football grounds. During the Exhibition summer of 1900 the athletic portion of the "Amateur World Championships called Olympic Games" would be held there.

Meanwhile, in 1883, students of the Lycée Saint-Louis, who had been informally running and training in the Luxembourg Gardens, founded the Stade Français, which became the Racing's great Left-bank rival. It was after a cross-country race in 1887 that the two clubs joined in a federation of running clubs that soon turned into the more comprehensive Confederation of French Athletic Sports Clubs (USFSA). This organization incorporated tennis, cycling, football, rowing, and similar activities; facilitated the international competitions that were beginning to take place; encouraged and spread the gospel of sport; organized national competitions; and kept fans in touch.

Among the USFSA's many sports, football gradually gained prominence. It seems to have come to France several years before it reached Germany. A list of provincial teams in the *Almanach des Sports of 1899* confirms the English game's predictable lines of penetration: the ports; the north (and Lyons), with their textile connections; the highway from Normandy to Paris; and Paris itself, with its large Anglo-Saxon colony. Across the Channel, the Football Association had been set up in 1863, but it took some years to make up its mind how the game should be played. By 1871, however, Association football and Rugby football had become clearly separate and autonomous in England. About the same time, the game entered France through Le Havre, where the Havre Athletic Club (HAC) was born in 1872. Founded by Oxford and Cambridge men, its colors combined the light blue of the latter and the dark blue of the former. It is not very clear what game the HAC played, but its early teams do not seem to have known, or cared about, the rules finally laid down in England. They played a "combination" game probably close to rugby until 1891, when the Club finally set up distinct rugby and soccer sections—one of the first French clubs to do so.

For a long time French football was dominated by the HAC, or, if not by the club itself, then by the English sailors, clerks, and students who colonized both soccer and rugger until about 1914. When HAC won the French championship in 1899, six of its players were English. All the earliest Paris soccer clubs were also started by Englishmen. The Paris Football Club (1879–1884), which lapsed for want of rivals, was succeeded in 1890 by the Football Association Club, founded by the personnel of two English firms. Yet, though in 1894 the national soccer championship was won by a team composed of one Frenchman and ten Englishmen, by 1899 Association football boasted some threescore clubs in the Paris area alone, and French teams were beginning to participate in international competitions. These, especially the ones played against the English, tended to end in catastrophic scores: 15–0 in 1906, 12–0 in 1908, 11–0 in 1909, 10–1 in 1910. In 1911, with a loss of only 3–0, the tide began to turn and, by 1921, French soccer marked its first victory against England: 2–1.

But this was in the future, and popular interest in ball games even farther off. Sports were the preserve of an elite that could afford them, and elitism was a crucial element of contemporary sporting effort. The Racing accepted only amateurs, as defined in 1866 by the English Amateur Athletic Club in a formula that banned professionalism or the possibility of gain, stressed the fact that the amateur is a "gentleman," and excluded "mechanics, laborers and artisans." When the first article of the USFSA's rules barred all but amateurs from membership, it eliminated not only any athlete who had ever competed in an open race, or for money, or for pay, or for a share of the gate receipts, or against professionals, but also specifically, anyone "who has ever been, at any time in his life, a paid teacher or monitor of physical exercises."

The latter were professionals, hence barred from activities that gentle-men not only pursued but regulated. The true sporting spirit, as the general secretary of the USFSA explained to a provincial prefect, con-sisted in opposing "professionalism, money prizes, and betting, in a word, all that paralyzes the beneficent effects of sport."

No man could devote much time, let alone his life, to sport without a private income and not be in some way a professional. But the pioneers of pure sport addressed themselves to an audience who did not need to face this problem. Their determined stand against profes-sionalism would play its part in the development of twentieth-century sports—and more immediately in the rival fortunes of Rugby and Association football.

Rugby, the favorite game of English public schools, was the form of football that most students adopted, especially in Paris. It is striking to find Charles Péguy, who in the early 1890s had introduced Association football in his lycée at Orleans, moving to the *cagne* at Lakanal and there taking up rugby because it was the game that Paris lycéens played.

Thus rugby spread, carried by the hazards of student life, to univer-sity towns and sometimes to other areas—like Nantes, where Parisian influences inspired the Stade Nantais as early as 1886, or Perpignan, where, in 1889, a boy who had played the game at the Lycée Michelet in Paris founded the Union Athlétique du Collège Perpignanais, seed of the great Catalan rugby school. Altogether, after 1899, all but six of the national pennants were won by clubs located south of the Loire. The south, above all the southwest, remained rugby country, partly because of the USFSA's prejudices, partly because of the English in-fluences radiating from Bordeaux, Bayonne, Biarritz, and Pau.

Soccer appeared as a kind of Cinderella: "Latecomer, faced with a cold reception . . . The wealthy clubs showing no interest, there was no publicity for its matches . . . School clubs, that is, the bourgeoisie, keep away for ten years. Rugby alone seems noble, fascinating."[28] When, in 1909, the Douanier Rousseau painted his *Joueurs de Football*, the play-ers were obviously rugby players, as were those of later painters who depicted ball games—André Lhote, Albert Gleizes, Robert Delaunay. Equally revealing, the illustrated cover of the *Revue des Jeux Scolaires* showed two young men in sports costume, one wearing cycling knick-ers, the other football shorts and carrying a rugby ball under his arm.

"It seems as if Association football is essentially popular, and rugby the preserve of an elite," an observer mused, adding that rugby's future depends wholly on how it does in secondary schools.[29]

By 1900, when Association football appeared south of the Loire, established clubs were controlled by rugby players and a local tradition had grown up. Soccer teams and clubs were set up and flourished in larger places. Association football became the great spectator sport of industrial urban centers, drifting to professionalism as a direct result of the role it played, the masses to which it catered, and the resources it commanded. But the small towns and small urban centers of Midi and Languedoc, which lacked both the industrial concentrations that furnished the public of professional soccer and the resources for a variety of sports, remained faithful to the amateur game with which they identified. Rugby remained true to the ideals that the first sporting clubs embodied: elitism, amateurism, the educational value of sporting activities, and what is found in the writings of men like Pierre de Coubertin, whose name remains linked to the Olympic Games he was responsible for reviving in 1896. Coubertin, whose efforts played a major role in the spread and acceptance of sporting activities in the late 1880s and 1890s, considered athletics and games as key educational activities, able to produce all-round men and to free French youth from moral and physical inertia.[30] What he had not bargained for was that the athletic revival that he did so much to bring about also made a great contribution to the nationalist revival of the pre-1914 years.

Before the turn of the century the *Almanach des Sports* already was celebrating the martial virtues of the team games. "*Le football*," for instance, "is a veritable little war, with its necessary discipline and its way of getting participants accustomed to danger and to blows." In 1913 Agathon's well-known inquiry into the mood of middle-class youth noted the effect of sports on "the patriotic optimism of youth" and praised "the moral benefit of collective sports, like football, so widespread in our lycées," which "develop and maintain a warlike atmosphere among young people."

Coubertin himself had little use for such conclusions. But he quoted with approval an article in which journalist Pierre Mille described what his young contemporaries had learned from sport: "They quite often consider a possible war as a match that must be played as well as possible, after having trained for it scientifically. You hold on, keeping your composure and your breath to the end. And if you win, you win; if you lose, you lose. It is no dishonor. A game is a game, and that is all."

Going beyond the advantages of preparedness, competitive games offered a means of channeling and regulating violence, especially the savage violence of adolescence. To individuals too ready to follow some subversive drummer, games provided opportunities for self-assertion and sometimes also for indulging in competitive violence in any number of ways that society condemns off the battlefield. Theodore Roosevelt, a great supporter of Coubertin, preached the value of sport as a source of energy and as a way of channeling excess energy into socially acceptable directions. That the concrete possibilities of this function of sport were soon noticed, and generally approved, can be seen from an essay printed as an appendix to Agathon's inquiry, in which a sports writer praised *l'éducation sportive* for preparing its subjects to be "the right *and contented* man in the right place."[31] Another contributor described how the practice of football and cross-country running had taught him and his friends the competitive nature of life, persuaded them that men were unequal, and turned them away from socialism with its false ideas of equality, fraternity, and pacifism. "Sport enlightened me on myself and on my real feelings."

Whether socialism and sport could coexist was not as yet quite clear. The Socialist Youth International took a generally positive view; and we have seen that in 1907 the Socialist Party endorsed sport, especially cycling. But some socialists complained that games were a diversion from true revolutionary activities. In 1910 the Italian Federation denounced all sport as a bourgeois plot, likely to cripple young people's health, and conducive only to competitiveness and nationalism. Such contagion was avoided when the Fédération Sportive Athlétique Socialiste was set up in 1908, catering only to members of the Socialist Party (SFIO). Though this counterexclusivism was quickly abandoned, sporting activities for class-conscious workers remained at the mercy of political fluctuations and counted for little until the 1930s. At the other end of the spectrum, the very idea of sporting activities for the common people evoked laughter when raised in a municipal council. And when great department stores like the Bon Marché in Paris or the Dames de France in Bordeaux sponsored their own football and rugby teams, these seem to have played mostly against their own kind.

There were of course the *patronages*, well-intentioned enterprises designed to improve the character and body of the deserving poor. The name reflects a paternalistic and, eventually, patronizing inspiration. Not that, from a contemporary perspective, there was much wrong in this, except that the patronages themselves served ulterior ends, while their activities, far from bringing sporting enthusiasts closer together, emphasized their divisions. Since the 1870s many English clubs founded in churches, chapels, or Sunday schools had grown to national prominence. But whereas in England such enterprises were "an innocent source of pleasure and satisfaction for the masses," in France they were too often mere rods to beat a foe. Thus, and especially in those western regions where political divisions were fiercest, many small towns had two sports clubs where one would have been ample— one Catholic, the other Republican; one for the Right, another for the Left; centers of their party's activities and focus for hostility toward the other side. In the first decade of the twentieth century, especially after the December 1905 law separating Church and State, Catholics made very serious efforts to expand and organize the scattered activities of their parish groups and thus regain some of the influence forfeited with the loss of so many teaching establishments. An increasing number of parish patronages, deliberately oriented toward physical activities that appealed to the young (Les Jeunes de Saint Bruno, de Saint Genès, de Saint Roch) were grouped in regional gymnastic and sporting union; these in turn were affiliated to the Fédération Gymnastique et Sportive des Patronages de France, founded in 1898.

When a federation of patronages was officially registered in 1907, its directors naturally insisted that it had no political aims, but the authorities were skeptical. "There can be no doubt," a police report noted, "that their true purpose is to gather together the greatest possible number of young Catholics in order to maintain their confessional hold upon them." Such Catholic zeal spurred the foundation or reanimation of secular competitors: patronages laïques, some founded by private enterprise; others (patronages scolaires) extracurricular enterprises undertaken somewhat halfheartedly by primary schoolteachers at the urging of the Ministry of Education. In 1909 the southwest counted ninety-nine such patronages scolaires, mostly devoted to gymnastics, shooting, or premilitary training. But the local school inspector bewailed the inability of such "Republican and secular" patronages to meet the challenge of Catholics and "enemies of the secular spirit." "Religious or reactionary patronages," he reported, "open and operate on all sides, grabbing our pupils when they step out of school and seeking to destroy that which we have sought to raise in their minds."

Lay and religious patronages sometimes clashed over access to playgrounds; the latter better served, as a rule, by the generosity of private sympathizers, the former clamoring for the support of the republican authorities. Neither side lost sight of its ultimate purpose, which the inspector quoted above recalled in his report: the children were the electors of tomorrow. But, whatever their inspiration, it is clear that patronages must have provided some of the first—and few—playgrounds and sporting activities available to the young of the poorer classes, excluded by regular sporting clubs.

Not that the leaders of the USFSA wished to ignore the lower classes. Like other pursuits (including war), sport can suggest that its rules are applicable to the rest of life, that the sense of comradeship and fair play developed on the playing field may be appropriately indulged elsewhere. This would favor ideas of social justice. Coubertin, for one, was always keen to bring sports to the workers. But his hostility to professionalism, his indifference to the cost of athletic pastimes, small to the rich, but prohibitive to the poor, were as good as barriers. When in due course the stadiums were opened to the masses, it would be less down in the arena than up on the tiers. Indeed, those sporting associations that catered first to the petite bourgeoisie and later, in the 1920s and 1930s, to the working classes, showed less interest in participation and disinterested competition than they did in prizes, professionalism, and spectator sports. Explicit or implicit, elitism ensured that "athletic sports" would remain the privilege of a minority. Social exclusivism could manifest itself in the clubhouse and on the playing field. The elitist aspiration of athletic enthusiasts could be enlisted to meaner ends. "An elite alone can accede to this intensive culture of the muscles," declared an Aquitainian enthusiast. Student clubs in particular tended to exclusivism. Thus, when the Bordeaux Université Club, founded in 1897, encountered the financial difficulties usual to its kind, it decided to merge with the powerful Stade Bordelais. In the debates that preceded the merger, a speaker warned that the Université Club was a society "of young men with a similar education, stemming from the same milieu, sharing common tastes," and hence more likely to get on together than with the mixed crew they would encounter in the larger club. It is true that the membership of the Stade Bordelais, though generally described in police reports as "comfortably off" and benefiting from a "bonne éducation primaire," did include a fair number of clerks, shopkeepers, shop assistants, commercial travelers—even a waiter and a shoemaker. Such were no fit company for wellborn youths. No wonder the merger soon dissolved, the students taking their leave in 1903 to found the Bordeaux Etudiants Club, explaining that "students who wish to engage in sports are tired of turning to clubs where they must mix with young persons of diverse professions and ages."

Such attitudes elicited the tacit or overt support of the first sportsmen themselves, whose views may be found in the authoritative *Les Sports Athlétiques*. Concluding a series of articles on the popularization of physical exercises, the organ of the USFSA opposed the idea of clubs where workers and members "of the ruling classes" would mingle: "We strongly reject mixed associations." Such contact between rich and poor would be bound to create frictions that were best avoided. Besides, it explained, many young people would never consent to mix with workers, sharing the games of a class they did not know and from whom they were separated by prejudices of birth, wealth, and upbringing. The article quoted "one of our finest runners," who waxed indignant at the thought of measuring himself against opponents "from the ranks of the people." That, it affirmed, was how three-quarters of the membership of all athletic societies felt. Evidently "the hour of popular sports was not yet." Despite the fact that Georges Bourdon, historian and veteran of the *Racing*, writing in 1906, rejoiced that "athletic education, having transformed the youth of the lycées, is beginning to touch the sons of the people," the negative evidence of his remark is more convincing than the wishful thinking.

A simple list of dates is enough to tell how far sporting activities could affect the people or their sons. The ten-hour working day was introduced in 1900; a law of July 13, 1906, established one day of rest per week; another of April 23, 1919, cut the working day from ten to eight hours; finally, the official forty-hour-week for both sexes was introduced in 1936. Obviously before 1919 there was little free time for games.

Cycling apart, the early history of organized sport in France had narrow scope: schoolboys, foreigners, young men of good family. Most of its protagonists were lycéens and collegians. And there were, in the 1880s and 1890s, only about 52,000 lycéens and 160,000 young people in all secondary establishments, both clerical and lay. These students represented something like 5 percent of their age group. Few of them took an interest in organized games. But, then, there were not really many who enlisted in nationalism, or syndicalism, or in the more passionate pursuit of the arts, and it is always the active minorities that attract our attention, because they influence—or in some way reflect—the rest.

*

From this perspective it is not inappropriate to compare sport and politics, both at this time evolving from the practice of an elite, both beginning as the preserve of amateurs, before becoming accessible to the multitude and being turned into spectacles run by professionals and destined for mass consumption. Like football today, politics for most is usually a spectator sport. This should not confuse us about the role of sport in its early days, when it was confined to amateurs—that is, quite literally, to those who participated in it purely for love of the sport. The role sports played in encouraging the physical regeneration of a "decadent" nation, or at least in suggesting a new image, raising national spirits, and expressing a new kind of confidence, has received deserved attention. It should not blind us to the fact that sports began as games, inspired above all in the fun participants could have, the excitement they and their public shared, the sense of liberation enjoyed on the playing field.

If we carry this a step further, we glimpse the possibility that, even then, sports *could* offer escape from lives too far removed from the clear-cut situations of the playing field, an excuse for not trying to resolve the complexities of the outside world, a refuge in the simpler, more limited world of club and game. Seen from this point of view, games are the ultimate antiutilitarian pursuit: quite useless in the material sense, unproductive, gratuitous. Free, separate, uncertain, regulated, fictitious, games are ends in themselves. They leave behind no harvest, no gain, no work of art, not even any ruins. And none could be more gratuitous or nonutilitarian than the sport of fencing on horseback that Coubertin spent his life trying to get accepted by the Olympic committees which he headed.

If we consider that games are excellently suited to the consumer society about to dawn upon the Western world, being simply the accumulation and expenditure of disposable effort, we may understand that sports were a commodity suitable for the consumption of the rentier class that flourished in late-nineteenth-century France. Such leisure activity was characteristic of a particular moment when the economic slump, or stagnation, of the 1880s and 1890s liberated the time and energies of the upper and middle classes, or at least of their young. Lower prices; higher relative incomes, especially for the rentier class, members of the liberal professions, and persons on fixed salaries; and a combination of medical advances and economic retrenchment that kept old men alive longer, slowing or blocking possibilities of advancement—all this meant fewer opportunities or temptations in the traditional directions to which young men who did not really need to work could turn. A higher proportion of the leisured young could wait, or chose to wait, a relatively long time before engaging in money-earning activities. Many sought careers in less traditional directions: literature, the arts, politics, and overseas ventures.

The rash of little reviews that marks the fin de siècle, the rising interest in colonial adventure, and the expansion of sports where they had been ignored before were reactions against a society often condemned as sclerotic; they were also reactions against its products: the symptoms of a hardening and aging of social issues. The growing favor and significance of nonutilitarian activities in social circles that once had scorned them was evidence of a pathological condition—and perhaps also a token of its cure.

Pierre de Coubertin's aim was to form (or to re-form) a moral being, inner-directed, autonomous within an ever-more-encroaching world. If this resembled an ideal prototype rather than an actual person operating in a recognizable social context, that too was very much in fin de siècle style. Reading Coubertin, his ideal sporting type appears as real (or as related to reality) as Huysmans' Des Esseintes. Although the figures of the ideal sportsman and the superaesthete seem very distant from each other, the rise of organized sports in France *was* contemporary not only with the development of aestheticism and art for art's sake, but with Nietzsche's formulation of the aspiration to go beyond laws and standards, to enlist effort and will to create superior humans, to become supremely human, a kind of language that Coubertin could easily accept. A kind of language, too, that could be found in a whole tide of writings beginning to attract attention in the 1890s, where young dilettantes found a new and "passionate taste for human energy" and "the constant effort to create oneself, to the point of substituting one's own conception of the world for conventional reality."[32] A good description of current aesthetic attitudes, as of one aspect of organized games: refuge from, remedy for, or attempt to reshape an unsatisfactory world. Recall Knute Rockne's remark: "After the church, football's the best thing we've got."

Sports played an important part in what Coubertin described, in a fencing term, as possible *parades* (parries) against the industrial civilization that he disliked and feared. Industrial civilization stood for the four Sancho Panzas of the Apocalypse: greater comfort; specialization; exaggerated nationalism; and the triumph of democratic homogenization. Sport and education could provide remedies to these evils and foster a human progress which Coubertin, like many contemporaries, conceived as the unlimited development of individual capacities. Such development could come only after the young had been converted: to sport, to games, to exercise, and to a self-discipline which alone could forge sound characters in healthy bodies. If the idea strikes us as naive (as it did some contemporaries), that may be because decency, loyalty, fair play, and healthy minds in healthy bodies were not then, as they are not now, commonplaces of daily experience.

The more reason, thought Coubertin, to lure the young onto the playing fields. This, he believed, could be done only through the example of champions, by the glamour of achievements that many would wish to emulate. Great exploits would fire the imagination of the young, attract them to the stadium, the track, the court, the swimming pool. It was not that Coubertin wanted to recruit players and athletes in great numbers to seed out champions, but that he sought champions, heroes whose influence would inspire the young to play. The individual exploit was a recruiting agent. What better stage for such exploits than competitions on an international level, surrounded by all the excitement and publicity of great official functions, colored by the glory and prestige of ancient deeds? Rereading Coubertin's *Souvenirs*

232 • Faster, Higher, Stronger

d'Amérique et de Grèce, published in 1897 in the wake of the first Olympic Games of 1896, we are tempted to see in it the greatest of Coubertin's parades against intrusive modernity, the most astute publicity move for the expansion and popularization of sports.*

Reactionary? Not in contemporary terms. To the current elitism of the contemporary upper classes, Coubertin and those who thought like him opposed another kind of elitism, more in tune with the times because more activist, more competitive, and also, at least potentially, more open and accessible. Competitive games reflected a society that increasingly stressed competition. In an age of high productivity and high performance—measurable and ever more precisely measured, sporting games confirmed ruling social norms and further structured the anarchic old order of things. Sports adopted and perfected the exploit achieved within precise and measurable standards, provided proof of progress by records that ceaselessly outdid previous records: performances in which men (and, in due course, women) measured themselves not only against each other but against the impersonal scale of time. In an age of mass entertainment they proposed spectacular diversions, first for the few, then for the many. Vulgarized, commercialized, sports were rapidly becoming politicized, even beginning to show traces of chauvinism. Something had to be done to save them from what some votaries perceived as degradation, revalue games before they had time to become devalued.

England, first to accept the competitive principle in economic life, first to introduce it in the recruitment of its bureaucracy, had also been the first to idealize it in sport, to ennoble it with notions of sportsmanship and fair play, to turn it into a social convention. Other modern societies had to follow suit or face grave risks. Competition, if not limited by some counterideal, can prove destructive. At the end of Balzac's *Père Goriot,* Rastignac's apostrophe to Paris, "Et maintenant, à nous deux," is that of a player about to enter the ring, a player determined to win whatever the means, whatever the effect on the game, on the rules, on the others. Rastignac is the professional champion, for whom the game is a means rather than an end; the values he represents, or at least accepts, are precisely those that Coubertin and his friends

---

*"Faster, Higher, Stronger," the title of this chapter, echoes the Olympic slogan: "Citius, Altius, Fortius."

wished to counteract. The games they sponsored were intended to provide such satisfactions that play should prove its own justification: good ends for once pursued by the best means.

A society where competition ruled in business, elections, examinations, and *concours,* where winning at any price appeared essential but where the dice too often were loaded, discovered a mitigating factor in the regulated competition of sports. Aleatory in the real world, the rewards of effort and of merit were codified and (almost) assured in the reconstituted world of track and field, where ideal, sheltered conditions permitted official values to be honored in the observance rather than the breach. And, lest even these conditions should prove too hard to bear, the proviso was added in the famous address to the participants in the London Olympic Games of 1908, that "it is less important to win than to take part." A sentiment more memorably quoted by Grantland Rice:

For when the One Great Scorer comes to mark against your name,
He writes—not that you won or lost—but how you played the Game.[33]

12

"The Best of Times"

---❊---

The Hachette *Guide* to the Universal Exhibition, published in Spring 1900, described the century ending that year as "the most fertile in discoveries, the most prodigious in sciences" that the world had known and spoke of a "revolution in the economic order of the universe." *Le Vélo* reached the same conclusion. There had been a miraculous revolution, magnificent and diverse: not just mechanical and industrial, but physical also—hence moral too—achieved by men determined to master matter and, foremost, their own bodies in order to prepare not merely stronger, healthier, handsomer human beings, but better ones.[1] The conjunction of healthy minds within healthy bodies was as debatable then as now, but the general sense of overall improvement is evident. Even more so, was the sense of revolutionary change. The world, Péguy wrote only a few years later, "has changed less since Jesus Christ than it has changed in the last thirty years." Not just the world, but people and things, ordinary people and ordinary things, and the gestures of life, and the rhythms of work, and the values one lived by, and the problems one faced.

It had happened before. History is a litany of change. But never before to the same degree. We have seen plenty of other crises, said Péguy, and I could say with the song

> "I have forgotten plenty
> I shall forget this too."

One has to admit, said Péguy, "this race has seen plenty. It has never seen as much. It has never seen anything like it. It will get over it."[2] It will forget this too. Nothing is so readily forgotten as the unforgettable. Nothing is as uncertain as experience, as peculiar as perspective, as personal and diverse and subject to [re]interpretation as lives that have been lived side by side. The future of the past is never very sure. The only certainty is that the past will be what we make it, that what we choose to note about the present, to remember about the past, will change as our own concerns change.

What matters is not whether Péguy was right, but how his apprehension fitted an epoch less impressed by continuity than by rapid change. There was nothing very exceptional about the fin de siècle. Its two or three decades did see the culmination of certain secular trends, like the impression of decadence, as well as the birth of activities and techniques characteristic of the century that followed: movies and driving, popular access to leisure, mobility, news, and sports, a preoccupation with speed and the conquest of space, the massive spread of facilities and civilities hitherto reserved for the very few. But every age has its novelties and its fulfillments. We could locate the origins of developments this book has touched on in other places, other times. What makes the fin de siècle interesting is its unexceptional nature: the way it reflects the nineteenth century to which it belongs; the way it announces the twentieth century already taking shape; the continuities it affirms in the midst of change; the changes it experiences amid persistent continuity.

Consider the scientific revolution. On Christmas Day 1900, in a village near Angers, an old man was stabbed to death, then fiercely kicked and trampled by two young farmhands. "The sorcerer had cast a spell on our cattle, which he caused to perish."[3] The young murderers presumably had attended those very schools to which Péguy attributed so much of the radical change he lived, the schools that glorified (or, if they were Catholic, deprecated) the triumphs of nineteenth-century science. But stronger forces held them in their grip. The old world passed away more reluctantly than we are sometimes told—even by those who lived through its passing. Experience, our own and that of others, is like the yellow pages: we find what we look for. The triumphs of science produced as much doubt and confusion as they instilled confidence. Were hypnotism and magnetism evidence of knowledge advancing, or of its treading water? Scientific discoveries in domains that appeared close to occultism, the *Petit Parisien* warned, suggest that one should be prudent about what scientists affirm and what they condemn.[4] In January 1901 the International Psychological Institute opened its doors with a lecture by Emile Duclaux, eminent chemist and head of the Pasteur Institute: "If we admit that an instrument—a sort of metallic ear—installed at Versailles, can perceive and register waves coming from Paris, why not admit that an individual with human ears can similarly perceive and register other waves directed toward him by another person?"[5]

Even without such uncertainties, the effects of the scientific revolution were not all of one piece. It prolonged life, commented Emile Faguet of the Académie Française, but it also saved and protracted the life of a greater number of invalids and weaklings who burdened society. The technology that science spawned had helped create great nations, "but this merely juxtaposed giants armed to the teeth, made wars more deadly and armed peace ruinous." It permitted Europe to conquer the world, but the shrinking of our planet by new means of communication and the arming of the conquered peoples with new modern arms, "has brought to our gates, threatening us either as industrial and commercial competitor or as military foe, a whole world, hitherto barbarous and distant, which tomorrow will weigh down upon us."[6]

Perhaps, Faguet speculated, the rhythm of change would now slow down, the tumult of transformation quiet: "everything suggests that the speed of communications will not continue to increase." There were limits, after all. The electric telegraph would operate no faster fifty years hence. "True, we travel ten times as rapidly from Paris to Marseilles as we did fifty years ago, but fifty years hence we will not travel ten times faster than we do today."[7] A relatively quiet century, Faguet mused, may follow the agitated one that was about to end.

Even as Faguet wrote, Max Planck was preparing to publish his quantum theory of energy (a mysterious force, jumping mysteriously from one state to another) and unsettle what was left of the stable, consistent, harmonious image of the world. Within five years Einstein had formulated his first theory of relativity ("the geometric nature of our world is fashioned by mass and speed"). Two more and the cover of L'Illustration could carry two photographs of "flying men": one machine taking off, the other actually in flight.[8]

For some reason airplanes struck the popular imagination more sharply, more vividly, than balloons, which had been around for over a century (a balloon would be used to film Paris for a cinerama show during the 1900 Exhibition), and certainly more than the obscure theorizing of foreign scientists. As far as the popular imagination went—and by then it could go pretty far—even native theorizers remained relatively confidential, even Henri Bergson, appointed to the Collège de France in 1900, to whose courses intellectuals and society people flocked as flies to honey. Péguy went to hear Bergson ("Friday at quarter to 5—the best hour of my week"), as did Georges Sorel. So did Jacques Maritain, who later converted to Catholicism and attacked Bergson's philosophy as the root of all modern intellectual heresy.[9] Of course, Bergson's thought was nothing like the root of modern intellectual heresy, but its manifestation. Or, rather, the imaginative expression of the growing sense that "there are more things in heaven and earth, Horatio, than are dreamt of in your philosophy."

In his attempt to rebuild the bridge between metaphysics and science, this very French son of a Jewish musician and an Englishwoman called attention to instinct and the unconscious. Bergson set the cat among the pigeons by talking about spontaneous vital forces, about mind acting on matter—something new and unpredictable among what contemporaries regarded as rigid laws of nature. Reminiscent of Emile Duclaux and of Max Planck? But also of the trend away from rationalism and moderation, to action, to activism, to vitalism; of Fauves and Futurists, wild clash of colors, exalted appeals to energy, intuition, and spontaneous action symbolized by roaring cars, snapping propellers, and a lot of verbiage. When Maurice Barrès noted, "Intelligence, what a small thing on the surface of our selves," he did not think that many of his admirers were busy proving him truer than he knew.

Jules Claretie, a favorite chronicler of Paris life, testified to the coincidence between Futurist references and fin de siècle novelties: "A Paris both practical and fantastic, revised by Robida [the science fiction writer and cartoonist] . . . The Paris of *pétrolettes and bicyclettes* . . . and of that sort of pocket-locomotive called *automobile*." That too was "progress . . . tenfold liveliness . . . shortened distance . . . assured hygiene."[10]

There were other changes. Opening the Universal Exhibition, the President of the Republic, Emile Loubet, spoke about Justice and Human Kindness. His Minister of Labor, the Socialist Alexandre Millerand, talked of Justice, Kindliness, and Solidarity. Justice had been the password of the Dreyfusards, now in power, but kindliness (*bonté* can also mean goodness, but here it was used in the sense of benevolence and goodwill) introduced a rather novel note in authoritative pronouncements. An influential senator, Ernest Millaud, who heard the two men, insisted on the new spirit of their speeches: "And what praise of labor! what thrust of folk toward emancipation, toward enlightenment, toward a fairer distribution of social wealth!"[11]

The Exhibition opened in the wake of the lacerating discords of the Dreyfus Affair and, more immediately, of a long string of bitter strikes. Accordingly, we must take the benevolence with the grains of salt that appropriately season political language. But the tenor of public discourse was indicative. It seems fair to admit that Loubet and Millerand spoke about aspirations and priorities they believed in and that they shared with their kind. As they spoke, a good deal remained to be done on behalf of Justice, let alone kindliness, in French society. Though more now suffered from guilty consciences, few thought it improper to earn their living by the sweat of someone else's brow. The mutation from Empire to Republic confirmed H. L. Mencken's observation that politics consists of the delusion that change in form means change in substance. Governments changed, but the style of government persisted. Administrative formalism concealed arbitrariness behind equalitarian legalisms, affirming that the general interest could not be imposed without some particular injustice. Anatole France, converted to socialism by the Dreyfus Affair, would write *Crainquebille* in 1901 to remind the better-off how absurd this was, and how brutal. Not much seemed to have changed from the perspective of the weak and poor, who would have understood Mayor Daley's assertion (after the 1968 Chicago riots) that "the policeman isn't there to create disorder. The policeman is there to preserve disorder."

Nevertheless, more had been achieved than the regime's critics admitted, then as now. Moderate like Loubet's, radical like Millaud's, socialist like Millerand's, the politics of men like these were the quintessence of what two generations described as "republican" or decried as "opportunist" (which meant belief in reforms when the time was ripe for them: *en temps opportun*). Jean Touchard has described this stance with reference to his grandfather, Republican deputy of the Finistère. It meant, "above all . . . that one refused to consider a certain social order as ineluctable, indestructible, and indefinitely satisfactory . . . that one believed in change as possible, in a certain degree of modernization, in modern progress."[12] Not very thoroughgoing, admittedly, and hardly satisfying to those who continued to suffer, let alone to those who suffered for those who suffered. Yet, as Touchard points out, the local railway lines for which his grandfather worked hard profoundly changed the face of Finistère. So did his refusal of a religious faith founded on authority and obedience. So did his confidence, and that of men like him, in the high value of dispensaries and clinics, schools and free school lunches. It was good to have fire-eaters like Clemenceau and Jean Jaurès point out that republican or moderate or opportunist achievements, and even their programs, did not go far enough. But it was also good that somebody had made a start in going anywhere.

Railways and schools and anticlericalism apart (and these were all of one piece in the panoply of progress), the Republicans of those years left France with a powerful myth, based on the Dreyfus Affair. The Affair, not as it happened, but as it was swiftly foreshortened and rewritten to serve as reference and inspiration to the Left.[13] Mythological history recorded no socialist indifference, no radical hesitations, just a spontaneous mobilization for the Republic, innocence, and justice against militarism, chauvinism, and anti-Semitism—hitherto no strangers to the Left, but henceforth, at least officially, anathema. Against clericalism too, which was taken to represent not just hostility to progress but also the equivalent of a political party: the only organized political force in the land until, precisely as the new century began, a national Radical Party (1901) and a unified Socialist Party (1905) could be cobbled together.

The Dreyfus Affair provided more than a persistent myth and a significant turning point in political polarization. (Before it, the presence of a socialist in government would have been unthinkable.) It reaffirmed the crucial role of intellectuals or, at least, men of letters in politics, a little lost from sight after 1850; and what François Furet describes as a tendency to fill political gaps with literary references, and to pretend that opinion counts for more than power does. This last— and here again the Affair served as a *révélateur*—would be confirmed by the powerful role of print, which functioned, as Rivarol had put it a hundred years before, as the artillery of thought, or at least of passion, establishing what the twentieth-century world would learn to take for granted: the association of high thinking and low reporting. "Without *l'Aurore* and Zola, Dreyfus would perhaps have been left in prison," Jean-Denis Bredin comments in the latest of many books on the Affair.[14] "But without Drumont and the *Libre Parole,* would he have been sent there?"

Bredin reminds us of the crucial role that the press now played, not just in politics but in fin de siècle society. Periodicals, even dailies, had been the prerogative of a small cultivated elite. As mass-circulation dailies came into their own and the number of their readers soared, opinion became increasingly public and more receptive to the impressions that print and image forcefully conveyed. The 1880s and 1890s saw the press replace Parliament as the chief site and instrument of public debate, frightening politicians even more than it impressed the general public, but affecting the public by its capacity to communicate, magnify, and manipulate the notions, scenes, and bits of information that it brought very close to home. Would the star of Boulanger have flared and crashed but for the "American" publicity he got? Would there have been a Dreyfus "Affair" without the press—an arrest in 1894, let alone a retrial in 1899? The coincidence was striking. It was Sadi Carnot (1887–1894) who had begun to invite the press to public functions and to accompany him on presidential tours around the country. Before his time journalists had fended for themselves. Thereafter, they were given special facilities, board, lodging, transport. The more they got, the more they wanted. Loubet's head of staff found them perfect pests. At Toulon, in April 1901, the press corps numbered fifty, "making as much noise as a hundred." At Compiègne that September, during the Tsar's visit, they were an even greater nuisance: *encombrants, inoportuns.*[15] But presidents who henceforth subjected themselves to their harassment had little choice: the Fourth Estate was not to be gainsaid.

The presence of a Socialist minister at Loubet's side, the weakening and discrediting of parliamentary institutions, the affirmation of new collectivist organizations, parties and unions, also reflected a significant change. Nineteenth-century men had worked to accomplish an eighteenth-century vision of freedom for individuals as for markets and for politics. What we might regard as partial success could appear quite futile from some contemporary perspectives. "The failure of liberal-

ism," Faguet wrote in November 1900, "may well be the special characteristic of the nineteenth century"; future textbooks might describe
the period by that title.[16] The contradictory ideals of liberty and equality had clashed, and the former had shattered. Under the circumstances, thought Faguet, not only France but all of Europe was well on
its way to despotism: "We are going to pass through a period of
discord and disorder, as equalitarianism tries to assert itself fully." That
sort of threat was more evident from the top of the social pile (where
most of its articulate expressions were forged) than from the bottom,
where equality of opportunity, status, or condition seemed impossibly
far away. The poor, that is, the many, perceived more pressing priorities than sheer equality.

Whether we consider it progress or not, the modern world was built
by hard labor, its greatest enemy idleness, seen as a threat to productivity. From Benjamin Franklin to Henry Ford, work was the condition
of economic, social, and moral well-being and emancipation. It was
only during the fin de siècle that some work began to be perceived as
overwork, leading to excess fatigue, jadedness, exhaustion—not just
for the better-off, but for all. In 1880 Paul Lafargue argued for *The
Right to Idleness,* that is, not only to work, but also to leisure and rest.
In 1900 John Rae's *Eight Hours For Work* (London, 1894) would be
translated into French. It argued that fewer hours of work made for
higher productivity, but the argument was really about leisure and
dignity. After 1900 the struggle for shorter working hours became the
center of industrial action, and after 1906 the eight-hour day became
the major theme of frightening May Day demonstrations. There was to
be no eight-hour day until after the First World War, but many settled
for a nine-hour day, or for the "English Week" that allowed a half-day
on Saturdays. What testified to progress more than the slow and un-
even improvements in working conditions were the evolving methods
of claiming these improvements. From rioting to demand the right to
work, industrial labor progressed to strikes for higher wages and, now,
for better conditions in and outside the workplace. Even the powerful
myth of the General Strike, supposed to overturn bourgeois society,
looks as if it had been designed to avert more murderous encounters by
replacing the possibility of barricades with less immediate conflicts.

The anarchist turbulence that bloodied the 1890s may have been the
last hurrah of the old desperate insurrectionist tradition, now losing

ground to more up-to-date kinds of confrontation. Violence continued, and the prewar years saw strikes as serious as any in the nineteenth century. But fewer of them turned to riot, and bloodshed became exceptional. The future lay with action in the context of the newly legal, organized and increasingly effective unions and political parties. Even the question of vagrancy, which so obsessed the times, may have loomed larger because society was growing more settled; temporary migration, no longer part of normal craft rhythms, more exceptional; the vagabond less familiar; and improved dress among the lower classes made tramps stand out more sharply.

Economic strife, far from abating, may have become more intense as it became more broadly organized, more self-conscious, less fractured. But it also became more structured, developing rituals and accepting rules in keeping with participation in an increasingly civil society. Civility, however condescending, was becoming a democratic right, something that all could, or at least should, share. Witness the views of that ultimate authority on good manners, the Baroness Staffe, who wrote benignly about the "equalitarian courtesy" of the present generation, which "already practices an *almost* equalitarian politeness, that is to say, applied to *almost* everybody. The time is not far off when courtesy will spread to all, with no more distinction of caste, position, or fortune, prejudices which *tend* to disappear."[17] The Baroness Staffe welcomed this evidence of progress as proof that fraternal feelings were gaining ground. She was premature, perhaps even mistaken. Nevertheless, easier access to bourgeois respectability was bolstering self-respect, hence respect for others, that was fostering a new tone of discourse and debate. Though no less astringent, it recognized that interlocutors might detest but had to tolerate each other.

That too testified to democracy. Now that it had been established, opined Faguet, unafraid of prophecy (or self-contradiction), "history might well become less checkered, less picturesque, less dramatic."[18] His views were not exceptional. The growing concentration and integration of international capital suggested that national concentration might lead to international integration. Personal ambitions, like national ones, would henceforth focus on success through the peaceful arts of science and industry. That was what the great Exhibition was all about. But even the Exhibition bore witness to more ominous possibilities. It had been President Loubet who, as Prime Minister in

1892, decided that there should be an exhibition in 1900. He did so to steal a march on the German Emperor, who had been planning a Universal Exhibition for Berlin.[19] Like international sporting events in later times, such great displays tended less to amplify international harmony than to stress international rivalry. This could be confirmed by reading the official Catalog, especially the section devoted to military display. "After thirty years of peace," the "Introduction to the Retrospective Exhibition of Land and Sea Armies" explained, "it seemed indispensable to revive in all minds [the memory of] the wars of the past." War was "natural to humanity . . . a school of the highest qualities of man . . . Peace fructifies the arts, trade, and industry, [but] also develops those states of mind called selfishness, pessimism, nihilism, egoism." To recall the warlike virtues of our fathers was "a patriotic action which would bear fruit in the masses visiting these halls, restore the lofty virtues that seem to be fading, raise their spirit, and given them new heart."[20]

Less than a year later, visiting the naval base at Toulon, the presidential party embarked "on a narrow plank 45 meters long and with a little kiosk in the middle," France's first submarine.[21] Within a few years more, the first flying machines would sputter through the skies. In 1909 Emile Pouget, syndicalist prophet of the ultimate strike, included them and the bombs they would drop in his account of the Revolution to come.

No wonder Faguet concluded his discussion of the twentieth century by insisting that the only alternative to European solidarity was European decadence: progress or disaster.[22] We tend to pay more attention to those who predicted the worst, because we know it came. Contemporaries, though, could be forgiven for entertaining a different point of view. Mankind, the *Petit Parisien* declared on December 29, 1900, could greet the coming century "with cries of gladness." It would bring, there was no doubt, the alleviation of many pains, the further perfection of the democratic and humanitarian beginnings started in the nineteenth century.[23] The *Petit Parisien* was right. It merely forgot that every silver lining comes attached to a cloud.

By the turn of the century the access of decadence had largely passed away. Rather, it sparked a counterlurch into revivalism. Roger Martin du Gard, born in 1881, made his *Jean Barois,* the quintessential Dreyfusard and rationalist intellectual, face the vitalist representatives of this reaction, more interested in solving the problems of practical life than in "intellectualism" and "sterile abstractions."[24] The tension between the two points of view would become another leitmotif of the twentieth century. For the moment, however, *Le Vélo,* agent and beneficiary of the vitalist revolution, declared that France was on the verge of a brilliant Renaissance.[25]

When Talleyrand in his old age recalled the Ancien Régime in which he had grown up, insisting that those who had not known the 1780s had not known the real joy of life, he was talking nonsense—revealing nonsense. Similarly, an old lady who had lived, loved, and been loved a lot, recalled her life at the turn of the century: "I have been a frivolous woman. I lived in frivolous times. Frivolous nations are happy nations."[26] Thoughtless, insensitive words, characteristic of a thoughtless, insensitive few, protected and spoiled and of a turn of mind that would scarcely dare express itself today. Yet true. Frivolous people are not necessarily happy, but they are harmless to most, sometimes even to themselves. But the frivolous can prove misleading.

In 1912 the first volume of Marcel Proust's *Remembrance of Things Past* was rejected for publication. André Gide, the publisher's reader, had not even bothered to untie the parcel of the manuscript, considering, he later admitted, the author to be "a snob, a dilettante, and a man-about-town (*mondain*)," too worldly for the serious business of literature.[27] Yet worldliness can be a way to get to know the world. What is *Remembrance of Things Past* but the profound account of a profoundly frivolous world? A fin de siècle history of the fin de siècle, always remembering Proust's view that Clio was the muse who gathered in everything that the loftier muses of Philosophy and Art rejected, everything not founded on truth—contingent, uncertain, accidental, incidental, and ultimately dependent on the evanescent impressions and the distorting memories of men. In history, as in Proust, observation depends on the observer's point of view, claims to objectivity can be misleading, all we can do is to suggest connections.

It is not irrelevant to remember that when, in 1892, Proust's cousin Louise Neuburger married Henri Bergson, the twenty-one-year-old Marcel acted as best man (*garçon d'honneur*); and that the title of the English translation of his greatest work does not quite render the French *A la recherche du temps perdu*, which would translate more clumsily, "In Search of Time Lost"—or, if you like, "Forgotten." The work is about the narrator's quest to recover and comprehend past feelings and experience, figures and lives, forfeit to time and to resurrect them in a book that would provide a link between lost past and present. Memory wanes, but the books we write about it may live on. We too may live in and with them, as Bergotte does: the famous writer, perhaps Anatole France, who had so influenced Marcel in his youth.

> They buried him, but all through the funeral
> night, in the lit shop windows, his books
> arranged three by three watched like angels
> with outspread wings and appeared, for him
> who was no more, the symbol of his resurrection.[28]

Notes

---

* * *

For books published in Paris, the notes will show only the date of publication.

Introduction

1. Georges d'Avenel, *Le Nivellement des jouissances* (1919; 1st ed., 1913), 207–208.
2. Georges d'Avenel, *Les Français de mon temps* (1910), 1.
3. Charles Maillier, *Trois journalistes Drouais: Brisset, Dujarier, Buré* (1968), 47–48.
4. Rudyard Kipling, *Souvenirs of France* (London, 1933), 37.
5. Quoted in Peter Quennell, *Customs and Characters* (London, 1982).
6. Paul Vidal de La Blache and Camena d'Almeida, *La France* (1915), xii.

1. Decadence?

1. *Gazette des Tribunaux* (hereafter cited as GT), January 20, 1889.
2. A. Claveau, *Fin de siècle. Pile ou face* (1889), vii.
3. GT, April 20, 1891. In 1892 a provincial newpaper describes a local priest as wanting to be fin-de-siècle, for attempting to write in the press and join in political debates. Paul Fesch, *Souvenirs d'un abbé journaliste* (ca. 1900), 171.
4. GT, December 3, 1891, reviewing Bérard des Glajeux, *Souvenirs d'un Président d'Assises* (1891).
5. "Préfecture 'fin de siècle,'" *L'Avenir républicain d'Auch,* March 7, 1891; *Gazette du Palais* (hereafter cited as GP), May 4, 1892.
6. "Un Mari fin-de-siècle," GT, November 5, 1892.
7. Paul Desachy and René Dubreuil, *Fin de siècle, monologue en vers dit par F. Galipaux du Palais-Royal* (1891).
8. Quoted in Fernande Zayed, *Huysmans, peintre de son époque* (1973), 517.
9. Francis de Jouvenot and H. Micard, *Fin de siècle, pièce en quatre actes* (1888). Jouvenot was the author of another classic, *Cloaca maxima.* Humbert de Gallier, *Fin de siècle* (1889).

10. *Fin de Siècle. Journal Littéraire, Illustré* (hereafter cited as FS), January 17, 1891.
11. Ibid.
12. See GT, June 24 and July 1, 1893.
13. FS, August 19, 1897.
14. Arthur Lautrec, *La Fin du monde prochaînement. Arguments décisifs* (Lyons, 1901); Jean Rocroy, *La Fin du monde en 1921, prouvée par l'histoire* (1904). Jeannin, who saluted Drumont, decried the decadence of the times.
15. Octave Uzanne, *La Femme à Paris. Nos contemporaines* (1894), ii.
16. Alfred Legoyt, *De la Prétendue dégénérescence physique de la population française comparée aux autres populations européennes* (1863); H. A. Depierris, *Le Tabac* (1876), 3.
17. Maurice de Fleury, *Les Grands symptômes neurasthéniques* (1901), 4; Lucien Grelley, *Nevrosés et décadents* (Macon, 1913), 3, 14; Pasteur Vallery-Radot, *Mémoires d'un non-conformiste* (1966), 86–87: "I fed on *A Rebours*. I was des Esseintes . . . I went to hear Pelléas, my nose in an orchid. It was the rage, in 1910, to delight in melancholy."
18. O. Uzanne, *Le Miroir du monde* (1888), 57.
19. A. Mabille de Poncheville, *Vie de Verhaeren* (1953), 168.
20. André Derain, *Lettres à Vlaminck* (1955), 32. Curiously, this echoes Alfred Fournier's treatise, *La Syphilis héréditaire tardive* (1886), 23: "Venereal disease is a breeding ground for all corruptions." But one should bear in mind Vlaminck's warning, p. 13, about the fundamental mood in which judgments like Derain's were passed: "Le lecteur se tromperait s'il pensait qu'un être dégouté de la vie s'exprime, s'il y voyait les lamentations d'un neurasthénique, s'il croyait y respirer une atmosphère de lassitude" (The reader would be wrong to take them for the views of a man disgusted with life, to read in them the laments of a neurasthenic, or to detect there a sense of weariness). This must hold true for many expressions of despair inspired by a moment's boredom or simply by the spirit of the times.
21. Paul Cambon, *Correspondance, 1870–1924* (1940), I, 372. Cambon, who saw it in May 1894, when Antoine was on tour in Constantinople, found the play "boring and repulsive."
22. Charles Féré, *Dégénérescence et criminalité. Essai physiologique* (1888) 130; Dr. Legrain, *De la Dégénérescence de l'espèce humaine* (1892) l; Paul Robin, *Dégénérescence de l'espèce humaine. Causes et remèdes* (1905), l; H. Thulié, *La Lutte contre la dégénérescence et la criminalité* (1912), 4, 7, 15.
23. Jean Lacouture, *François Mauriac* (1980), 64.
24. For a rich account of these aspects, see Albert Boime, *Thomas Couture and the Eclectic Vision* (New Haven, 1980), esp. ch. VI. Boime also notes (160–61) the influence of Suetonius' *Lives* and of the *Satyricon* of Petronius, with its description of Trimalchio's feast and its song of impending civil war.
25. Houssaye, *Les Confessions,* II (1885); quoted in Boime, *Couture.*
26. Pierre Guiral, *La Vie quotidienne en France à l'âge d'or du capitalisme* (1976), 18. Edmond de Goncourt noted with horror the silver bidets in the *cabinet de*

toilette of a parvenu house: *Journal* (1956), IV, 512. In the same connection, J. E. C. Bodley's essay on "The Decay of Idealism in France" remarked on the French invention of the term *arriviste,* a neologism that Littré, who died in 1881, ignored, "but that most reflects the spirit of the age." *Cardinal Manning and Other Essays* (London, 1912), 165–66.

27. Alexis de Tocqueville, *Oeuvres complètes* (1968), VIII, 3, 105; Comtesse Jean de Pange, *Comment j'ai vu 1900* (1965), III, 59; Paul Adam's Jean Stival in *La Force du mal* (1896).

28. Gustave Flaubert, *Correspondance,* VI (1928), letter 1206; Eugène Sue, *Les Mystères de Paris* (1963), 288; Goncourt, *Journal,* I, 209. Gautier already distrusted "the routines and the bad instincts of the crowds." In his preface to *Mademoiselle de Maupin* (1835), an early manifesto of art for art's sake, he insisted that "nothing is really beautiful except those things that are no use for anything. All that is useful is ugly, for it is the expression of some need, and the needs of man are ignoble and disgusting."

29. Baudelaire's description; quoted in Williams, *Horror of Life,* 12–13.

30. See Georges Sorel's ideas on "Grandeur et décadence," app. I in 1910 edition of *Les Illusions du progrès,* esp. p. 333, where democracy = mediocrity and parliamentarism = democracy.

31. G. Paul-Boncour and J. Phillipe, *Les Anomalies mentales chez les écoliers* (1905): "Tant que l'instruction n'était pas obligatoire, ces refractaires ou incapables passaient facilement inaperçus . . . Mais aujourd'hui il n'en peut plus aller de même" (As long as schooling was not compulsory, the rebellious or unfit were easily ignored . . . Today it is no longer so). Cited in Francine Muel, "L'Ecole obligatoire et l'invention de l'enfance anormale," *Actes de la recherche en sciences sociales* (January 1975), 69.

32. Pierre Giffard, *Les Grands bazars* (1882), 157.

33. Louis Gérard-Varet in a Chamber debate of 1908, quoted in Robert A. Nye, *Crime, Madness and Politics in Modern France* (Princeton, 1984), 307. Yet even ill winds blew some good, as the makers of the Elixir Dieudonné, the only one to afford a real cure for fin de siècle maladies, could testify; or those of the Dragées du Roi David, which offered to restore the strength of those weakened or exhausted by contemporary stress. See FS, September 1898, April 1900.

34. See Marc Bloch, "Le Salaire," in *Mélanges historiques* (1963), II, 898, 900; and Eugen Weber, "The Secret Life of Jean Barois," in John Weiss, ed., *The Origins of Modern Consciousness* (Detroit, 1965), and "Inheritance and Dilettantism: The Politics of Maurice Barrès," *Historical Reflections* (Summer 1975).

35. Denounced by Benedetto Croce as quoted by Richard Drake, "Toward a Theory of Decadence," *Journal of Contemporary History* (January 1982), 81.

36. By then, Lombroso's much reedited and translated study of genius and madness had become *L'uomo di Genio* (1888) in which (inter alia) Symbolist poetry was linked to neuropathology and madness. It was to be translated into French the following year. The preface to this French edition, by Dr. Charles

Richet, quoted Moreau as saying that genius and madness are closely related. Brooks Adams' "essay on history," *The Law of Civilization and Decay* (1st ed. London, 1893), appeared in an American edition (New York, 1895) at the same time as A. E. Hake's *Regeneration. A Reply to Max Nordau* (New York, 1895), with an introduction by Nicholas Murray Butler. By the time Arthur Balfour delivered his Henry Sidgwick Memorial Lecture at Cambridge in 1908 on Decadence, he was addressing a commonplace.

37. Goncourt, *Journal,* II, 592; Ferry, *Lettres* (1914), December 8, 1871.
38. *Annuaire de l'économie politique* (1876), *Annuaire statistique de la France* (1883).
39. Hippolyte Taine, Introduction, *Histoire de la littérature anglaise* (1863). He also admired the English for having succeeded in building character where the French had failed: *Notes sur l'Angleterre* (1872).
40. Like the successful prank of publishing the poems of a mythical Adoré Floupette, under the significant title, *Les Déliquescences* (1885).
41. *Le Décadent,* no. 1, April 10, 1886. To put such activities in contemporary perspective, one Sunday in 1885 a third-year student at the Ecole Normale d'Institutrices of Rouen, caught smoking during a walk outside the school, tried to poison herself out of shame and despair at her expected expulsion. Archives Nationales, F. 17 9614, Ecole Normale d'Institutrices, Rouen, Directrice to Inspecteur de l'académie, January 15, 1885 (with thanks to Anne Quartararo).
42. Goncourt, *Journal,* III, 831.
43. Guy Thuillier, "Paul Valéry et la politique," *Revue Administrative,* no. 90 (November 1962), 617.
44. Marie-Thérèse Eyquem, *Pierre de Coubertin* (1966), 58. Edmond de Goncourt (*Journal,* IV, May 11, 1894), notes a visit to Mme. de Bonnières, surrounded by "all the young poets, symbolists, decadents, *altruists.*" Somebody suggesting that they must court her, "Oh! she replied . . . there is no danger. They've all been rejected for military service."

2. Transgressions

1. See Alfred Fouillée, *Psychologie du peuple français* (1914; 1st ed., 1898), 358 and passim; Gabriel Désert in Paul Dartiguenave et al., *Marginalité, déviance et pauvreté en France, XIVe–XIXe siècles* (Caen, 1981), 255.
2. Robert Sherard, *My Friends the French* (London, 1910), 116.
3. GT, December 24, 1898, Haute-Marne Assizes; see also GT, June 17, 1886, Aveyron Assizes.
4. GT, February 18, 1892, Calvados Assizes.
5. GP, February 22, 1900, Tribunal Civil, Beauvais: "l'ivresse notoire publique de l'un des époux constitue . . . une injure grave de nature à motiver le divorce" (the notorious and public drunkenness of one spouse constitutes an offense serious enough to justify divorce).
6. GT, March 12, 1899, Savoie Assizes; GT, September 14, 1902, Tribunal

Correctionnel, Quimper; L. Landouzy, *De l'irrationnel et de l'insuffiisant dans l'alimentation des ouvriers et des employés parisiens* (1906), 3.

7. GT, March 15, 1906.
8. Emile Goudeau, *Paris qui consomme* (1893), 8.
9. H.-A. Depierris, *Le Tabac qui contient le plus violent des poisons, la nicotine, abrège-t-il l'existence? Est-il cause de la dégénérescence physique et morale des sociétés modernes?* (1876), 19, 218–22, 366–67. Depierris pointed out that in the late 1870s France's more than 30,000 *débits de tabac* numbered more than half of its 50,000 bakeries (459), that state revenue from taxes on tobacco had almost quintupled in the previous half-century (353), and that over a billion [gold] francs were going up in smoke every year (492). A French Association Against Tobacco Abuse had been set up in 1868 (437). E.-V. Veauclin, *La Question du paupérisme* (Bernay, 1887), 15, denounced the "disquieting symptoms" of such abuse, especially in the case of poor children between eight and twelve years old, often seen making their way to school with a cigarette between their lips. Some let the nails of thumb and index grow inordinately long, in order to smoke their fags to the end (Depierris, 490).
10. Depierris, *Le Tabac,* 150, 163–65, 166–67. Cigarettes, fashionable among the fashionable by the late 1880s, were few. Paul Sébillot, *Le Tabac dans les traditions, les superstitions et les coutûmes* (1893), talks of pipes, cigars, snuff, and chewing tobacco, but never mentions cigarettes.
11. Depierris, *Le Tabac,* 81, 124.
12. Ibid., 228–29, and ch. xii passim; John Grand-Carteret, *La Femme en culotte* (1899), 11. Francis Jourdain, *Né en 1876* (1951), 186, tells us that the wife of a successful painter, Albert Besnard, was a heavy smoker, something contemporary protocol prohibited in public: "thus, at parties she had to take refuge on the landing in order to gratify her passion."
13. Goudeau, *Paris qui consomme,* 34.
14. Charles Braibant, *Felix Faure à l'Elysée* (1963), 61.
15. Maurice Talmeyr, *Les Possédés de la morphine* (1892), 1–2; Paul Poiret, *En habillant l'époque* (1930), 67; Jean-Paul Crespelle, *Les Maitres de la Belle Epoque* (1966), 26. For an overview, see Jean-Louis Brau, *Histoire de la Drogue* (1972).
16. Brau, *Drogue,* 175; Goudeau, *Paris qui consomme,* 44–45; Emilien Carassus, *Le Snobisme et les Lettres françaises* (1966), 431; "Tout-Paris" in *Le Gaulois,* September 14, 1897.
17. Brau, *Drogue,* 290, citing Freud's *Correspondance générale* (1966).
18. Marie-France James, *Esotérisme, occultisme, franc-maçonnerie et christianisme au XIXe et XXe siècles* (1981), passim.
19. Michel de Lézinier, *Avec Huysmans* (1928), 193; Zayed, *Huysmans,* 432. Huysmans was a credulous man. See Gustave Boucher, *Une Séance de spiritisme chez J.-K. Huysmans* (Niort, 1908), for one occasion when he witnessed the materialization of the deceased General Boulanger. Edouard Drumont was credulous too. See Eugen Weber, *Satan Franc-Maçon* (1964), 16.
20. *L'Année Littéraire,* 1887, reviewing Mlle Hucher's *Spirite; Fin de Siècle,* June

20, 1891; "mysticisme, le dernier cri de la nevrose"; *Le Figaro,* April 23, 1891; *Le Mondain,* April 6, 1895 (Eric Satie had written a "fanfare de la Rose Croix de M. le comte de La Rochefoucauld"); *Vie Parisienne,* January 19, 1895; Carassus, *Le Snobisme,* 394, 397; Jules Bois, *Le Noces de Sathan* (1890), *Les Petites religions de Paris* (1894).

21. Charles Richet, *Traité de métapsychique* (1922), preface; for quotations below, see 9, 10, 785.

22. J. Maxwell, M.D., *Metapsychical Phenomena* (London, 1905), 184–85.

23. A. E. Waite, *Devil Worship in France* (1896), vi.

24. For the story of Taxil's hoax and its incredible success, see Weber, *Satan Franc-Maçon.*

25. André Billy, *Stanislas de Guaita* (1971), 153, 163–64; Adolphe Retté, *Au pays des lys noirs. Souvenirs de jeunesse et d'age mur* (1913), 36–37. See also Jules Giraud, *Testament d'un haschischéen* (1912), by a *fouriériste* and occultist addicted for 45 years (use of drugs was not illegal); Edouard Schuré, *Les Grands initiés* (1889); Jules Boissière, *Fumeurs d'opium* (1896; posthumously republished in 1910); Ernest Raynaud, *En Marge de la mêlée symboliste* (1936), 136. Zayed, *Huysmans,* 464, 455, appears to agree with Guy Michaud in considering occultism the key to Symbolism; she cites the names of Nerval, Barbey d'Aurévilly, Rimbaud, Villiers de l'Isle-Adam, Catulle Mendès, Lautréamont, Charles Cros, Tristan Corbière, Jean Lorrain, Maurice Rollinat, Jean Richepin, Maeterlinck, Léon Bloy, Huysmans (of course), and also Alfred Jarry and Apollinaire.

26. Brau, *Drogue,* 29–31; Theda Shapiro, *Painters and Politics* (New York, 1976), 52; Fernande Olivier, *Picasso and His Friends* (New York, 1965), 49, 73, 133–34; Charles Douglas, *Artist Quarter* (London, 1941), 35, 59.

27. Talmeyr, *Les Possédés,* 234, 247–48; Maurice Donnay, *J'ai vécu 1900* (1950), 13.

28. Talmeyr, *Les Possédés,* 95–98.

29. Yvonne Deslandres, *Le Costume. Image de l'homme* (1976), 244; J. J. Coulmann, *Réminiscences* (1862), I, 61.

30. Sébastien Commissaire, *Mémoires et souvenirs* (Lyon, 1888) I, 52; GT, August 20, 1836; *Petit Journal,* January 1, 1897; GT, December 4, 1889; GT, November 7 and 8, 1910.

31. Ernest Raynaud, *Souvenirs de police* (1923), 119; Préfêt, Eure, to Ministre de l'Intérieur, November 27, 1892, Archives Nationales (hereafter cited as AN) F712.944.

32. Grand-Carteret, *XIXe siècle (en France). Classes, moeurs, usages, coutumes, inventions* (1893), 125: Mme. Marc de Montifaud à la Bibliothèque Nationale; 127: Léonide Leblanc en homme; 136: Etre homme: ô rêve doucement caressé: ô joie suprême; 240: une bicycletteuse; 241: chauffeuse en ourson; 247: culotte, and so on.

33. General Legrand-Girarde, *Un Quart de siècle au service de la France* (1954), 154; Liane de Pougy, *Mes Cahiers bleus* (1977), 201; Rachilde, *Portraits d' hommes* (1929), 21.

34. GT, March 5 and 21, 1885, Seine Assizes; January 16, 1886, Mayenne Assizes; December 23–24, 1889, Aveyron Assizes; March 20 and 21, 1903, Seine Assizes. See also GP, February 18, 1892; G. Guilermet, *Comment devient-on criminel?* (1913?), 93.

35. Yvette Guilbert, *La Chanson de ma vie* (1927), 77, 106, 170–71; *Fin de Siècle*, 1891 (see "Filles de Lesbos," December 23, 1891); Goudeau, *Paris qui consomme*, 213; André Germain, *Les Fous de 1900* (1954), 58.

36. GP, May 1, 1900.

37. Germain, *Les Fous de 1900*, 57.

38. Gabriel Tarde, *Essais et mélanges sociologiques* (1895), 211, 217–19, 220–21; J.-C. Chesnais, *Les Morts violentes en France* (1976), 35–36, 58. For statements following, see GT, January 1, 1892, and April 28, 1901; Jacques Bonzon, *Le Crime et l'école* (1896); G. Guilhermet, *Comment se font les erreurs judiciaires* (1911), 109.

39. GT, February 6, 1885; August 10, 1887; January 16 and 17, 1911.

40. Emile Levasseur, *La Population française* (1891), II, 456; Denis Szabo, *Crimes et villes* (1960), 39–40.

41. Gabriel Désert in Dartiguenave et al., *Marginalité*, 226, 236–37, 233, 261.

42. GT, June 29–30, 1891, Morbihan Assizes; GP, November 27–28, 1904; for alteration of goods, Vilbert in Dartiguenave et al., *Marginalité*, 197.

43. Tarde, *Essais*, 221.

44. "Hooligan," *L'Auto*, July 30, 1906.

45. Tarde, *Essais*, 108.

46. For some mentions of interpreters in court, see GT, July 22 and October 24, 1883, July 21, 1887 (Finistère), March 12, 1890 (Morbihan), June 17, 1893 (Nord), August 3, 1895 (Côtes-du-Nord), August 10, 1899 (Gard).

47. Such mentions, the latest of many more, may be found in GT, October 5, 1891, April 23, 1892, March 15, 1894, January 19, 1896.

48. GT, November 14, 1890, Haute-Vienne Assizes; Henri Dabot, *Calendriers d'un bourgeois du Quartier Latin, 1888–1900* (1905), August 2 and 5, 1900.

49. GT, July 17, 1884.

50. GT, August 5 and 8, September 2, 1883; Karl Baedeker, *Paris et ses environs* (Leipzig, 1900), xxx; GT, November 9, 1899 (Finistère).

51. Olivier, *Picasso*, 123.

52. GT, October 30, 1889, Var Assizes; February 6, 1891, Meuse Assizes; September 7, November 23 and 26, 1892, Gironde Assizes; March 3, 1895, Pas-de-Calais Assizes; GP, July 30, 1904, Berry Assizes.

53. Alexandre Vexliard, *Introduction à la sociologie du vagabondage* (1956), 90–93; Ferdinand Dreyfus, *Etudes et discours* (1896), 151, 152; *Misères sociales* (1901), 97–98.

54. Emile Fourquet, *Les Faux témoins* (Chalons-sur-Saone, 1901), 22.

55. Sherard, *My Friends*, 162–63. See also A. Buwyd, Gendarme en retraite. Ancien chef de poste à Pégomas, *Les Bandits de Pégomas* (Nice, 1913), for bucolic doings in a village near Cannes, 1906–1913.

56. The first page of Alphonse Daudet's *Numa Roumestan* (1881) mentions the

game of strangle-cat in the context of a Provençal urban celebration that he places in 1875. GT, April 7, 1883, mentions a sadistic young Norman weaver who killed a goat by skewering it alive on a pole; that was not what brought him to court. Jean-Paul Chavent, *La Vie quotidienne en Périgord au début du siècle* (Limoges, 1978), 61, prints the Prefect's decree of May 15, 1913.

57. GT, September 5, 1912. The Court of Appeals increased this to three months and 50 francs each for involuntary homicide, but still ignored the deliberate killing of the animal.
58. December 12–13, 1898, Morbihan Assizes; February 23, 1893, Isère Assizes.
59. GT, September 3, 1896, Basses-Pyrénées; August 29–31, 1898, Ille-et-Vilaine; November 14, Vert (Seine-et-Oise); July 7, 1884, Finistère; March 28 and April 3, 1900, Paris.
60. GT, November 13, 1889, Meuse Assizes.
61. GT, October 25, 1889, Mayenne Assizes; January 1, 1883, Gironde Assizes.
62. GT, February 21, 1887 Lot Assizes; July 1, 1888, Aveyron Assizes; September 18, 1889 and January 7, 1897, Manche Assizes. A horrid picture emerges from the proceedings of a case tried before the Loire Assizes (GT, September 17, 1884). The husband beat the wife, his third, and starved her; she, when too hungry, sometimes stole his bread. The husband ate alone in the barn, either because he did not want to share his food, or because he was afraid to be poisoned, as he eventually was.
63. GT, June 9, 1883, Basses-Pyrénées; December 23, 1883, Vosges.
64. GT, February 16, 1890, Ille-et-Vilaine.
65. For notaries, see Sherard, *My Friends,* 198–99. Cases cited in order: GT, January 5, 1883, Tarn; August 5, 1886, Alpes-Maritimes; January 1, 1890, Côtes-du-Nord; September 8, 1892, Charente; June 3, 1910, Puy-de-Dôme.
66. Louis Desprez, *Autour d'un clocher. Moeurs rurales* (Brussels, 1884), 22–23, 41–47, 36.
67. GT, February 12, 1893, Finistère; May 14, 1894, Côtes-du-Nord; November 30, 1893, Alpes-Maritimes; October 27, 1910, Doubs; James E. McMillan, *Housewife or Harlot* (Brighton, 1981), 18.
68. Michel Bernard, founder of the Sharecroppers' Syndicate in the Bourbonnais, to Emile Guillaumin, April 1905; quoted in Daniel Halévy, *Visites aux Paysans du Centre* (1978), 63. Bernard's description, of his fellows, their "coeurs durcis par les peines, la crainte, la peur" (hearts hardened by grief, anxiety, fear), might well be compared to that in J.-A. Delpon, *Statistique du département du Lot* (1831), I, 202–03: "abruti par les besoins . . . peu affligé par la mort de ses proches . . . Jamais il n'est sorti de lui-même par le sentiment de sympathie" (stupefied by need . . . scarcely touched by the death of his near ones . . . He has never forgotten himself in a feeling for others).

3. How They Lived

1. Jean Follain, *L'Epicerie d'enfance* (1938), 31.
2. George Dupeux, *La Société française* (1972), 19. The census of 1901 showed

29.1 percent living in towns of 10,000 or more. J. C. Toutain, *La Population de la France* (1963), 66.

3. Gustave Tarde, *Les Lois de l'imitation* (1890), 245–46; H. P. Clive, *Pierre Louÿs, 1870–1925* (Oxford, 1978), 23; Paul Adam, *La Force du mal* (1896), 18; Germaine de Maulny, *Les Bottines à boutons* (1978), 149.

4. E. and J. de Goncourt, *Journal* (1956), III, 133, Nov. 11, 1881. For Huysmans, see F. Zayed, *Huysmans,* 147, 350, 357, and his own *En Rade* (1887) based on time spent at Jutigny (Seine-et-Marne), near Provins; for the Nord, Bernard Auffray, *Pierre de Margerie, 1861–1942,* (1976), 35–36; for Vendée, Dr. E. Boismoreau, *Coutûmes médicales et superstitions populaires du Bocage vendéen* (1911), 97; for magistrate, Antoine Baumann, *Le Tribunal de Vuillermoz* (1896), 43–44, and *La Vie sociale de notre temps* (1974), 146–48; Philippe Gratton, "Grèves agricoles en France, 1890–1935," *Mouvement Social* (April 1970), 26, quoting Compère-Morel at the SFIO Congress of 1909. Equally, Clifford H. Bissell, *Les Conventions du théatre bourgeois contemporain en France, 1887–1914* (1930), 122.

5. Ginette Guitard-Auviste, *Jacques Chardonne* (1984) 31; E. Delorme, *Nos Garnisons de France, d'Algérie et de Tunisie. Guide de l'officer d'infanterie,* passim. George Mallet, *Mes Souvenirs sur la vie abbevilloise à la fin du XIXe siècle* (Abbeville, 1950), 39, 41.

6. Elysée Reclus in 1881, quoted in Maurice Agulhon, ed., *Histoire de la France urbaine* (1983), IV, 53; Mallet, *Mes souvenirs,* 13, 16, 20; Hugues Lapaire, *Le Pays berrichon* (1908), 20.

7. Raymond Abellio, *Mes Dernières mémoires* (1971), I, 65–66.

8. Henri Bachelin, *Sous d'humbles toits* (1913), 41.

9. GT, February 28, 1883, Gironde Assizes: "My parents . . . sat by the fire, never lit a candle." Antoine Sylvère, *Toinon, Pays d'Ambert* (1980), 4: in 1888 his grandparents' lamp consisted of some threads floating in nut oil inside a scooped-out potato. Henri Bachelin, *Les Manigants* (1907), 12: "neither candle nor lamp," the flame in the fireplace cooks the soup and lights the room. (See also Gason Moreau, *L'Eclairage dans le Baugéois* (Baugé, 1954), 5–6.) Elisabeth de Clermont-Tonnerre, *Mémoires, I. Au Temps des équipages* (1928), 138.

10. Martial Deherrypon, *La Boutique du charbonnier* (1883), 82; GT, September 5, 1884. For similar instances, see GT, January 19 and February 4, 1985, Dordogne; January 21, 1887, Somme; and May 4, 1887, Orne; September 13, 1888, Aveyron.

11. GT, February 3, 1886, Conseil de Préfecture de la Seine.

12. Emile Rivoalen, *Révolution de l'architecture* (1883), 174.

13. Goudeau, *Paris qui consomme,* 63–65; Robert Fleury, "L'Eau à Paris," *Revue des Deux Mondes* (September 15, 1982), 385.

14. Henri Monod, *Le Choléra. Histoire d'une épidemie—Finistère, 1885–1886* (1892), 58.

15. See Maurice Agulhon, "Imagerie civique et décor urbain," *Ethnologie française,* V (1975), 34.

16. Henri Chardon, *Voyage et voyageurs dans le Maine du XVIe au XXe siècle* (Le Mans, 1906), 15–16; Jean-Louis Malaviale, *Le Journal de Villefranche et la presse d'arrondissement en Bas-Rouergue* (1965), 22.

17. Serge Chassagne in François Lebrun, ed., *Histoire d'Angers* (Toulouse, 1975), 231; Emile Aron, *Tours en 1880* (1981), 52; Roger Marlin in Claude Fohlen, ed., *Histoire de Besançon* (1966), 356, 411 (for lead poisonings at Vitré, Ille-et-Vilaine, see GT, September 3, 1901); Goudeau, *Paris qui consomme,* 68.

18. Sylvère, *Toinon,* 174; Aron, *Tours,* 110, *Recueil des travaux du Comité Consultatif d'hygiène publique en France,* tome 22e, année 1892 (Melun, 1893), 282–83.

19. GT, March 20, 1896, Tribunal de simple police, Auch; March 11, 1899, Tribunal Correctionnel, Chateauroux.

20. Pierre Bouchardon, *Souvenirs* (1953), 10–11; Jean-Joseph Escande, *Histoire de Sarlat* (1912), 441–42; Annie Merlin and A.-Y. Beaujour, *Les Mangeurs du Rouergue* (1978), 105.

21. Marlin, *Besançon,* 411; Janne Janinard, *Le Printemps du siècle à Langres* (Langres, 1983), 43; Jacques Roussel, *Vivonne* (Poitiers, 1977), 79 ff.; GT, February 17, 1912, Tribunal de simple police, Paris.

22. Monod, *Le Choléra,* 61; Bichambis, *Ingénieur, Narbonne* (Narbonne, 1926), 114 ff.; Henri Dabot, *Calendriers, 1872–1888* (Péronne, 1903), January 15 and 26, 1884; for *tout-à-l'égout,* GP, May 14, 1892; GT, May 15, 1896, January 21, 1901, and G. d'Avenel, *Le Mécanisme de la vie moderne* (1903), III, 101.

23. Antoine Baumann, *Souvenirs de magistrat* (1899), 16, notes a *juge suppléant,* the freshness of whose linen made him stand out from afar to all who passed.

24. Comtesse de Pange, *Comment j'ai vu 1900* (1968), 245. See also 102, and Elinor Glyn, *The Visits of Elizabeth* (London, 1901), 68. Pauline de Broglie, who married Jean de Pange in 1910 and left us her memoirs under her married name, was born in 1888, just as the Eiffel Tower began to grow. Her grandfather, the Duc Albert de Broglie, was the grandson of Madame de Staël.

25. Marquis de Bonneval, *La Vie de château* (1978), 15, 37.

26. For the price of carried water, Avenel, *Le Mécanisme,* III, 97. The Bonnevals of course would not need that; a mansion like theirs would use tap water, which was a great deal cheaper. Avenel, *Le Nivellement des jouissances* (1913), 210, explains that under Napoleon III a successful medical man living in the center of Paris paid his waterhauler 72 francs a year for 14,000 liters of water; at the turn of the century the same sum paid for 206,000 liters of tap water. Yet (*Histoire de la France urbaine,* IV, 326, 336) in 1906 two lodgings out of three had no lavatory; in 1940, in towns over 30,000, one-third still have neither water nor electricity and only one-tenth boast a bathroom.

27. "Le Bain," reproduced in *Le Parisien chez lui au 19e siècle, 1814–1914* (Archives Nationales, 1976), 116.

28. GT, April 5, 1900, "Chronique," for the owner of a café in the place Clichy suing his tormentors.

29. Pange, *1900,* 195–96.
30. Maulny, *Les Bottines,* 14–16; Glyn, *Visits of Elizabeth,* 144–47. Elizabeth, coming from England, did not know that upper- (and middle-) class standards of propriety precluded spouses seeing each other naked, or ever sharing the same room. In 1890 Goncourt received a letter from married friends in Burma, where the heat was such that they went to bed naked: "Nous pensions, Daudet et moi, que cette coucherie sans chemise devait joliment tuer le respect du mari pour la femme et ne plus lui faire voir dans l'épouse qu'une maîtresse" (We thought, Daudet and I, that this intercourse with no chemise must have pretty well killed the husband's respect for the wife and led him to consider her as no better than a mistress); (*Journal,* III, 1211). A French innkeeper would assume that a wife who slept in the same room as her husband was a woman of easy virtue. (Glyn, *Visits of Elizabeth,* 84. See also Goncourt, *Journal,* 581.) After twenty years of marriage, Zola's Comte Muffat "n'avait jamais vu la comtesse Muffat mettre ses jarretières" (had never seen his wife put on her garters); (*Les Rougon-Macquart,* II [1961], 1213). Hence his fascination with Nana's body and also, perhaps, the number of vaudevilles where one spouse does not recognize the (disguised) other, even when making love. Hence also no doubt the envious fascination with lower-class (and colonial) sexuality that bourgeois and bourgeois writers felt.
31. Glyn, *Visits of Elizabeth,* 104.
32. G. Vacher de Lapouge, *Les Sélections sociales* (1896), 316; Jacques Thibault, *L'Influence du mouvement sportif sur l'évolution de l'éducation physique* (1972), 33, quotes a hygienic treatise of 1906 to the effect that, in one provincial town at least, the public baths were heated only on the eve of the day of the prefect's annual ball.
33. Comtesse de Pange, *Confidences d'une jeune fille* (1966) 149–50; this was in 1905. See also Colette's *Claudine à l'école* (1900).
34. Marcel Jouhandeau, *Mémorial* (1948), I, 160, 166–68, for the *coiffeuses* who did his mother and other *commerçantes* before these women opened their shops in the morning. After 8, "on pomponnait les grandes dames qui se rendaient aux messes tardives" (one titivated the great ladies who went to Mass later). As Pange suggests, none of these women knew how to do her own hair.
35. "And their feet black with filth for, during the three months they were there, no one had them washed." Jules Renard, "Poil de carotte. Les Poux," in *Oeuvres* (1970), I, 712–15.
36. Jules Renard, *Journal, 1887–1910* (1965), 849: "On peut faire toutes les boutiques de Corbigny sans trouver une lime à ongles, une brosse à dents, et il n'y a des éponges que pour les voitures" (You can go through all the shops of Corbigny without finding a nail file or a toothbrush, and there are sponges only [to wash] carriages). This in 1903. In the 1920s Pierre-Jakèz Hélias, with a scholarship to the lycée de Quimper, wonders, and his family with him: "Qu'est-ce que c'est, un gant de toilette? Et une pâte dentrifice?" (What's a wash cloth? And tooth paste?).

37. For one example among many, see Paul de Kock, *Le Cocu* (1925 ed.), 18.
38. Renard, *Oeuvres,* II, 468, 470 (1913); *Journal,* 946, 945 (1905).
39. Alain Corbin, *Le Miasme et la jonquille* (1982), 174.
40. See Stephen Kern, *Anatomy and Destiny* (New York, 1975), ch. 5. For Nietzsche, p. 45. In 1885 a French biologist, Ernest Monin, published a catalog of body odors, *Essais sur les odeurs du corps humain,* steadily reedited until 1903. In popular parlance the term *se dégrossir* (to become more polished or civilized) was used for washing or cleaning up (Marcel Jouhandeau, *Mémorial* (1955), V, 77.
41. *Histoire de la France urbaine,* 414, 547, 550.
42. Daudet, *Souvenirs d'un homme de lettres* (n.d.), 204–14. See also, Alis Levi, *Souvenirs d'une enfant de la Belle Epoque* (Rome, 1970), 14–15. For a different view, see Anne Martin-Fugier, *La Place des bonnes* (1979), 11, 28, 30.
43. See George Rocal, *La Science de gueule en Périgord* (Saint Saud, 1938), 13; Georges Haussmann, *Mémoires du Baron Haussmann* (1890), I, 74; Henri Bachelin, "Les Sports aux champs," *Cahiers du Centre* (February 1911), 38. Compare Denis Chapman, *The Home and Social Status* (London, 1955), 19–20.
44. Quoted in Pierre Guiral and Guy Thuillier, *La Vie quotidienne des domestiques* (1978), 70.
45. Jules Verne, *Les 500 millions de la bégum* (1879), 172.
46. L. Landouzy, *La Tuberculose, maladie sociale* (1903), 27, passim.
47. *L'Illustration,* August 20, 1887, praised a painting, *La Douche au regiment,* not only for the painter's talent but for the "interest and novelty" of the subject. Charles de Freycinet, *Souvenirs, 1878–1983* (1913), 407, recalled how, as Minister of War in the 1880s, he acted to combat typhoid fever in the army. With the support of the Ministry of the Interior, municipalities were encouraged to purify and filter their waters. Where they did not, barracks installed their own filtering systems. By 1890 this had produced significant improvements. The "Palais des armées et de l'hygiène" that one could visit at the Paris exhibition of 1900 glorified the beneficial effects of military concerns on the broader public welfare.
48. Monod, *Le Choléra,* 39; *Recueil des Travaux du Comité d'hygiène.*
49. Jacques Léonard, *Les Médecins de l'Ouest au XIXe siècle* (1978), III, 1179; Donald R. Hopkins, *Princes and Peasants. Smallpox in History* (Chicago, 1983), 315, 96.
50. *La Nouvelle Mode,* March 18, 1900.
51. Pasteur Vallery-Radot, *Pasteur inconnu* (1954), 190; *Correspondance de Pasteur* (1951), III, 19; IV, 35, 81, 286–87.
52. Avenel, *Les Mécanismes de la vie moderne* (1902) I, 157. By 1913 his *Nivellement des jouissances* (52, 46, 50, 41) gave even more encouraging figures, but went beyond the level of necessity (59, 99). The industrial cultivation of strawberries, Avenel claimed, allowed "the humblest proletarian to eat for a few sous the dessert that only the well-off could afford in 1860s." Fresh vegetables and salads were far cheaper than in the 1870s because market gardeners grew

much more of them. Rice, once a luxury, sold for 25 centimes a kilo, a third of its price of 1875; milk, also 5 sous the liter, had almost halved in price in half a century.

53. Jacques Desportes, *Essai démographique sur le département des Côtes du Nord, 1801–1911* (Arras, 1913), 110

54. Pierre Gascar, *Terres de mémoire* (1980), 29.

55. Jules Renard, "Ragotte," in *Oeuvres* (1956), II, 327; Claude Franchet, *Les Trois Demoiselles Colas* (1946), 31; Annie Merlin and A.-Y. Beaujour, *Mangeurs du Rouergue,* 162–63.

56. Goudeau, *Paris qui consomme,* 75–77; Daniel Goulle, "Le Petit Commerce," *L'Aurore,* April 29, 1902; Alain Faure, "L'Epicerie parisienne au 19e siècle," *Mouvement Social* (July 1979), 117, 124. For one case of meat poisoning that killed three, see GT, September 20, 1899.

57. Henri Dabot, *Calendriers, 1888–1900* (1905), December 29, 1896; Charles Rulon, *Images du passé. Bain-de-Bretagne (Ille-et-Vilaine)* (1966), 163.

58. Unless otherwise indicated, data in this and subsequent paragraphs is drawn from Guy Thuillier. *La Monnaie en France au début du XIXe siècle* (Geneva, 1983), which includes an invaluable section on coins in late-nineteenth-century France, 329–40.

59. GT, January 29, 1888, Tribunal Correctionnel, Paris.

60. GT, January 29, 1888; January 25, 1890, Cour d'Appel, Caen; October 4, 1890, Aisne Assizes.

61. Lequin, *Histoire de la France urbaine,* IV, 499. This is confirmed in Jeanne Gaillard, "Les Migrants à Paris," *Ethnologie Française* (April–June 1980), 133, who tells us that, in 1861, 63.3 percent of Paris's population lived in the primitive furnished lodgings called *garnis;* by 1896 only 7.05 percent. By then the number of indigents, seven or eight times fewer than at the end of the Second Empire, accounted for less than 2 percent of the capital's population.

62. Grand-Carteret, *XIXe Siècle,* 155–56.

63. Alfred Robida, *Le XIXe siècle* (1888), i, 369–70.

64. Gustave Flaubert, *L'Education sentimentale* (1869), pt. 3, ch. 1.

65. John P. McKay, *Tramways and Trolleys* (Princeton, 1976), 60, 72, 113–17, 135, 139–40, 202, 226. And also putting an end to the *vinaigrette,* the two-wheeled vehicle similar to a sedan chair but drawn by a man. Public transport, rejoiced a publicist, offered complete comfort and security. Paris trolleycars were not only very *select,* but carried far more pretty women than before. Pierre Giffard, *La Vie au théâtre* (1888), 177.

66. Bonneval, *Vie de château,* 95; Elisabeth Hausser, *Paris au jour le jour, 1900–1919* (1968), 40; McKay, *Tramways,* 161; Avenel, *Les Mécanismes,* V, 162. A few years later, in *Le Nivellement,* 317, Avenel, ever the enthusiast, saw the métro offering every Parisian proletarian the unheard-of luxury that only a millionaire like the Count of Monte Cristo once could enjoy: a carriage ready for his orders at any hour of the day.

67. For electricity, see Catherine Bertho, *Télégraphes et téléphones* (1981), passim; Aboilard, GT, January 17, 1885.

68. Avenel, *Les Mécanismes,* II, 108, 111–12.
69. Pieter Spierenburg, *The Spectacle of Suffering* (Cambridge, 1984), 88.
70. GT, January 8, 1899.
71. In October 1888 the Seine Assizes judged the first "vol au téléphone."
72. *Lettres de Jules Ferry* (1914), 245–46. Pierre Giffard, *Le Téléphone expliqué à tout le monde* (1878), 10–11: "In France, nobody believed it. The invention came from the land of mediums; and there is truly something mysterious, unexpected, about Graham Bell's discovery that recalls the sort of extranatural phenomena that the Yankees like." Soon thereafter, his *Téléphonie domestique* (1880), 53, sought to assuage fears of the problems that telephone wires might cause. Would they come to obstruct thoroughfares? Would they obscure the sunlight? Giffard thought such concerns unwarranted.
73. Bertho, *Télégraphes,* 194, 197; Ithiel de Sola Pool, ed., *The Social Impact of the Telephone* (Cambridge, Mass., 1977), 43, 97, 103; for Proust, see Carassus, *Le Snobisme,* 532; see also Levi, *Souvenirs,* 11; police, GT, May 22, 1912.
74. Grévy in Bertho, *Télégraphes,* 183; Greffulhe in Goncourt, *Journal,* IV, 251 (May 14, 1892); Degas in Paul Valéry, *Degas Danse Dessin* (1938), 110.
75. Bertho, *Télégraphes,* 200–61; Jacques Attali, in Pool, *Social Impact.*
76. Alfred Robida, *Le Vingtième siècle. La Vie électrique* (1892), 35–36, 123; and an excerpt published separately: *Voyage de fiançailles au XXe siècle* (1892).
77. Avenel, *Les Mécanismes,* I, v, xiii.
78. "L'Argent," in Charles Péguy, *Oeuvres en prose, 1909–1914* (1961), 1103–04.
79. Renard, *Oeuvres,* II, 73.
80. Georges Lecomte, *Ma Traversée* (1949), 60; GT, November 26, 1887 (Paris), and January 2, 1888 (Savoie); Robert Sherard, *Twenty Years in Paris* (London, 1905), 76–77; André Siegfried, *Tableau politique de la France de l'Ouest* (1913), xvii.
81. *Journal,* III, 623.
82. Ragotte in Renard, *Oeuvres,* II, 336 (a bigger mirror is given her by her daughter, a servant in Paris, "habituée à la délicatesse, là-bas," 334). For Duroy, who had been unable to see himself full-length in his shaving mirror, see *Bel Ami* (1885), ch. 2. In a French château in the 1880s, "there isn't a decent dressing-table mirror, only one in an old silver frame about eight inches square, and that is sitting on the writing table." Glyn, *Visits of Elizabeth,* 67.
83. Gustave Flaubert, *Madame Bovary* (1857), ch. 4. Contemporaries of Flaubert confirm his evidence. In a bourgeois household of the Midi, described in Hyppolite Babou, *Les Payens innocents* (1858), 17, the daughter of the house "did her hair before half a mirror." In the midcentury country vicarage sketched in Ferdinand Fabre, *Mon Oncle Célestin. Moeurs cléricales* (1881), 24, the priest has only "a mirror narrow as a hand." Even that was often lacking in the countryside, where young peasant girls are shown, "using each other as mirrors," by their reflection in the other's eyes. Mme. Louis Figuier, "Le Franciman," in *Nouvelles languedociennes* (1860), 123.
84. Preface to *Pierre et Jean* (1887).

85. Louis Marcelin, ferblantier, to his son, in Paul Marcelin, *Souvenirs d'un passé artisanal* (Nîmes, 1967), 44.
86. Pierre-Jakez Hélias, *Le Cheval d'orgueil*, 507.

4. Affections and Disaffections

1. Pierre Gascar, *Terres de mémoire* (1979), 24, 32.
2. Nicole Morin, *Mari et femme autrefois en Poitou* (Poitiers, 1982), 127; Lorenz von Stein, *The History of the Social Movement in France, 1789–1850* (Totowa, N.J., 1964), 308, quoting Flora Tristan; Martine Ségalen, "Le Mari et la femme dans les proverbes du Sud de la France," *Annales du Midi*, (July 1975), 279.
3. Harry Eckstein, "Civic Inclusion and Its Discontents," *Daedalus* (Fall 1984), 128–31. Sylvère, *Toinon*, 16, 18, 51; Maurice Toesca, *Le Lycée de mon père* (1981), 44, 45; Abellio, *Dernières mémoires*, I, 84. Remember Balzac's remark: "Rien ne forme l'âme comme une dissimulation constante au sein de la famille" (Nothing tempers the spirit like constant dissimulation in the bosom of one's family); in *Une ténebreuse affaire*. In this context it is worth noting that of 1579 divorces granted in 1896, 779 affect day laborers (*journaliers*), and half of these were initiated by the wife. Jeanne Gaillard, "Les Migrants à Paris," *Ethnologie française* (April–June 1980), 134.
4. Ségalen, "Le Mari et la femme," 283; J. de Mouxy de Loche, *Histoire d'Aix-les-Bains* (Chambéry, 1900), I, 15.
5. Laisnel de La Salle, *Croyances et légendes du Centre de la France* (1875), II, 14. At Miramas, near Marseilles, young mothers were still being churched after the First World War. Bonnie Smith, *Confessions of a Concierge* (New Haven, 1985), 50. Guy Thuillier avers that pious ladies of Nevers continued to make their amends through the Second World War.
6. GT, March 2, 1847, Loire Assizes; Samuel Pyeatt Menefee, *Wives for Sale: An Ethnographic Study of British Popular Divorce* (New York, 1981), 269 n. 2, 31; *Lemouzi*, no. 48 (1967), 184–85.
7. Grand-Carteret, *XIXe Siècle*, 182–83.
8. Ségalen, "Le Mari et la femme," 285–86; Morin, *Mari et femme*, 144–45; for beaten husbands, ibid., 151; GT, April 1, 1896, Cour d'Appel, Bourges.
9. GT, October 11, 1884, Finistère Assizes. Eight years later a Breton veterinarian who had beaten and kicked his wife to death was condemned to serve six months in jail; GT, January 7, 1892, Ille-et-Vilaine. About the same time, a husband denounced by his wife for attempted poisoning, was forgiven by her in court, "à cause des enfants," and acquitted by the jury. GT, March 6, 1892. Note that the wife battered to death in Finistère would have poisoned her husband if she could. He beat her to it.
10. Jehan Rictus, *Le Coeur populaire* (1914), 54.
11. Alan Ryan, "The Domestic Trap," *Times Literary Supplement* (London), August 13, 1982, 872.
12. GT, February 2 and June 7, 1885.

13. For sensation, see Dabot, *Calendriers,* July 30, 1884 (at Saint Severin, there even opened a Brasserie du Divorce); for ratio, see S. C. Hause and A. R. Kenney, *Women's Suffrage and Social Politics in the French Third Republic* (Princeton, 1984), 22, and Désert in Dartiguenave, *Marginalité,* 235, who points out the steep rise of prosecutions for adultery, when it appeared that divorce claims could benefit from a judgment against the errant spouse.

14. *Journal,* IV, 373, March 15, 1893.

15. Sherard, *My Friends,* 204–16; De Maulny, *Les Bottines,* 32. In another vein, see GT, September 1, 1889, "Coupeur de nattes de cheveux."

16. Marcelin, *Souvenirs,* 28.

17. Danielle Delhome, Nicole Gault, and Josiane Gonthier, *Les Premières institutrices laïques* (1980), 229; Eugène Delard, "Les Dupourquet. Moeurs de province," *Revue des Deux Mondes,* December 15, 1891.

18. Ludovic O'Followell, *Bicyclette et organes génitaux* (1900), 8; Ménie Grégoire, *Telle que je suis* (1976), 141.

19. Guitard-Auviste, *Chardonne,* 15.

20. Ibid., 152, 154, 155. One might add the view expressed by Georges d'Avenel, *Les Français de mon temps* (n.d.), 217: "Though very prominent in imaginative literature, love plays a small part in the lives of normal men." As if to confirm this, Georges de Porto-Riche's successful play *Amoureuse* (1891) is about a man who has "sought refuge in the port of marriage," and who bids his wife to leave him in peace and satisfy her need for love in someone else's arms.

21. Hause and Kenney, *Women's Suffrage,* 22; Morin, *Mari et femme,* 63, 111, 163.

22. Georges Friedmann, ed., *Villes et campagnes* (1953), 344; Henri Boutet, *La Parisienne d'à présent* (1897), 111–12.

23. Henry James, *A Little Tour in France* (Boston, 1907), 90; Sherard, *My Friends,* 26–27.

24. Benjamin F. Martin, *The Hypocrisy of Justice in the Belle Epoque* (Baton Rouge, La., 1984).

25. See Marcel Thomas, *L'Affaire sans Dreyfus* (1961), 34–37. Significantly, one of Estherhazy's complaints was his wife's sensual attachment to him: "of all forms of love the lowest and least lasting."

26. When not otherwise indicated, the discussion in the following paragraphs owes much factual information to Hause and Kenney, *Women's Suffrage,* and James E. McMillan, *Housewife or Harlot* (Brighton, 1981).

27. Tribunal Correctionnel, Château-Thierry, February 6, 1903, in Henry Leyret, ed., *Les Nouveaux jugements du Président Magnaud* (1904), 80–86.

28. GP, January 14, 1905.

29. Edmée Charrier, *L'Evolution intellectuelle féminine* (1931), 301; Léonard, *Médecins de l'Ouest,* II, 999–1001; Guy Thuillier has attracted attention to the mounting tide of women clerks and to the revolution in everyday office life this brought. See Georges Lecomte, *Les Cartons verts* (1902), 47: "tout un frémissant peuple enjuponné, qu'on emploie à la place des hommes, par économie" (rustling, petticoated small fry employed in place of men for economy's sake); "sourde rancune contre les femmes appelées récemment à des

emplois jusqu'alors réservés aux hommes" (muffled resentment against women recently admitted to jobs hitherto reserved for men), 67.

30. Anne Delbée, *Une femme* (1982), 106.

31. See *Le Temps,* May 13 and 15, 1897; *Paris,* May 15, 1897; and Florence Baker, "Life and Education of Women Art Students in Paris, 1870–1914," ms 1984.

32. Charrier, *L'Evolution,* 296; Dabot, *Calendriers,* December 12, 1888, and January 24, 1889.

33. Hause and Kenney, *Women's Suffrage,* 24; GT, November 25 and December 1, 1897, March 22 and November 21, 1898, December 1, 6, 20, 1900, December 21, 1910; Dabot, *Calendriers,* November 14, December 4, and 9, 1900.

34. *La Nouvelle Mode,* December 23, 1900.

35. *La Science du Monde* (1859), 5; quoted in Philippe Perrot, *Les Dessus et les dessous de la bourgeoisie* (1981), 167.

36. H. Despaigne, *Le Code de la mode* (1866), 58. For fascinating glimpses of dressmakers' bills and prices, see GT, January 7, 1891; January 8, 1899; April 29, August 9, and October 9, 1901; GP, January 7, 1892. For normal women, see Marcel Jouhandeau, *Mémoires* (1951), II, 39–40.

37. Ly'onell, *L'Art de relever sa robe* (1862), 70; Eugène Chapus, *Manuel de l'homme et de la femme comme il faut* (1862), 138.

38. Grand-Carteret, *XIXe Siècle,* 340.

39. Octave Uzanne, *Les Modes de Paris* (1898), 194, 200–202, 224.

40. Yvonne Deslandres, *Le Costume. Image de l'homme* (1976), 245. All evidence suggests that it was foreign girls, especially English ones, who inspired French women to greater freedom of action. Margaret Betham-Edwards, *Anglo-French Reminiscences, 1875–1899* (London, 1900), 18: "No lady of independent means walks out unaccompanied in Provincial France, the thing is not to be thought of." Uzanne, *Les Modes,* 210, refers to the "intrusion" of foreign girls destabilizing schools and society. In their *Vie quotidienne des professeurs de 1870 à 1940,* Pierre Guiral and Guy Thuillier quote a school inspector's remarks in 1907: "Having spent a long time in England, Mlle B has adopted the free manners of English *misses.* She dares to walk alone on the ramparts. All Langres is scandalized, and her Principal lives in terrified expectation of an unpleasant incident."

41. Octove Uzanne, *Le Miroir du monde* (1888), 128, concludes the chapter on food with the sad note that meals are getting less important and sobriety is on the rise: "on s'observe, on craint les représailles de la digestion, on met quelque peu son estomac en interdit." (We watch ourselves, fear the reprisals of digestive processes, place the stomach under an interdict.)

42. Maulny, *Les Bottines,* 21.

43. *Petit Journal,* January 5, 1897; GT, April 11, 1900.

44. *La Nouvelle Mode,* January 9, 1898. See also Uzanne, *Les Modes,* 225, and Perrot, *Les Dessus et les dessous,* 282; Pierre Dufay, *Le Pantalon féminin* (1906), 303–304.

45. Uzanne, *La Femme à Paris* (1894), 10–11, Morin, *Mari et femme,* 25;

Madame Celnart, *Manuel des dames ou l'art de l'élégance* (1833), 37; quoted in Corbin, *Le Miasme*, 210; precept quoted in Dr. Goulin, *La Mode sous le point de vue hygiènique, médical et historique* (1846), 81–82. Pierre Bouchardon, *Souvenirs* (1953), 69, who tells the Forain story, adds that of the Guérèt lawyer who never bathes, explaining: "Simple. I sweat." Reminiscent of the Saintongeois who do as much: "Nous aut'pésants, j'attrapons de bonnes suées, o vous nettoie le corps!" (Us peasants, we work up a good sweat—it sure cleans the body!) Eugen Weber, *Peasants Into Frenchmen* (Stanford, 1976), 149.

46. Association des anciennes élèves du collège d'Aurillac, *Du Cours secondaire de jeunes filles d'Aurillac au lycée d'Etat de jeunes filles, 1905–1970* (Aurillac, 1972), 13. *Fin de Siècle*, June 17, 1897, printed a story about a bride on her wedding night, shocked at being approached by her lightly clad husband. "Didn't your mother warn you?" he asked. "She warned me not to take off my stockings if my feet weren't clean."

47. "Tuyaux de modestie," Uzanne, *La Femme*, 38; Yvette Guilbert, *Gil Blas Illustré*, October 30, 1892; Dufay, *Pantalon féminin*, passim.

48. Dufay, *Pantalon féminin*, 217, 272.

49. Louis Helly, *Cent ans de ski français* (Grenoble, 1968), 56, makes it clear that even women skiers benefited from this. In 1896 their recommended wear was the *culotte bouffante* used for cycling. This was followed by trousers held tight round the ankle to keep the snow out and, after 1918, by *le golfe*, kin to the earlier cycling pantaloons. Women's ski pants (*fuseaux*) were finally accepted in the 1930s.

50. *Fin de Siècle*, July 18, 1891. For the other side, see *Le Figaro*, January 2, 1892: "Les peintres, sculpteurs, médicins, reprouvent-ils . . . l'usage disgracieux, malsain et trompeur du corset?" (Do painters, sculptors, and medical men reprove the graceless, unhealthy, and deceptive use of the corset?)

51. Perrot, *Les Dessus et les dessous*, 281; Ludovic O'Followell, *Le Corset* (1905), 220.

52. Collette, *Mes Aprentissages* (1936), 19–20.

53. Dr. Gaches-Sarraute, articles of July and September 1895, quoted in her *Le Corset* (1900), 113, 125–31.

54. Ludovic O'Followell, *Le Corset. Etude Médicale* (1908), 253, 280–83.

55. See Diana Festa-McCormick, *Proustian Optics of Clothes* (Stanford, 1984), 11, 54, 75–76.

56. Poiret, *En habillant*, 63. For the charm of complications without practical utility or evident necessity, see "Le Monde de Marcel Proust," in Madeleine Delpierre, ed., *De la mode et des lettres* (1984), 60–68.

57. *La Nouvelle Mode*, October 28, 1900.

5. The Endless Crisis

1. A. Mabille de Poncheville, *Vie de Verhaeren* (1953), 363.

2. Albert Malet and Jules Isaac, *La France de 1789 à la fin du XIXe siècle.*

Enseignement primarie supérieur. Deuxième année (1910), 252. Albert Malet, *Histoire de France. 3e année. Enseignement secondaire des jeunes filles* (1907), 500.

3. Emile Boutmy, *The English People: A Study of Their Political Psychology* (London, 1904), is a translation of the original French version of 1901. See also Victor Dujardin, *Histoire du Valois* (Céret, 1888), 162: "L'Angleterre et l'Allemagne, voilà les deux ennemies de la France!" And *Le Vélo*, November 6, 1898, "L'Ennemi séculaire," which focuses on Britain alone.

4. Malet, *Histoire de France*, 500.

5. Lille, July 6, 1887; Douai, February 10, 1890; Sceaux, April 1, 1898; GT, January 14, 1900, Tribunal Correctionnel, Boulogne-sur-Mer.

6. Cambon, *Correspondance*, I, 430.

7. Ibid.; J. E. C. Bodley, *France* (London, 1898), I, 29–30.

8. Camille Mauclair, *Servitude et grandeur littéraires* (1922), 64; Sherard, *Twenty Years in Paris*, 114.

9. Bernard Auffray, *Pierre de Margerie* (1976), 28.

10. Clermont-Tonnerre, *Mémoires* I, 55; GT, November 8, 1897, Trouville; see also GT, August 20, 1883, Cour d'Appel, Chambéry.

11. Henry James, *Parisian Sketches: Letters to the New York Tribune, 1875–1876* (New York, 1957), 78; Fidus (Eugène Loudun), *Journal de dix ans* (1886), II, 37; Jules Clarétie, *Candidat!* (1887), 18.

12. Goncourt, *Journal*, II, 819 (May 31, 1871); Jeanne Bouvier, *Mes Mémoires* (1983), 74; Dabot, *Calendriers*, March 20, 1883.

13. Dr. Rommel [Alfred Pernessin, fils], *Au Pays de la Revanche* (Geneva, 1886), 85.

14. James, *Parisian Sketches*, 77; Cambon, *Correspondance*, I, 73.

15. Denis Brogan, *The Development of Modern France* (London, 1947), 183.

16. Louis Lépine, *Mes Souvenirs* (1929), 78–79; Charles Braibant, *Félix Faure à l'Elysée* (1963), 62.

17. See Bodley, *France*, II, 282, 293.

18. GT, February 3, 1888, and August 6, 1888; Pierre Daubert, *Du Port illégal de costume et de décoration* (1904), 76.

19. Brogan, *Modern France*, 202; Cambon, *Correspondance*, I, 319; General Zurlinden, *Mes Souvenirs depuis la guerre, 1871–1906* (1913), 159.

20. Maxime du Camp, *Souvenirs d'un demi-siècle* (1949), II, 235; Pierre Decharme, *Les Petites coupures de billets* (1911), 34; Braibant, *Félix Faure*, 61–62.

21. GT, March 31, 1889, and through the summer of that year.

22. Bodley, *France*, II, 273.

23. Jean Bousquet-Melon, *Louis Barthou et la circonscription d'Oloron* (1972), 83; Brogran, *Modern France*, 284.

24. Bodley, *France*, II, 178, 180.

25. GT, December 18, 1892; E. de Marcère, *Entretiens et souvenirs politiques* (1894), II, 217, 327; see also Goncourt, *Journal*, IV, 338 (December 24, 1892).

26. Cambon, *Correspondance*, I, 362–63; Freycinet, *Souvenirs*, 464–55.

27. GT, November 20, 1887, Aisne Assizes; March 22, 1888, Loire Assizes; February 15, 1890, Allier Assizes; passim.

28. Dabot, *Calendriers*, March 28, June 25, 1892; GT, July 6, 1890, ff., "Affaire des nihilistes russes," for Ravachol, GT, April 27, 1892.

29. GT, April 25–26, 1892, Seine Assizes; June 23, 1892, Loire Assizes.

30. Ernest Raynaud, *Souvenirs de police* (1923), 305 ff.; GT, December 9, 1893, January 11, April 28, 29, 1894.

31. See the Paris press, February–April 1894, GT, March 31, for fish at Easter, July 7 and August 4 for Caserio's trial. Within a few hours of Carnot's murder, Italian shops and cafés in Lyons were being ransacked and Italians had to be protected by the army. See Maître Bermann, *L'Assassinat de Sadi-Carnot* (Lyons, 1962), 20–24. Cambon, *Correspondance*, I, 377, noted the next day: "Il n'est pas mauvais qu'on le [Caserio] suppose anarchiste, mais j'imagine qu'il y a là tout simplement quelque vendetta d'Aigues-Mortes" (It's not a bad thing to have [Caserio] taken for an anarchist, but I imagine that it's no more than some vendetta from Aigues-Mortes). There, shortly before, Italian workingmen had been attacked by French workingmen.

32. GT, February 28, 1894, Seine Assizes.

33. Léauthier, GT, February 24, 1894, Seine Assizes. See also May 31, 1894, Nord Assizes, and June 29, 1894, Compiègne (Oise).

34. GT, January 12, 1887; M. Bérard des Glajeux, *Souvenirs d'un Président d'Assizes, 1880–1890* (1892), 108.

35. GT, November 4, 1889, Seine Assizes, April 30, 1893, Alpes-Maritimes, May 27, 1893, Seine. There were intellectual justifications for what afficionados described as "individual repossession." Elysée Reclus's nephew Paul, writing in *La Révolte*, Nov. 21, 1891, explained that in existing society there was no essential difference between work and theft, and denounced "the groundless claim that there is an honest way to earn a living, work; and a dishonest way, robbery."

36. Ernest Raynaud, *Souvenirs* (1926), 46.

37. Edward Lockspeiser, *Débussy. Sa Vie et sa pensée* (1980), 273. At that time, both Vlaminck and Derain proclaimed anarchist sympathies.

38. Adolphe Retté, *Au Pays des lys noirs* (1913), 168, 170; Ernest Raynaud, *En Marge de la mêlée symboliste* (1936), 129; Carassus, *Le Snobisme*, 387; Laurent Tailhade, *Commérages de Tybalt* (1914), 200. But *L'Anarchie*, May 9, 1912, "Des hommes," had compared the gangsters' moral beauty to that of Spartans.

39. Emile Goudeau, *Paris qui consomme* (1893), 274, gives the menu of a "Festin bomboidal": "Potage à la nitro-glycérine, Hors d'oeuvres avariés, Glandes de veau mélinite, Canetons au sang de Beaurepaire [after the Public Prosecutor, Quesnay de Beaurepaire], Langouste explosible, Bombe Ravachol."

40. Léon Blum, *Au théatre* (1909), II, 179; *Figaro*, June 19, 1891.

41. For Adam, see his *Critique des moeurs* (1893), 255–60, *Le Soleil des morts* (1897), and *La Ville lumière* (1904). See also, Carassus, *Le Snobisme*, 379, 383. Note Goncourt's view of the "parti de l'anarchie, en train de recruter tous les ratés, tous les cocus, tous les bossus, tous les mécontents physiques et

moraux de la vie" (party of anarchy, busy recruiting all the failures, all the cuckolds, all the misfits, all the physical and moral malcontents), in *Journal*, IV, 241 (May 1, 1892).

42. Sylvain Bonmariage, *Le Sang des pharisiens* (1939), 86; Camille Mauclair, *Servitude et grandeur littéraires*, 107–08, 112–23, esp. 115. This also applies to paragraph following.

43. Retté, *Au Pays des lys noirs*, 52, quotes "the iconoclast hymn": "Les rois sont morts, les dieux aussi / Demain nous vivrons sans souci / Sans foi ni loi, sans esclavages / Nous sommes les briseurs d'images."

44. Emile Zola, *Paris* (1898), 37–38, 444, 402.

45. Ibid., 602.

46. General Legrand-Girarde, *Un Quart de siècle au service de la France* (1954), 123, 124.

47. Maurice Baumont, *Au Coeur de l'affaire Dreyfus* (1976), ch. I, "L'Espionnite"; Francine Amaury, *Le Petit Parisien* (1972), II, 888; *Petit Parisien*, June 8, 1895, "La Réforme du code militaire"; GT, July 11, 1884, Conseil de Guerre, Lille; Dabot, *Calendriers*, December 23, 1894: "Tout le monde s'écrie 'Comment! on ne l'a pas condamné à mort?'" (Everyone cries out: "Why has he not been condemned to death?").

48. Dabot, *Calendriers*, November 20 and 21, 1897.

49. Legrand-Girarde, *Un Quart de siècle*, 133, 142, 162, 196; Braibant, *Félix Faure*, 139; Zurlinden, *Mes Souvenirs*, 212–17. René Rémond, *L'Anticléricalisme en France de l'ancien régime à nos jours* (1976), 201.

50. Michel Robida, *Ces bourgeois de Paris* (1955), 150; Legrand-Girarde, *Un Quart de siècle*, 148; Cambon, *Correspondance*, 436–37; André Bellesort, *Le Collège et le monde* (1941), 31; Poiret, *En habillant*, 45.

51. Of the Third Republic's fifteen heads of state, only four served out their full terms: five resigned, two were murdered, one went mad, one died in office, one was forced out of office, and the last died in prison.

52. GT, February 24, 1899 commented: "il ne faut rien exagérer" (let's not exaggerate).

53. Abel Combarieu, *Sept ans à l'Elysée* (1932), 3 ff. See his notes for February 18 and July 31, 1899.

54. Cambon, *Correspondance*, II, letter of September 12, 1899; Legrand-Girarde, *Un Quart de siècle*, 232–33; Emmanuel Berl, *Interrogatoire* (1976), 23; Douglas Johnson, *France and the Dreyfus Affair* (London, 1966), 179; Henry de Bruchard, *1896–1901. Petites mémoires du temps de la Ligue* (1912?), 267.

55. GT, January 1–3, 1900, Seine Assizes; January 27, 1901, Tribunal Correctionnel, Paris.

56. GT, February 11, 1906, Tribunal de Château-Thierry (Aisne).

57. In *Rural Society and French Politics* (Princeton, 1984), Michael Burns argues convincingly that it was neither very much nor very far.

58. Combarieu, *Sept ans*, 56 ff.

59. Ibid., 14, 67; GT, February 2, 1898; Octave Aubert, *De l'Histoire et des histoires* (1943), 60, 78; Bousquet-Melon, *Louis Barthou*, 114; Jules Huret,

Tout yeux, tout oreilles (1901), 310–83, esp. 372–83: "Une commune drey-fusarde," Lédignan (Gard).

60. Paul Adam, *Le Mystère des foules* (1895), I, 2.

61. Legrand-Girarde, *Un Quart de siècle*, 207. See also Braibant, *Félix Faure*, 178, and Combarieu, *Sept ans*, 40.

62. Dabot, *Calendriers*, November 15, 1899; Daniel Halévy, *Pays parisiens* (1932), 177–78.

63. *Revue des Deux Mondes*, November 1, 1901, 232; Combarieu, *Sept ans*, 228–29, conversation with Delcassé on February 22, 1903; Jacques Aubert et al., *L'Etat et sa police en France* (1979), 211.

64. Maurice Lucas, *Luttes politiques et sociales à Douarnenez, 1890–1925* (Morlaix, 1975), 84; Alexandre Charbin, *La Vie chère* (Lyons, 1912), 164.

65. E. Pataud and E. Pouget, *Comment nous ferons la Révolution* (1909); E. Pataud, *Demain* (1911?); Ernest La Jeunesse, *Des Soirs, des gens, des choses* (1911), 175–76.

66. André Bernardy, *Remontons la Gardonnenque* (Uzès, 1961), 10–11.

6. A Wolf to All

1. Alan Mitchell, "Contre-espionage et mentalité xénophobe," *Revue d'histoire moderne et contemporaine* (July–September), 489, passim.

2. Theodore Louveau, director of the *Théatre des Variétés* went under the name of Fernand Samuel, the better to compete with other theater managers. See Lockspeiser, *Débussy*, 222. Henri Bataille, in *La Femme nue* (1908) alludes to a certain Bertrand who calls himself Arnheim, "pour mieux épouvanter le marché" (the better to scare the competition). Clifford H. Bissell, *Les Conventions du théatre bourgeois contemporain en France* (1930), 106. Also Sylvain Bonmariage, *Catherine et ses amis* (Gap, 1949), 95.

3. Alexandre Hepp, *Paris tout nu* (1885), 169; Lockspeiser, *Débussy*, 224.

4. Anti-Semites early adopted a national-socialist stance familiar to the twentieth century. Their relations with the anarchists are not so well remembered. Yet when, in 1890, the most forceful of anti-Semites, the Marquis de Morès, ran for election to the Paris Municipal Council, he worked closely with the anarchists, helped them with money, and was hauled into court for his activities on the first of May. GT, June 5, 1890. In 1892 Marius Tournadre, unsuccessful candidate in the Gaillon [Opera] district, who had distinguished himself by the invention of a "procreative mattress," ran as an Anti-Semite Anarchist, supporter of Malthusianism and Women's Emancipation. Roger Girard, *Journal d'un Auvergnat de Paris* (1982), 171, 178.

5. Amaury, *Le Petit Parisien*, 888; Girard, *Journal*, 198.

6. Julie Manet, *Journal, 1893–1899* (1979), 255.

7. Doris Bensimon-Donath, *Sociodémographie des Juifs de France et d'Algérie* (1976), 166 ff.; Rabi, *Anatomie du Judaisme français* (1962), 67; David Cohen, *La Promotion des Juifs en France à l'époque du Second Empire* (Aix, 1980), II, 420.

8. In December 1897 one Auvergnat was hauled into court for hitting a man who had called him "Auvergnat." The court refused to admit attenuating circumstances; nevertheless, the term clearly was considered insulting. Girard, *Journal*, 246–47.

9. For working-class xenophobia in 1848, see, among many others, Lord Normanby, *Une année de révolution* (1858), 122, 169, 239–40, for hostility to English workmen, 300 for hostility to Savoyards. For the 1880s and 1890s, see Girard, *Journal*, 120, 246, and Paul Gemähling, *Travailleurs au rabais. La Lutte syndicale contre les sous-concurrences ouvrières* (1910), 200–201.

10. For Alsatians, see GT, July 17, 1883. For Italians, see Anne-Marie Faidutti-Rudolph, *L'Immigration italienne dans le Sud-Ouest de la France* (Gap, 1964), I, 19–20.

11. For some instances, see GT, October 9, 1884, Var Assizes; April 22, 1885, Meuse; May 20, 1885, Aube; September 27–28, 1886, Isère; January 19, 1888; November 25, 1888, Aisne; October 2, 1889, Marne; December 28, 1893, Charente; January 3, 1894, Chambéry; May 11–12, 1896, Haute-Savoie; May 2–3, 1898, Conseil d'Etat on violence in Meurthe-et-Moselle; June 10, 1898, Savoie; Yves LeFebvre, *L'Ouvrier étranger et la protection du travail national* (1901), 14; Faidutti-Rudolph, *L'immigration italienne*, I, 210; and A. Andréani, *La Condition des étrangers en France et la législation sur la nationalité française* (1896), for the law of August 8, 1893, designed to "protect national labor."

12. GT, May 20, 1885, Aube Assizes; LeFebvre, *L'Ouvrier étranger*, 7, 11; Gemähling, *Travailleurs*, 223, passim; Georges Deherne, *Les Classes moyennes. Etudes sur le parasitisme social* (1912), 104–06. For Gambetta, see Edouard Drumont, *La France juive* (1888 ed. by Société générale de Librairie Catholique), xxvii.

13. Bodley, *France*, I, 204.

14. *Journal de Fidus sous la République opportuniste* (1888), 133.

15. Quoted by Bodley, *France*, I, 159.

16. J.-H. Réveille-Parise, *Physiologie et hygiène des hommes livrés aux travaux de l'esprit* (1837), I, 97.

17. Balzac, *Le Curé de Tours*; quoted in Francois Lebrun, ed., *Histoire des Pays de la Loire* (1972), 377; Armand Audiganne, *Les Populations ouvrières et les industries de la France* (1854), I, 241; Charles-Louis Philippe, *Dans la petite ville* (1910), 56.

18. Bodley, *France*, I, 199; *L'Economiste français*, February 9 and March 29, 1884; Rommel, *Au Pays*, ch. 4, esp. 74–75. Sherard, *Twenty Years in Paris*, 179, tells the story of Edison, in Paris for the Exhibition of 1889, struck by "the absolute laziness of the people over here. When do these people work? What do they work at? . . . People here seem to have established an elaborate system of loafing." This is unjust, but characteristic of some consistent foreign impressions.

19. Emile de Saint-Auban, *L'Idée sociale au théatre* (1901), 14.

20. Bodley, *France*, II, 366.

21. The chapter on owls is even shorter.

22. *Souvenirs du Baron de Frénilly* (1908), xii. Whatever its origin, fear seems to have played a part in its appeal, as it did for the proscript's son crying "To the guillotine!" as prisoners were being herded to the guillotine. "At least keep quiet," one of his father's friends advised. And he: "But I'm afraid."

23. Leonard A. Morrison, *Rambles in Europe* (Boston, n.d.), 347; Clermont-Tonnerre, *Mémoires*, I, 47.

24. Deherme, *Les Classes moyennes*, 12, and introduction.

25. Guitard-Auviste, *Chardonne*, 178.

7. The Old Arts and the New

1. See Joëlle Caullier, "Musique et décadence," *Romantisme*, 42 (1983), 143, and *Revue des Deux Mondes* (February 15, 1872), 843, for a violent attack on German musical imperialism.

2. In 1874, the *Grand Dictionnaire* of Pierre Larousse described *phonographe* as a kind of phoneticist, "auteur qui s'occupe de prononciation figurée" (author who works on questions of figurative pronunciation). Larousse's supplement of 1877 noted Edison's marvelous invention—"une des inventions les plus étonnantes de l'esprit humain" (one of the most astounding inventions of the human mind)—but questioned whether the instrument could ever become practical and be brought into general use.

3. Jacques de Lacretelle, *Face à l'événement* (n.d.), 76.

4. In Marcel Prévost, *Les Demi-vierges* (1894), 39, the fashionable company is off to see *Die Walkyrie* at the Opera. One lady declares it is not a *spectacle convenable* for her daughters. These obviously know the libretto perfectly, but the performance is a public one, "and others see what we hear."

5. See Caullier, "Musique," 141; she also notes the contemporary popularity of funeral music, whether from Berlioz, Beethoven, Wagner, or Strauss (139).

6. Goncourt, *Journal*, February 23, 1893, IV, 368.

7. September 18, 1886.

8. Zayed, *Huysmans*, 341; Gustave Coquiot, *Le Vrai J.-K. Huysmans* (1913), 4; Gabriel A. Fauré, *Mallarmé à Tournon* (1946), 20; see also 118.

9. On politics, see Louis Bertrand, *Hippolyte porte-couronnes* (1932), 145; J.-H. Reveille-Parise, *Physiologie*, II, 65. On money, see H. P. Clive, *Pierre Louÿs, 1870–1925* (Oxford, 1978), 28; Lucie Delarue-Mardrus, *Mes Mémoires* (1938), 95; Camille Mauclair, *Servitude*, 51–52, 61–62.

10. Clive, *Pierre Louÿs*, 120.

11. Gabriel Vicaire and Henri Beauclair, *Les Déliquescences d'Adoré Floupette* (1911), first published in 1885. Rémy Saint-Maurice's *Décadents et Detraqués* (n.d.), 800, argues that the crazed gang of "alcoholics and rachitics" would never have received any notice were it not for the "véritable coup de tam-tam" of les Déliquescences. Yvette Guilbert, *La Chanson*, 205–206, includes a song written for her about this time by Jean Lorrain, "Décadente," that begins; "Je suis une jeune fille symboliste / Aux bandeaux plats et frèle et triste / Je rêve

tout le long du jour / Cherchant des consonnances rares / Et des prosopopées bizarres / Symbolisant le mot 'amour' " (I am a maiden symbolist / With flattened plaits and frail and triste / Dreaming all day of a way / To discover harmonies rare / And personifications bizarre / That symbolize the word for love).

12. *Le Décadent* (now a monthly) December 1887: "Ballade pour les Décadents": "Quelques uns dans tout ce Paris / Nous vivons d'orgueil et de dêche / D'alcool bien que trop épris / Nous buvons surtout de l'eau fraiche / En cassant la croûte un peu sêche."

13. *Le Décadent,* December 15, 1888.

14. A. Baju, "Le Fumisme," *Le Décadent,* September 4, 1886.

15. February 15, 1889.

16. See Mauclair, *Servitude,* 15, and René Doumic, "Littérature et dégénérescence," *Revue des Deux Mondes* (January 15, 1894), 445.

17. Doumic, "Littérature."

18. Jules Huret, *Enquète sur l'évolution littéraire* (1891).

19. Victor Brombert, *Victor Hugo and the Visionary Novel* (Cambridge, Mass., 1984), 75.

20. Ibid., 67.

21. Philip Gilbert Hamerton, *French and English. A Comparison* (Boston, 1891), 188–89: "the general rule is that a Frenchman will profess to admire what he thinks he ought to admire."

22. Bernard Knox, "Visions of the Grand Prize," *New York Review of Books,* September 27, 1984, 21.

23. Eugenia W. Herbert, *The Artist and Social Reform: France and Belgium, 1885–1898* (New Haven, 1961), 41; Jacques Lethève, *Vie Quotidienne des artistes français au XIXe siècle* (1968).

24. Alfred de Foville, *La Transformation des moyens de transport* (1880), 301; Maurice Talmeyr, *La Décadence au XXe siècle* (1907), 14.

25. Vicomte d'Avenel, quoted in *Histoire de la France urbaine,* IV, 433.

26. Jacques de Lacretelle, *Les Vivants et leur ombre* (1977), 8; GT, October 1, 1897, Tribunal de Commerce de la Seine.

27. AN, F17 11630, July 31, 1912.

28. Even catalogs and calendars, however, spread Paris fashions, aspirations, and points of view to rural realms that they had never reached before. So did photographs and picture postcards, which revealed France, and themselves, to the French. See Henri Chardon, *Voyages et voyageurs dans le Maine* (Le Mans, 1906), 5.

29. *La Décadence esthétique* (1888), 32, 48–49, 56–57.

30. Albert Robida, *Le XIXe siècle* (1888) tells the story of Renoir's asking Challemel-Lacour to publish an article in *La République française* on the Impressionist Exhibition of 1881 and being told: "We can do nothing for you; you are revolutionaries." Gambetta intervened and the article was written.

31. Crespelle, *Les Maîtres,* 41; Dabot, *Calendriers,* March 9, 1897.

32. Bonmariage, *Mémoires fermés* (1951), 271.

33. Camille Mauclair in *Le Figaro,* quoted in Crespelle, *Les Maîtres,* 35. Vlaminck confirms that the subversive character attributed to his paintings was not unfounded. In *Portraits avant décès* (1943), 110, he indicates that his use of pure color was for him the equivalent of throwing a bomb. "Given its individualistic and libertarian tendencies, if anyone personified Fauvism, it would be Ravachol."

34. Crespelle, *Les Maîtres,* 35. Similarly, Vlaminck, *Portraits,* 75–76, recalls that a provincial politician bought one of his canvases and one of Derain's for 100 francs each to present to his son-in-law whom he detested.

35. But Sisley himself died poor in 1899. See Albert Boime, "Les Hommes d'affaires et les arts en France au 19e siècle," *Actes de la Recherche en sciences sociales,* 28 (June 1979), 64–67; *La Nouvelle Mode,* September 16, 1900, about "le modern style." The latter appears to have caught on some years before: Marcel Prévost's *Demi-Vierges* (1894), 11, begins with the description of a room in a Paris apartment whose furniture reflected "ce goût d'outre-Manche, amusant et un peu faux, ou se réfugie l'élégance moderne" (that taste from across the Channel, amusing and a bit spurious, in which modern elegance takes refuge).

36. See Crespelle, *Les Maîtres,* 191–92. But Derain (*Lettres,* 173) wrote to Vlaminck in 1907: "As-tu vu les *Indépendants*? . . . Je ne pense pas . . . que c'est par les Indépendants qu'on peut arriver. C'est bien entre gens de métier. Mais pas pour le public, ni l'étranger" (Have you seen the [exhibition of the] Independents? . . . I don't think . . . that's the way we'll forge ahead. It's all right for professionals. But not for the public, or for foreigners). The latter, he thought, were more likely to buy paintings than were the French.

37. Valéry, *Degas,* 106.

8. Theater

1. Pierre Giffard, *La Vie au théatre* (1888), 2. "If you really want to be known in literature, you have to be on the stage," insisted Goncourt in 1892, "because the theater is all the literature a lot of people know"; *Journal,* IV, 186.

2. Antoine, *Le Théâtre* (1932), I, 264–65.

3. Ibid., 293–94, 307; Lockspeiser, *Débussy,* 130–31. One wonders about the role of wealthy patrons with artistic aspirations. Thus, Count Stanislas Rzwuski, whose one-act play *Comte Witold* was staged by the Théatre Libre, was a large Polish landowner fascinated by gambling and the theater. Gustave Guiches, *Le Spectacle* (1932), 44–46.

4. Antoine, *Théatre,* 322; René Peter, *Le Théatre et la vie sous la 3e République* (1947), 80, 107.

5. Peter, *Le Théâtre,* 290; Antoine, *Théatre,* 341. Roger Shattuck, *The Banquet Years* (New York, 1968), 209, claims that "this single performance assured Jarry's celebrity far beyond literary circles." One wonders just how far beyond. When Jarry died ten years later he was still unknown beyond the avant-garde, his celebrity remained a confidential affair.

6. Peter, *Le Théâtre,* 158–61.

7. *Le Figaro,* which loved the play, described it as *du sublime aimable* (amiable sublimity), which may strike some as a contradiction in terms. Jacques de Lacretelle, *Face à l'évènement,* 136.

8. Antoine, *Théatre,* 350. "At last we shall be able to talk about another love than that of humanity," wrote Jules Renard to Mme. Edmond Rostand, after he had seen the general rehearsal of *Cyrano. Correspondance* (1954), 154, December 28, 1897.

9. Antoine, *Théatre,* 419, 486.

10. Clifford H. Bissell, *Les Conventions du théatre bourgeois contemporain en France, 1887–1914* (1930), ch. III, "L'amour, sujet principal du théatre bourgeois contemporain." But see also 86, and compare Peter, *Le Théatre,* 34, 292 and Guiches, *Le Spectacle,* 268.

11. Peter, *Le Théatre,* 50.

12. This, presumably, would save all the trouble of living for themselves.

13. Georges Moynet, *Trucs et décors* (1893), 402.

14. Michael Booth, *Victorian Spectacular Theatre, 1850–1910* (London, 1981), 9; M. J. Meynet, *L'Envers du théatre* (1874), 3.

15. Meynet, *L'Envers,* 153 ff.; Percy Fitzgerald, *The World Behind the Scenes* (London, 1881), 91.

16. Fitzgerald, *Behind the Scenes.*

17. Meynet, *L'Envers,* 138; Fitzgerald, *Behind the Scenes,* 101, 242; Booth, *Victorian Theatre,* 58, 28; quoting Henry James, "After the Play," *New Review,* I (June 1889), 34–35. One recalls Henri Heine's view that since French political life absorbs the best comedians, only mediocre talents are left for real theater. *Lutèce* (1861 ed.), 40–41.

18. Fitzgerald, *Behind the Scenes,* 41.

19. Booth, *Victorian Theatre,* 3, passim.

20. Terence Rees, *Theatre Lighting in the Age of Gas* (London, 1978), 8; Meynet, *L'Envers,* 109.

21. Fitzgerald, *Behind the Scenes,* 29–30; GT, November 17, 1887, ff. After the fire, the Undersecretary of State for Fine Arts was alleged to say that his daughter never went to the theater without a silk ladder rolled under her coat. Giffard, *La Vie au théatre,* 89. The fire that charred the Théatre Français in 1900 would be caused by a short circuit.

22. Fitzgerald, *Behind the Scenes,* 15, 19; Georges Favre, ed., *Correspondance de Paul Dukas* (1971), 12; Emile de Saint-Auban, *Un pélérinage à Bayreuth* (1892), 57, 336.

23. André de Lorde, *La Galérie des monstres* (1928), 54, tells of running into apaches one night when returning from the theater, and being spared: "I often go to the Grand Guignol and I've often seen your phiz [face] on the program," says *la Terreur de Barbès.* In 1907 an English import, *Raffles,* would initiate a successful series of detective plays, soon imitated by Maurice Leblanc with his *Arsène Lupin* (1907).

24. Bernard Shaw in the *Saturday Review,* January 1, 1898; Fitzgerald, *Behind the Scenes,* 3–4; Peter, *Le Théatre,* 113 ff. Antoine, *Théatre,* 294, 297, glumly

notes that while in 1893 the Théâtre de l'Art's single matinée of Maeterlinck's *Pelléas et Mélisande,* though an artistic sensation, went over with a dull thud, *Miss Dollar,* the operetta by Messager, filled the Nouveau Théâtre for eighteen months, "thanks to seven dancers executing a ballet in the air while hanging by wires from the highest tier."

25. Quoted in Bissell, *Conventions,* 93.

26. Bernard Auffray, *Pierre de Margerie* (1976), 26; Marquis de Bonneval, *La Vie de château* (1978), 104. Giffard, *La Vie au théâtre,* 75, gives slightly lower prices for everyday shows: a seat 5 francs; a loge 10–15,000 francs per year, for one night a week. He also describes, 139–40, the common people in the gallery, "sallow, vicious, and ugly," throwing down apple cores, orange peel, and even benches. "Let a panic break out [presumably from a fire], and they'll rob you blind."

27. Haussonville, "Le Combat contre le vice," *Revue des Deux Mondes* (January 1, 1887), 133–34; Georges Deherme, *Les Classes moyennes* (1912), 156.

28. Lucien Descaves, *Souvenirs d'un ours* (1946), 10; Paul Marcelin, *Souvenirs d'un passé artisanal* (Nimes, 1967), 20.

29. Antoine, *Théâtre,* 419. For instances of an ill-known subject, see Sirius Ravel, *Les Enfants de la balle. Histoire d'un théâtre ambulant* (Toulon, 1936); Max Dearly, *Mémoires* (1946), 86; and GT, July 19, 1888, about the *theatre forain de M. Papillon,* still showing *Geneviève de Brabant.*

30. Guy Bechtel, *1907. La Grande Révolte du Midi* (1976), 30–31; and AN, F^7 12794, Préfêt Hérault, May 1907, on Albert's career.

31. GT, October 1, 1890, Tribunal Civil, Rennes; GT, April 14, 1892, Tribunal Correctionnel, Toulon; Marcel Jouhandeau, *Mémorial* (1950), II, 72.

32. Frederic LeGuyader, *Quimper-Théâtre. Esquisse d'histoire locale* (Quimper, 1904): "Désormais, grace aux soins du plus zélé des Maires, / Puisque Quimper n'a pas des troupes à séjour, / Paris nous fournira les Nouveautés du jour."

33. A.-J.-A. Lobry, *Les Provinciaux* (1921), 132; Alfred de Foville, *La Transformation,* 414; Francisque Sarcey, *Souvenirs de jeunesse* (1885), 53; Henri Boutet, *Almanach pour 1899. Les Heures de la Parisienne* (1899), 81.

34. *Magazin pittoresque,* quoted in *Histoire de la France Urbaine,* IV, 467. They also provided a new danger of death. In May 1897 the fire that killed 120 people at the Bazar de la Charité resulted from the new attraction. The assistant operator had struck a match which had ignited fumes, the film had caught fire, and within a few minutes the whole hall was ablaze.

35. See, for example, Jean Cruppi in *Revue des Deux Mondes* (January 1896), 121; GT, June 8, 1912, on an execution at Riom, which attracted some six thousand spectators, and not just peasants and workmen. "Des autos et des cars ont amené durant toute la première partie de la nuit de Clermont et de Vichy un public élégant . . . venu comme pour une fête, avec des paniers de champagne et de provisions" (through the night, buses and motorcars brought an elegant public from Clermont and Vichy . . . come as to a festival, with baskets of food and champagne).

36. Archives départementales, Indre, M2866, Commissaire de police, Chateau-

roux, December 29, 1880; Jacques-Charles, *Le Caf'Conc'* (1966), 200; Edmonde Charles-Roux, *L'Irrégulière* (1974), 119, 125; Guilbert, *La Chanson,* 79.

37. Talmeyr, *La Décadence,* 17–18; Guilbert, *La Chanson,* 56, 76.
38. Jean-Paul Chavent, *Limousin. Le Temps retrouvé* (Limoges, 1977), 74; Charles-Roux, *L'Irrégulière,* 119, 125.

9. Curists and Tourists

1. Pierre Larousse, "Touriste," *Dictionnaire universel du XIXe siècle* (1876). Like "touriste," whose use was popularized by Stendhal's *Mémoires d'un touriste* (1838), "curiste" is a nineteenth-century term invented to describe the growing number of visitors taking the waters or some other cure at a mineral spa.
2. Jean de Pange, *Comment j'ai vu 1900* (1965), II, 97 ff. Alfred de Foville, *La Transformation des moyens de transport* (1880), 407, quoting Edouard Laboulaye. Nor did this apply to the rich alone. Painted in the early 1880s, George Seurat's canvases of folk relaxing by the river at Asnières or La Grande Jatte show a mixture of classes. Another witness is even more explicit about the factory hands, office workers, shop assistants, working men and women, who pour out on Sundays to eat, drink, and get their fill of sky and shade, nature and fresh air in the woods of Vincennes and other beauty spots accessible to them. "For thousands of proletarians, the lakeshore was the only countryside they knew—a dreamland". Louis Besse, *La Débauche* (1898), 180.
3. *A Day in the Country* (Los Angeles Museum of Art, 1984), 81, 146; Abel Combarieu, *Sept ans à l'Elysée, avec le Président Emile Loubet* (1932), 33.
4. Baudelaire had already remarked that man likes man so much that, when he flees the town, it is to seek the crowd, that is, to recreate town life in the countryside (*Journaux intimes, mon coeur mis à nu,* xxxvi). A cartoon of the *Vie Parisienne* showed a couple, at Vichy, contemplating a villa for rent: "Here's a pretty cottage far from everything, on the river's bank. Shall we take it?" "God no! It would look as if we were in the country."
5. G. Bruno, *Le Tour de France par deux enfants* (1975 ed.), 239.
6. Even in the mid-1880s, W. Graham Robertson found Biarritz "hardly more than a village, in the midst of quite unspoilt country" and cork woods. *Life Was Worth Living* (London, n.d.), 101.
7. Etienne Chabrol, *L'Evolution du thermo-climatisme* (1933), 149; Armand Wallon, *La Vie quotidienne dans les villes d'eaux, 1850–1914* (1981), 20.
8. Gabriel Pérouse, *La Vie d'autrefois à Aix-les-Bains* (Chambéry, 1922), 177; Jean Kastener, *Le Passé de Plombières* (Plombières, 1958), 21.
9. Comte de Fortis, *Amélie, ou voyage à Aix-les-Bains* (Turin, 1829), I, 4; Jean Galup, *Le Mont-Dore et ses fantômes* (Aurillac, 1948), 41, 47, 168.
10. Galup, *Mont-Dore,* 83, 93, 118; Louis Laussédat, *Une Cure au Mont-Dore* (1868), 30; J. D. Haumonté, *Plombières ancien et moderne* (1905), 307; Jules de Mouxy de Loches, *Histoire d'Aix-les-Bains* (Chambéry, 1898), I, 387, 410; Pérouse, *Vie d'autrefois,* 268, 277.

11. Emile Vidal, *Rapport général sur le service médical des eaux minérales de la France pendant l'année 1884;* quoted in Wallon, *Vie quotidienne,* 94. But see *La Nouvelle Mode,* August 26, 1900, about the success of German and Bohemian spas: "Marienbad especially, where one loses weight—the dream!"

12. Wallon, *Vie quotidienne,* 119.

13. Ibid., 118. See also for the figures to be found in accounts of the court proceedings brought by the Compagnie Fermière de Vichy against Saint Yorre, in GT, April 6 and 7, 1894.

14. Rober Marlin, "Besançon, 1845–1945," in Claude Fohlen, ed., *L'Histoire de Besançon* (1966), II, 380–82.

15. Dr. Mével, *Les Seigneurs de la mer* (Saint-Brieuc, 1927), 114.

16. Louis Roubaudi, *Nice et ses environs* (1843), 44; Alain Huetz de Lemps, *Les Sables-d'Olonne* (Fontenay, 1951), 72; Amédée Achard, *Une Saison à Aix-les-Bains* (1850), 277: "Autrefois Chamonix était une vallée; aujourd'hui c'est un hôtel." *Mémoires du Baron Haussmann* (1890), I, 324; C. James Haug, *Leisure and Urbanism in Nineteenth-Century Nice* (Lawrence, Kan., 1982), 8, 15, 131, 139; *La Gazette des Eaux,* October 16, 1872. See also Georges Salamand, *Alphonse Daudet à Allevard. Numa Roumestan. Une cure thermale août 1879* (Grenoble, 1976), 77 ff.

17. For the history of Vittel, see P. Bouloumié, *Histoire de Vittel* (1925), and Lise Grenier, M.-Th. Comtal, Guy de la Motte-Bouloumié, et al., *Vittel, 1854–1936* (1982). For Contrexéville, see Alain Decaux, *Petite histoire et petites histoires de Contrexéville* (1954).

18. Hyacinthe Audiffred, *Quinze jours au Mont-Dore* (1850, 1853); H. Audiffred, *Une Saison à Salins* (1861); H. Audiffred, *L'Eté à Aix en Savoie* (n.d.); J. de Boisgrolan, *Guide-Roman. Au Mont-Dore* (1880); Ernest Ferras, *Jean Bonnet à Luchon* (Toulouse, 1890). Narcisse Gallois, *Un Rimeur aux thermes des Pyrénées* (1887), also sings the wonders of Luchon, its promenades, sumptuous hotels, splendid new bazaars, and the cures it offers to those suffering from skin diseases or rheumatism: "Qui n'a vu d'Etigny la remarquable allée? / De somptueux hotels, vrais palais enchantés / Avec des grands bazars enfermant les cotés . . . // Malades que le dartre a marqué de son sceau, / Ou qui du rheumatisme endurez le fléau, / Accourez tous ici . . ." For the importance of publicity, see A. Mazon, *Notice historique sur Vals-les-Bains* (Privas, 1896), 43–44, who mentions that the little spa which languished for centuries unknown beyond the Vivarais was launched by articles in the Paris press during the later 1860s.

19. Motte-Bouloumié, *Vittel,* 13, passim. Vittel developed the most important bottling plant in Europe, selling over three hundred million bottles a year in the 1960s, compared to just over half as many sold by Perrier. The latter water, incidentally, is not associated with a spa, but with a spring at Vergèze, about ten miles north of Alès in the Cévennes. First developed by a Dr. Perrier in 1903, it was marketed by the Société Anonyme de la Source Perrier, founded in 1936.

20. Vicomte G. d'Avenel, *Le Mécanisme de la vie moderne* (1905), V, 21; Karl Baedeker, *Le Midi de la France* (1892), xx–xxiii; GT, July 29, 1897.

21. *Journal,* IV, 820, July 17, 1895.

22. GT, October 7, 1897, Tribunal Civil, Bayonne.

23. G. Bardet and J. L. Macquarie, *Plages et stations hivernales* (1888), 103, passim; Gabriel Désert, *La Vie quotidienne sur les plages normandes* (1983), 82, 86, 90, 102–104; Wallon, *Vie quotidienne,* 136, 164–66, 202.

24. Wallon, *Vie quotidienne,* 142; Désert, *Vie . . . plages normandes,* 197–98; Jean and Françoise Fourastié, *Voyages et voyageurs d'autrefois* (1972), quote the Comtesse de Pange about the family's annual trip to Dieppe in a reserved first-class compartment, in a carriage without a corridor, so the party carried a rubber chamberpot. It also carried smelling salts, cologne, mint alcohol, fans, rubber cushions, blankets, and baskets of provisions. The luggage was checked through, or traveled with the servants in another compartment.

25. On Vichy, see Theodore Zeldin, *France, 1848–1945* (Oxford, 1977), II, 92–96; Grand-Carteret, *XIXe siècle,* 520.

26. See the long report of the Prefect of Hautes-Pyrénées to Minister of Interior, dated November 15, 1908, in A.N., F^7 12734.

27. Jouhandeau, *Mémorial* (1951), II, 39–40.

28. Désert, *Vie . . . plages normandes,* 118, 115–17.

29. Dr. Galtier-Boissière, "Villégiature et santé," *Revue Universelle* (1902), 369 ff.; quoted in Wallon, *Vie quotidienne,* 132.

30. Max O'Rell, *English Pharisees and French Crocodiles* (London, 1892), 124; Vidal, quoted in Francoise Cribier, *La Grande migration d'été des citadins en France* (1969), 38.

31. See Jean Viard, *Penser les vacances* (1984), 69–70, passim. A survey of 1893 suggests that one of every four employed workmen worked on Sunday as well.

32. Cribier, *Grande migration,* 41; Pierre Dassau, *Le Nord vu par la presse, 1860–1910* (Dijon, 1981), 40–41.

33. Paul Marcelin, *Souvenirs d'un passé artisanal* (Nîmes, 1967), 29–30.

34. Eugène Labiche, *Le Voyage de Monsier Perrichon* (1860); J. Collet, *Notice sur la société des touristes du Dauphiné* (Grenoble, 1892), 1–2; Henry Beraldi, *Cent ans aux Pyrénées* (1900), IV, 2–5.

35. Beraldi, *Cent ans,* V, 77, VI, 24, 142; VII, introduction. See also Maurice Gourdon, *Les Hautes montagnes du Comminges* (Saint-Gaudens, 1890), 2, for "la foule banale des touristes" (the banal crowd of tourists).

36. Beraldi, *Cent ans,* VI, 143.

37. E.-A. Martel, *Les Cévennes et la région des Causses* (1890), vii.

38. *La Nouvelle Mode,* August 19, 1900.

39. Cauterets set up a syndicat d'initiative in 1884, the province of Dauphiné in 1889, Annecy and Chambéry in 1894.

10. La Petite Reine

1. Théodore Deckert, *Ode au Véloce* (Bordeaux, 1890). The poet would also author a short story: *Le Tandem, conte cycliste* (Bordeaux, 1895).

2. Zola, *Paris,* 418. On the preceding page we find one of the heroes, the

unfrocked priest, Pierre Froment, riding a bicycle that could be bought for 150 francs at the Bon Marché.

3. Victor Dauphin, *Le Cyclisme en Anjou* (Angers, 1936), 9–10.

4. Jacques Thibault, *L'Influence du mouvement sportif sur l'évolution de l'éducation physique dans l'enseignement secondaire français* (1972), 143.

5. In 1907, now signing himself Leblanc, Maurice Le Blanc hit the jackpot with his creation of Arsène Lupin, the gentleman-crook and detective, which proved an instant success.

6. Their advertising already seized on every possible opportunity. A large cartoon of General Boulanger as a centaur, published by *L'Illustration* on July 16, 1887, referred to and carried the discrete image of a cycle company of that name, established at 24 avenue de la Grande-Armée, and of one of its delivery-tricycles.

7. Pange, *Comment j'ai vu 1900,* II, 125.

8. Richard Holt, *Sport and Society in Modern France* (London, 1981), 92–97. By 1899 France boasted three hundred velodromes. See Alain Ehrenberg, *Aimez-vous les stades?* (1980), 36.

9. Paul Poiret, *En habillant,* 28; Georges Montorgueil, *La Parisienne* (1897), 185.

10. Jacques Léonard, *Les Médecins de l'ouest au XIXe siècle* (1978), III, 1463.

11. Just Lucas-Championnière, *La Bicyclette* (1894), 10; Ludovic O'Followell, *Bicyclette et organes génitaux* (1900), 92–93.

12. GT, July 23, 1897, "La Bicyclette devant la loi."

13. Manet, *Journal,* 133.

14. Uzanne, *La Femme à Paris* (1894), 207, and *Les Modes de Paris* (1898), 212, 236; Henri Boutet, *Almanach pour 1899* (1899), 32.

15. O'Followell, *Bicyclette,* 63–64, 69, 174–75. See also *Fin de Siècle,* April 15, 1897, for a corset advertisement: "Les dames cyclistes ne veulent plus d'autre corset que le Corset Touring . . . grande commodité, irréprochable élégance" (Lady cyclists will accept no corset other than the Corset Touring . . . great comfort, unexceptionable elegance).

16. Lucas-Championnière, *La Bicyclette,* 12, 19; Montorgueil, *La Parisienne,* 186.

17. Montorgueil, *La Parisienne,* 186; Henri Boutet, *Les Parisiennes d'à présent* (1897), 14.

18. Beraldi, *Cent ans,* VI, 175, 176.

19. Henri Chardon, *Voyages,* 13; Baudry de Saunier, quoted in Georges Renoy, *Le Vélo aux temps des belles moustaches* (Brussels, 1975), 62.

20. GT, July 4–5, 1892, Tribunal Civil du Vigan; September 3, 1893, Tribunal correctionnel St. Etienne.

21. Lucas-Championnière, *La Bicyclette,* 45–47.

22. GT, January 6, 1894; September 23, 1898; May 17–18, 1901; for Académie, see Elisabeth Hausser, *Paris au jour le jour, 1900–1919* (1968), 34 (July 28, 1900).

23. Baudry de Saunier, quoted in Renoy, *Le Vélo,* 13.

24. Quoted in Jacques Ozouf, *Nous les maîtres d'école* (1967), 122–23.

25. Zola, *Paris,* 417; Renoy, *Le Vélo,* 33, 58.
26. Gerard Coulon, *Une vie paysanne en Berry de 1882 à nos jours* (Chateauroux, 1979), 121–22.
27. GT, February 12 and 13, 1912, Cour d'appel, Toulouse; Pierre Pierrard, *Lille et les Lillois* (1967), 249; Maurice Barrès, *L'Auto,* April 13, 1906.
28. Paul Gerbod, "Les Coiffeurs en France," *Mouvement social,* (January 1981), 81; Claude-Paul Couture, *Cinquante ans de cyclisme avec le Véloce Club Barentinois, 1904–1954* (Le Havre, 1955), 4–5, passim; Archives départementales, Indre, M3734: 3/1892, 10/1892, passim.
29. Thibault, *L'Influence du mouvement sportif,* 147.
30. Eugen Weber, "Gymnastics and Sports in Fin-de-Siècle France," *American Historical Review* (February 1971), 81.
31. F. Herbert, *L'Ouest automobile* (Le Mans, 1959), 7 ff.; Anthony Rhodes, *Louis Renault* (London, 1969), 12.
32. Rhodes, *Renault,* 19.
33. Jean Jolly, *Dictionnaire des parlementaires français* (1966), IV, 1455–57; Charles W. Bishop, *La France et l'automobile* (1971), 203.
34. Rhodes, *Renault,* 32.
35. Kipling, *Souvenirs,* 18. See Hausser, *Paris,* 146, for illustrations.
36. *La Nouvelle Mode,* May 6, 1900; Hausser, *Paris,* 88 (March 4, 1902); Géo Lefèvre in *Le Journal des Sports,* January 1, 1900.
37. *L'Auto,* July 10, 1903; *Journal d'Alençon,* July 20, 1909, "Une révolution alençonnaise."
38. Désert, *Plages normandes,* 70.
39. GT, December 2 and 14, 1899; February 4–5, 1900; November 23, 1912; Désert in Dartiguenave, *Marginalité,* 258.
40. Hausser, *Paris,* 78.
41. Airplanes remained in the realm of science fiction as the century ended. In 1904 Santos-Dumont's attempts to get his heavier-than-air machine off the ground at Issy-les-Moulineaux appeared "pathetic" to observers like Pauline de Broglie (Pange, *Comment j'ai vu,* II, 126). The enthusiasts who cheered him on were "des gamins en casquettes, des mecanos en salopettes bleues, toute la faune du quartier des automobiles avenue de la Grande-Armée" (lads in caps, grease monkeys in blue overalls, all the fauna of the motorcar quarter of the avenue de la Grande-Armée). Five years after this unimpressive performance, the Wright brothers were to prove these early believers right.
42. See *L'Auto,* July 15, 1904: "les incidents de la second étape ont singulièrement corsé l'intérêt de la grande épreuve" (the incidents that occurred during the second stage have remarkably sharpened public interest in the race).
43. Geoffrey Nicholson, *The Great Bike Race* (London, 1977), 53.
44. Ibid., 54–55.
45. See *L'Auto,* July 2–13, 1903 (the triumphant end came on Sunday, July 19).
46. Ibid., July 13, 1906.
47. Ibid., July 11, 1910.

11. Faster, Higher, Stronger

1. Victor Margueritte, *Le Goût de l'énergie* (1912); quoted in Bodley, *Decay of Idealism,* 139.
2. Henry Dartigue, *De l'état d'esprit de la jeunesse intellectuelle avant la guerre* (1916), 13.
3. Club Alpin Français, presidential address 1879, in *Annuaire* (1880), not paginated.
4. Helly, *Cent ans de ski français,* 10, 33–34. In 1903 Captain Clerc and Adjutant Transtour of the 159th Infantry Regiment published their *Rapport sur les expériénces de ski,* recommending the establishment of a national training school.
5. Archives départementales, Gironde, *Sociétés sportives.* See Weber, "Gymnastics and Sports," 72 ff.
6. Lermusiaux and Tavernier, *Pour la Patrie* (1886). The speaker was Octave Gréard, vice-rector of the Académie de Paris from 1879 to 1902.
7. M. Bernard et al., "Itinéraire," *Esprit* (May 1975), 710.
8. Here and for the paragraphs that follow, see Weber, "Gymnastics and Sports," 74 ff.
9. Archives départementales, Gironde, *Bataillons scolaires, 1881–1892;* Philippe Tissié, *L'Education physique* (1901), 6.
10. For salaries, see *Revue des jeux scolaires et d'hygiène sociale* (October 1908), 142, 144.
11. Quoted in Guy Thuillier, *Pour une histoire du quotidien au XIXe siècle en Nivernais* (1977), 66–67.
12. Georges Bourdon, *La Renaissance athlétique et le Racing Club de France* (1906), 126.
13. *Revue Blanche* (January 1984); *Oeuvres de Léon Blum* (1954), I, 204–06.
14. Leslie, *Bodley,* 378.
15. Sherard, *My Friends,* 62; René Valléry-Radot, *Journal d'un volontaire d'un an au 10e de ligne* (1874), 138–41.
16. Maillier, *Trois journalistes Drouais,* 107.
17. GT, May 16, 1895, Seine.
18. GT, August 11, 1887, January 14, 1888.
19. Pierre Daubert, *Du Port illégal de costume et de décoration* (1904), 81–82.
20. GT, November 13–14, 1899, Gironde; May 6, 1904, Seine (for Toulouse case). See also GT, June 26 and 27, 1888, Seine Assizes; June 23 and August 29, 1892.
21. Lockspeiser, *Débussy,* 237, 252–54.
22. Péter, *Le Théatre,* 132; GT, May 22–24, 1899. See also Guiches, *Le Spectacle,* 106–07, 243.
23. GT, October 24, 1900, Meuse.
24. Sherard, *My Friends,* esp. 78, where he mentions the high cost of an encounter, no less than 300 francs. Also Gabriel Tarde, *Etudes pénales et sociales* (1892), 31 ff., and Paul Morand, *1900* (1931), 128–31.
25. "Maupassant athlète," *La Culture physique,* 52 (March 1907).

26. Pierre de Coubertin, *Une Campagne de 21 ans, 1887–1908* (1909), 85; Marie-Thérèse Eyquem, *Pierre de Coubertin* (1966), 59.

27. This and the paragraphs that follow are taken largely from Weber, "Gymnastics and Sports," 82–96.

28. Raoul Fabens, *Les Sports pour tous* (1906), 127.

29. Edouard Pontié, *Le Football Rugby* (1905), 20.

30. The best book on this fascinating man is John J. MacAloon's *This Great Symbol: Pierre de Coubertin and the Origins of the Modern Olympic Games* (Chicago, 1981).

31. Agathon (Henri Massis, Alfred de Tarde), *Les Jeunes gens d'aujourd'hui* (11th ed., 1919; 1st ed., 1912), 139, passim; italics in original.

32. Maurice Barrès, *Du Sang, de la volupté, de la mort* (1894), 268. See also Eugen Weber, "Pierre de Coubertin and the Introduction of Organised Sport in France," *Journal of Contemporary History* (April 1970), passim.

33. Grantland Rice, "Alumnus Football," in *Only the Brave* (New York, 1941), p. 144.

12. "The Best of Times"

1. Paul Hamelle in *Le Vélo,* December 31, 1900.

2. Charles Péguy, *L'Argent* (1913), in *Oeuvres en Prose, 1909–1914* (1968), 1104, 1115.

3. "La Mort d'un sorcier," *Petit Parisien,* December 26, 1900.

4. "Les Magnétiseurs," *Petit Parisien,* October 16, 1900.

5. *Le Figaro,* January 31, 1901.

6. Emile Faguet, "Que sera le XXe siècle?" *Questions politiques* (1899), 302–03.

7. Emile Faguet, *Problèmes politiques du temps présent* (1901), xvii. Over half a century before, Henri Heine had exulted that "les chemins de fer font qu'un voyage de plaisir à Paris n'est plus qu'un saut. L'espace n'existe plus" (railways make a pleasure trip to Paris no more than a hop. Space no longer exists). *Correspondance inédite* (1877), III, 133, letter of July 9, 1848.

8. *L'Illustration,* November 2, 1907.

9. Péguy, *Compte-rendu de congrès* (1901), in *Oeuvres en prose, 1898–1908* (1965), 384; Jacques Maritain, *La Philosophie bergsonienne* (1914).

10. *Le Temps,* July 13, 1898.

11. Edouard Millaud, *Le Journal d'un parlementaire* (1914), IV, 79, dated May 29, 1900.

12. Jean Touchard, *La Gauche en France depuis 1900* (1977), 30.

13. To the Right as well, since the Action Française, its source of reference and its inspiration, was born of it in 1899. Charles Maurras, when condemned for collaboration in 1945, declared: "C'est la revanche de Dreyfus!" But new generations of the Right have dropped the Dreyfus issue. The Left, as Touchard observes, *Gauche en France,* 28, "has always been in search of a new Dreyfus Affair."

14. Jean-Louis Bredin, *L'Affaire* (1983), 476.

15. Combarieu, *Sept ans,* 126–27, 163.
16. Faguet, *Problèmes,* ii, xi.
17. Baronne Staffe, *Mes Secrets* (1896), 304–06; italics mine.
18. Faguet, *Questions,* 252–53.
19. Combarieu, *Sept ans,* 11. In April 1899 Loubet mused: "Were we right? I doubt it. These great shows bring no profit to the State and have awkward consequences for the country's general economy and finances."
20. Germain Bapst, *Exposition universelle internationale de 1900, Catalogue général officiel. Exposition retrospective des armées de terre et de mer,* 7.
21. Combarieu, *Sept ans,* 124–25.
22. Faguet, *Questions,* 335.
23. "Le Bilan du Siècle," *Petit Parisien,* December 29, 1900.
24. See Martin du Gard, *Jean Barois* (1913), ch. 12.
25. "Sommes-nous en décadence?" *Le Vélo,* July 5, 1903.
26. Quoted in Robert L. Delevoy, *Dimensions du XXe siècle* (Geneva, 1965), 13.
27. Jean-Yves Tadié, *Proust* (1983), 275. The fallacy principle that colors Proust's work, like much of his life, is illustrated by a letter he wrote in January 1901, in answer to New Year's greetings, "fully aware that my life is behind me." Marcel Proust, *Selected Letters, 1880–1903,* ed. Philip Kolb (New York, 1983), 217.
28. Marcel Proust, *A la Recherche du temps perdu* (1969), III, 188.

Acknowledgments

My thanks to UCLA and to UCLA's Senate Research Committee for unfailing research support; to the Fulbright Commission and the National Endowment for the Humanities for fellowships in 1983–1984; to the Ecole des Hautes Etudes en Sciences Sociales for a research appointment in 1985; to Ann Louise McLaughlin for inspired editing; and to my Paris colleagues Fernand Braudel, Emmanuel Le Roy Ladurie, and Guy Thuillier, for aid, amity, and inspiration.

Index

Designer   Marianne Perlak
Compositor   Achorn Graphic Services
Printer/Binder   Halliday Lithograph
Text   10½/13½ Linotron Galliard
Display   Tiffany Light